GARDENING
in your
GREENHOUSE

R.H. MENAGE

This edition produced exclusively for

WHSMITH

Acknowledgements

The publishers gratefully acknowledge the following persons, agencies and companies for granting permission for reproduction of the colour photographs:

Halls Homes and Gardens (pp. 17 (lower), 18 (lower)); the author (pp. 38 (top), 39 (lower), 81 (top), 83, 84, 101, 103 (lower), 113, 116, 133, 134, 135 (lower), 174 (top), 176); Unwins Seeds Ltd. (pp. 39 (top), 83, 102, 114, 115 (top)); Suttons Seeds Ltd. (pp. 40, 103 (top), 115 (lower), 153 (lower), 154); Murphy Chemical Ltd. (p. 32 (top)); Gillian Beckett (pp. 135 (top), 174 (lower)); Harry Smith Horticultural Photographic Collection (pp. 153 (top), 156 (top)); David Squire (pp. 155 (top), 175 (lower)); Pat Brindley (pp. 155 (lower), 173 (top)); and Clive Innes (p. 175 (top)).

The publishers also gratefully acknowledge Arthur Billitt of Clack's Farm in providing the locations for the following photographs: the back cover picture, the top right picture on the front cover, pp. 37, 38 (lower), 156 (lower), and Halls Homes and Gardens in providing locations for their greenhouses shown on the front cover (main picture) and on pp. 17 (top) and 18 (top). The Clack's Farm photographs were taken by Bob Challinor.

All line drawings are by Nils Solberg and were made from material supplied by the author. Some of the drawings have been published in similar form previously; these are acknowledged as follows:
Figs. 1 and 18 are after the illustrations which appeared on pp. 11 and 72 respectively in *Greenhouse Manual*, R. H. Menage, published by Max Parrish, 1964; Figs. 2, 7, 10, 11–13, 15, 16, 21, 21–23, 26–28 and 31 are after Figs. 1, 6, 7, 9–11, 12, 8, 4, 17–19, 3, 13, 15 and 14 respectively in *Woolman's Greenhouse Gardening*, R. H. Menage, published by Elm Tree Books/Hamish Hamilton, 1974.

© Ward Lock Ltd 1984

Produced especially for W.H. Smith & Sons by Ward Lock Limited, 82 Gower Street, London WC1E 6EQ, a Pentos Company.

House Editor Denis Ingram
Layout by Paul Saunders

Text filmset in Plantin
by Paul Hicks Limited, Burrington Way, Plymouth

Printed and bound in Spain by
Graficromo, Cordoba.

ISBN 0 7063 4267 4

CONTENTS

PREFACE

In recent years greenhouse gardening has become one of the most popular hobbies. There is no doubt that, as computers and robots take over people's chores, we shall have more leisure time – what could be better than spending some of this enjoying the many pleasures a greenhouse can offer.

One of the most important advantages is that you can grow plants the year round – however uncongenial the climate. The scope of growing also has many facets – fresh fruit and vegetables, flowers for pots and for cutting, and all sorts of ways to help the outdoor garden. A greenhouse can also be a very wise *investment*, since there are many ways it can save you money or at least earn its keep.

All can be exploited without much expenditure too. These days, a small greenhouse costs less than some of the common household luxuries and, with proper organization, there's no need to spend much on heating. Even an unheated house can have a diversity of uses.

This book, I hope, will provide an introduction to the numerous aspects of greenhouse gardening. It takes into account the fact that most home greenhouses are small and maintained at low winter temperatures to keep costs to the minimum. For this reason, I have excluded many exotics. A lot of these are best regarded as 'house plants'. They rarely stay happy in the average greenhouse over winter.

I have also tried to avoid discussing complicated or expensive equipment used by professional growers, but I hope the range of techniques described will give some idea of the horizons that can be explored.

Over the past few years tremendous strides have been made by plant breeders. Plants, at one time tricky for the home gardener, are now easy, thanks to the introduction of F_1 and similar hybrids. I have drawn attention to these whenever possible.

Many of the photographs are of plants grown in my own greenhouses by the methods suggested in the book. Most readers will be able to grow them as well, if not better!

R.H.M.

PUBLISHER'S NOTE

Measurements are generally cited in imperial followed by the metric equivalent in parentheses. In a few instances, owing to pressure on space, the metric equivalent has been omitted

GLOSSARY OF UNITS

Unit	Abbreviation	Unit	Abbreviations
British Thermal Unit	BTU	square metre(s)	sq m
centimetre(s)	cm	square foot (feet)	sq ft
foot (feet)	ft	cubic metre(s)	cu m
gallon(s)	gal	cubic foot (feet)	cu ft
litre(s)	l		
metre(s)	m		
watt(s)	W		

PART I
THE HARDWARE

1 INTRODUCTION: GARDENING WITH A GREENHOUSE

A LITTLE HISTORY

The greenhouse is by no means a modern idea. It seems to have been originated by the Roman Emperor, Tiberius (42 BC–AD 37). He was instructed by his Physician to eat a cucumber each day for at least a year. Even in the Italian climate this was a tall order. It was nevertheless accomplished by constructing pits in which to grow the plants, surrounded by trenches in which small fires were maintained. The pits were covered with sheets of the mineral mica which has good transparency, sheet glass not having then been invented. It worked. Not only did Tiberius get his cucumbers, but the idea was soon exploited and elaborated by wealthy Romans for out-of-season growing. Such structures were called Specularia. The cucumber treatment also seems to have been a success. Tiberius lived to a remarkably good old age for that period!

FINANCIAL ASPECTS

At one time greenhouse gardening was often regarded as a rich man's hobby. Today this is far from the truth. Indeed, the question is not 'Can you afford a greenhouse?', but 'Can you afford to be *without* one?' Apart from all the pleasure a greenhouse gives, it can be a real money saver and a sound investment. The initial cost can be quickly returned in the form of valuable produce. Anyone with a garden of moderate size will be thrilled with the cheap production from seed of otherwise expensive bedding plants alone. Then there is the abundance of a variety of food crops the majority being the type quite costly to buy in shops.

Fortunately, owing to mass production, ever-increasing demand and popularity, mod-ern prefabricated greenhouses are mostly modestly priced. They can well be cheaper than many domestic luxuries now found in the majority of homes, so there is no excuse to be without one!

WEATHER AND NATURAL HAZARD PROTECTION

The greenhouse is often thought of as a place to mainly shelter plants from cold, or to keep them comfortably warm. This may be true in some cases, but it can give other forms of protection just as important.

Often wind, torrential rain, hail, heavy snow, prolonged wet or waterlogged soil, and other kinds of extreme weather, can do enormous mechanical damage – even to quite hardy plants. In countries such as the British Isles – notorious for unreliable and changeable weather – a greenhouse can prove invaluable, if not indispensable, in acting as a 'buffer' against the elements. There are a few exceptions, but the very great majority of popular and favourite plants, grown in the average home greenhouse, do not need very high temperatures.

Other enemies of plants, such as wild animals, birds, domestic animals, pets and even small children, can be kept out of a greenhouse without much trouble. Pests and diseases are easier to control effectively too, provided prompt action is taken.

THE BENEFITS OF PERSONAL CONTROL

Outdoors our cultivated plants rarely get the sort of weather and growing conditions we ourselves would ideally choose for them.

However, the micro-climate of the greenhouse can be controlled by us to a great extent. We can influence temperature by artificial heating, ventilation, shading and damping down. We can choose the kind of growing medium or potting compost to give optimum results. We can apply just the right amount of water and plant foods to the roots or foliage. Light conditions can be adjusted by shading or even by special electric plant irradiation lamps. Everything can be done to keep the small environment clean and hygienic, and as free from plant predators as possible. Our environmental interference therefore enables us to grow a far wider range of top quality plants, perhaps out-of-season; a range that would be quite impossible in the same area if outdoors and unprotected.

RANGE OF PLANTS, APPLICATIONS AND SCOPE

To take up greenhouse horticulture is to enter a new world of gardening enchantment; the possibilities are enormous and fascinating. By keeping the greenhouse little more than frost-free, you can grow plants from almost the world over, and with a little extra warmth you can enjoy plant life that is really exotic. As well as a wealth of pot plants, you can also grow cut flowers, plants for the garden, and a delightful selection of fruits and vegetables. With some modest planning and care, it is usually possible to have something of interest to please the eye or palate all the year round.

The greenhouse enables you to grow many plants from the very beginning, from seed or cuttings. This gives great aesthetic satisfaction, and it is economic too. It can also be regarded as an invaluable 'garden tool' when used as a plant nursery, since it can then greatly influence the variety and quality of plants you can raise for subsequent outdoor growing. For example, you can make some exciting features with sub-tropical bedding and use the greenhouse to overwinter many plants that are pretty striking but just not hardy enough to survive outdoors.

The fact that a greenhouse can produce exquisite house plants may be well appreciated, but a lean-to with communicating door can become an integral part of the home,

perhaps the favourite place for relaxation. Earlier this century the conservatory, often rather grand, was a popular feature of wealthier homes. Nowadays a small structure is within the financial means of most people. The 'conservatory' proper was nearly always a greenhouse-like building with perhaps more attractive architectural design. A present-day substitute is often what is called a 'garden room' or 'home extension' when used for indoor plants too.

Despite the versatility of the greenhouse, certain groups of plants lend themselves particularly well to specialization. Some people therefore like isolating one subject for special attention. A beginner can, if preferred, start off by specializing in, for example, orchids, alpines, cacti, chrysanthemums, or foliage plants. However, the desire to specialize often comes after some general experience and the development of a form of favouritism. Growing one particular group to the exclusion of all others allows the ideal conditions of growth to be more easily and effectively maintained. You can achieve a far higher perfection and often build up a more extensive collection of species or varieties.

By having more than one greenhouse, or a compartmented one you can of course provide the ideal environment for the specialized subjects and still enjoy general growing.

PERSONAL COMFORT AND EDUCATION

Greenhouse gardening can be of enormous benefit to both young and old. Many schools, institutions, and therapeutic hospitals have found that greenhouse work for young people, and for people recovering from illnesses or being rehabilitated, can provide absorbing interest with excellent educational and psychological results. Many plant study 'laboratories' of colleges take the form of a greenhouse too.

The greenhouse has proved to be of tremendous value to disabled or infirm people, and the not-so-young. It is the absolutely ideal retirement hobby, and will solve many of the boredom and psychological problems that frequently arise when routine day employment comes to an end. Since, if necessary, much of the cultural work can be done at staging level (waist height), stooping and bending can be largely avoided. The weather protection a greenhouse affords will be greatly appreciated by those adversely affected by the cold and wet, or prone to rheumatic and similar troubles.

However, even the fittest should gain much pleasure from the role of the greenhouse as a winter garden. The dreary months of the year can be made cheerful with a gay colourful display of flowers which everyone will appreciate. Winter salads are well worth growing too not only for their flavour but also as a source of fresh vitamins.

GREENHOUSE GARDENING WITHOUT A GARDEN

Not having a garden is no excuse for not having a greenhouse. A small greenhouse can often be erected almost anywhere – even on roofs and large balconies. Certainly a concrete yard or paved area can prove an excellent site. The reason for this is that you do not have to have ground soil. In fact you are often far better off without it. Nearly all your plants can be grown in pots or other containers. In recent years growing bags, and the easily transportable lightweight growing 'boards', have made it possible to grow splendid flowers and crops anywhere. Other soil-less growing methods include hydroponics and nutrient film technique more suited to the experimenter and the enthusiast, and to school laboratories. See also information on siting the greenhouse, p. 23.

GREENHOUSE TEMPERATURE CLASSIFICATION

Greenhouses are often given a descriptive name according to the temperature range maintained. For example (winter temperatures):

Unheated house:	no artificial heat given
Cold house:	kept above freezing
Cool house:	4–7°C (40–45°F)
Warm house:	minimum 13°C (55°F)
Stove or hot house:	minimum 18°C (65°F)

The temperatures are only approximate and may vary over a range of a few degrees according to the requirements of the majority of plants in the greenhouse. There may also be a difference of about five degrees or so between the winter and summer minimum temperature maintained. Some people call the cool house described above a 'cold house', and the warm house an 'intermediate house'.

The vast majority of 'home greenhouses' come into the cool greenhouse category, but with the accent on fuel conservation in recent years there is greater effort to make do with cold house conditions in many cases. Sometimes it is a good idea to run your greenhouse as a cold house through the mid-winter months when high temperatures would prove expensive, and as a cool house from late winter through spring when there is enough natural warmth from the sun to supplement any artificial heating. Most of the popular plants grown by the home gardener make little winter growth or may be dormant – they do not need much warmth but must be kept frost free. From late winter onwards, there is much to be started into growth and to sow – extra warmth can then be very useful.

Very few home gardeners these days run warm or stove greenhouses. To heat even a small structure to the required minimum winter temperature is very expensive, unless you live in a country with relatively mild winters. Moreover, high temperatures are quite unnecessary, even decidedly undesirable, for nearly all the growing jobs the average home gardener wants to do. When extra warmth is needed for propagation or for a few special plants, it can be more economically confined to propagators or frames and cases. Both warm and stove greenhouses will need artificial heating in operation during the summer at times, especially overnight. With the desirable summer minimum temperature having to be about five Fahrenheit degrees higher than the winter minimum, the cost of heating is not to be undertaken lightly.

It will be appreciated that warm and stove greenhouses are intended for the large subtropical and tropical plants. Only if you are intent on growing these, and can afford the running costs, should these types of greenhouse be considered. This book deals only with plants suitable for lower temperature growing.

The unheated greenhouse tends to be for-

7

gotten – perhaps too many people think there is little use for it. This is a completely wrong assumption, as you will see by turning to p. 171. It is a good idea to have an unheated greenhouse as an extra in any garden.

IMPORTANT HINTS FOR BEGINNERS

Having read to this point in this chapter, it will probably be realized that, because the scope of greenhouse gardening is so great, some positive thinking and planning must be done at the start of your undertaking. It is obviously impossible to do everything in one average greenhouse of modest size. However, with proper planning it is astonishing just how much *can* be done. Some ideas and growing programmes are given on p. 45.

Failures and disappointments can often be traced to quite silly and avoidable mistakes. As a result quite good greenhouses have become derelict and demoted to the role of garden shed or store for junk.

A very common cause of problems is to collect a multitude of plants with widely differing cultural and environmental requirements. It is asking for trouble to mix plants like woodland subjects, sun lovers, desert cacti, tropical rain forest plants, and others all *widely different*, in the *same* (uncompartmented) greenhouse.

However, often the varied nature of a collection can be increased by careful siting of the plants. For example shade lovers may be happy under staging, plants preferring lower humidity could be placed near ventilators, and those liking moist conditions on capillary moisture matting. Plants expected to demand extremes are best avoided, or you must be prepared to give them special treatment.

It is often helpful to find out as much as you can about the natural environment of a plant, more especially if it is out of the more popular range. This may prove a useful guide to what sort of treatment should be given. Even so, there are quite a lot of exceptions. For example, many plants we commonly grow seem to thrive even when in conditions nothing like their natural habitat. Many that grow naturally in considerable warmth can be acclimatized to survive a cool greenhouse. I have drawn attention to a number of these exceptions in this book, so it is often worth experimenting.

Frequently lack of proper understanding in the matter of simple greenhouse routine is responsible for serious failure. Shading, for example, or rather the lack of it, can quickly ruin a greenhouse full of plants, so can lack of prompt attention to any pest or disease attack. If you have to be away from your greenhouse most of the day, some form of simple automatic watering may make all the difference between success and failure. Without automation, at least to some extent, greenhouse gardening may not be feasible for people who have to be absent for long periods. Fortunately modern methods have completely changed this formerly bleak outlook.

Gardening with a greenhouse

A small greenhouse, even if heated, can be an extremely valuable 'tool' in the cultivation of the outdoor garden. Indeed, it can have a quite dramatic effect in its improvement.

BEDDING PLANTS

A small greenhouse, or even some frames, can very quickly return the initial expenditure if they are used for raising bedding plants alone, although many other year-round uses can be found too.

Most bedding plants can be sown and grown as described on p. 71. If there is no heating sowing will have to be a few weeks later and more care taken over the hardiness of the varieties.

For bedding plants, the seedlings are best pricked out into large size plastic seed trays. Do not overcrowd them – about 24 seedlings to each tray (35×23 cm [14×9 in]) is usually adequate. By leaving plenty of space, and giving more potting compost to each plant, much better and stronger specimens than you can buy in the shop will result. Do not forget too, that you can take advantage of all the offers of new varieties and novelties that the seedsmen list each year.

If producing bedding plants on a large scale there is no need to keep the air of the greenhouse or the frames at a high temperature. It has been found that keeping the roots warm is far more important. By so doing, the roots are encouraged to make sturdy development, but the top growth is not; this means a much faster establishment when the plants are bedded out, and the top growth is not forced only to become checked when exposed to the rigours of the weather.

The most convenient way to grow the bedding plants is to plunge the seedling trays in a layer of moist peat spread over sand-covered warming cables. About 10W/90 cm² (1 ft²) should be allowed when distributing the cable. The greenhouse or frame air temperature need be only little more than frost free: 2–4°C (35–39°F) is certainly adequate. Often it is possible to enclose the warmed bench or area on which the seedlings are growing with transparent plastic film thus economizing in heating even further.

All bedding plants must be hardened off before planting out; this means gradually getting them accustomed to full exposure to the weather. It should be started about two to three weeks before the beginning of summer – before the time when all risk of frost has passed in the area where you live – this may vary by a few weeks from north to south. The hardening off is best done with frames, gradually increasing ventilation until the covers are left entirely off. At first, night cover must be given if there is risk of frost. Also at first frames may have to be slightly shaded if they are in a position of full sun. Use white Coolglass paint for this, gradually wiping it off by running a finger across the glass every few days. Remove the paint in lines, gradually increasing the width until the whole of the shading is removed.

SUB-TROPICAL BEDDING AND GARDEN FEATURES

This is where a greenhouse can really have a dramatic effect on the appearance of a garden. Ideally the most useful type of greenhouse for this job is a fairly spacious one but in most cases little more than frost-free conditions need be maintained in winter. In some mild areas no artificial heat may be necessary. A great number of the sub-tropical looking plants do, in fact, not demand tropical winter temperatures. The plants can be used in various ways. They can be plunged in beds or borders so that the pots are concealed, the pots can be slipped into slightly larger ornamental pots for standing on patios or terraces and the like or, in some cases, they can be permanently planted in ornamental containers which can be made mobile for easy moving in and out of the greenhouse. Tubs can be fitted with wheels, or wheeled stands made for other types of pot. Many garden centres are also now selling special pots fitted with castors. This is no doubt partly due to the latest fashion of patio gardening.

Some suitable plants to be found described in this book are the hardy, or almost hardy, palms (particularly *Phoenix carnariensis* which is a beauty and easy to manage; *Musa ensete*, not so easy but worth a try; *Grevillea robusta* and *Jacaranda mimosaefolia*, both from seed), cannas which are very popular and are used by many municipal gardeners (especially in sea-side resorts), neriums (usually pretty easy), *Ricinus communis* varieties also very popular, *Erythrina crists-galli* (easy but not so often seen), *Agave americana* which is bound to attract attention, and sometimes *Strelitzia regina* where the flowers will not be exposed to too much weather punishment. To this lot can be added the very beautiful *Phormium tenax*. This is hardy in some mild areas and will reach a considerable size. It makes a good pot plant and will survive well often in an unheated greenhouse. Two very lovely forms are 'Purpureum' which has purplish foliage and 'Variegatum' which has green leaves striped with cream. The foliage is erect and sword-shaped. *Cordyline indivisa* and *C. australis* also have sword-shaped sharp foliage, and are again quite easy to overwinter. They can be simply and cheaply raised from seed and, in their young stage, can make useful greenhouse foliage plants for the staging.

Among the easiest tropical-looking plants to grow from seed, and fast growers, are the various forms of ornamental maize, *Zea mays*. The varieties with cream, green, and rose-pink striped foliage are especially attractive, and can be raised along with the summer bedding plants. Another easy group is the amaranthus notable for richly coloured foliage. 'Red Fox' and the new more 'bushy tailed' 'Pigmy Torch' have quite eye-catching erect bold catkin-like reddish tails, and are easy half-hardy annuals.

All plants to be used as temporary features for beds and borders, with their containers plunged, should be given *clay* pots. These pots should have a layer of sharp sand at the bottom to discourage entry of earthworms (and some soil pests). Clay pots are porous and will allow moisture to reach the roots from surrounding soil – even so, watering must not be forgotten, All perennial plants must, of course, be taken up and returned to a greenhouse well before the first frosts.

For pots to stand above ground, it's best to avoid plastic, unless they are to be used as liner pots. Many plastics soon become brittle when exposed to sunlight; when you attempt to pick them up, they may fall to pieces or split! Before returning sub-tropicals to their winter quarters, make sure they are not harbouring any garden pests, and cut away cleanly any damaged or dying vegetation.

GENERAL PROPAGATION

Apart from bedding plants many choice perennials can be grown from seed and kept in a greenhouse until well established in their pots. The seedlings can be given a good start and protected from both weather and pests that often cause young subjects significant damage.

The vegetable garden can be made more productive by raising many vegetable seedlings and pot growing in the early stages in the greenhouse, provided the plants are not coddled. This way you also get much earlier cropping, e.g. sweet corn, sweet peppers and outdoor tomatoes.

Many of the favourite garden shrubs, trees, and other perennials can be propagated from cuttings. This work is also often best done in the greenhouse. Those gardeners especially interested in the more choice shrubs will find a mist propagation unit useful.

OVERWINTERING AND EARLY STARTING

A great many of the more tender garden plants need a greenhouse to survive the winter.

Pelargoniums, fuchsias, garden chrysanthemums, and dahlias are typical important plants benefiting from such accommodation. A greenhouse is essential for propagating the chrysanthemums which send up plenty of shoots from the cut-back plants to use as cuttings in early spring. As well as saving the old plants over winter, a greenhouse will allow cuttings of most types of pelargonium to be taken in late summer to autumn. These, overwintered in frost-free conditions will yield masses of new plants for bedding out the following summer.

Dahlia tubers can be started into growth in late winter and the shoots used as cuttings to increase stock. A trick for getting unusually early blooms – not generally known – is to pot up, in large pots, in early spring. Grow on the plants in the greenhouse to an advanced stage and until the beginning of summer when it is safe to plant out in permanent positions. Often the plants will start to bloom almost immediately and continue all the rest of the year until cut down by frost. By using this method you can enjoy these lovely flowers for the maximum period and they will enhance the garden enormously.

Terrace and patio pots can be kept colourful over a long period by growing the plants in 'liner pots' – plastic pots just large enough to fit *inside* the ornamental pot. The 'liner pots' can be planted up or sown with seed and kept in the greenhouse until ready to put out. Quick changes according to season can be made, resulting in a wide variety of colour.

GROWING YOUR OWN HOUSE PLANTS

Many of the more exotic house plants need congenial warmth, and often moderate humidity, to grow well and to maintain their attractive appearance. They do not make reliable long-term subjects for the average greenhouse with low winter temperatures. However, with the aid of a large warmed frame *in* the greenhouse as described on p. 26, you can use an ordinary cool greenhouse to grow many house plants from seed, or to propagate those you have, or from cuttings donated by friends.

To germinate seed of choice kinds a temperature of about 24°C(75°F) must be attainable if needed. Some, such as *Saintpaulia*, may be happy enough with several degrees lower. Similarly, to root cuttings quickly and well, a brisk 'bottom heat' is desirable. The frame should be large enough to accomodate seedlings or rooted cuttings until they are well established, and until the greenhouse temperature will be high enough for a transfer to the staging, where the plants can often be grown on further during the summer months, prior to being moved to the home.

Some house plants to raise from seed, freely available, are *Ficus elastica* and *F. benjamina* (*do not* cover the seed with compost when sowing); *Monstera deliciosa*; philodendrons; *Stephanotis floribunda*; *Anthurium scherzer-ianum*; *Crossandra infundibuliformis*; *Gardenia jasminoides* and *Ruellia macrantha*. You may also like to try seed of many tropical palms, bromeliads, cacti and other succulents, and warm climate fern spores.

By reproducing 'jungle-like' conditions in your warmed frame – sufficient heat and humidity – you can get most tropicals to root from stem and often leaf cuttings, very easily. Most of the begonias and members of the gesneria family, will root readily from their leaves. Those that form clumps can be propagated by simple division – marantas and peperomias, for examples. House plants are never particularly cheap to buy, so it's worth exploiting this possibility. The plants can be useful as gifts too.

2 DESIGN AND STRUCTURAL MATERIALS

HINTS ON BUYING

A study of this chapter may serve as a guide to buying a new greenhouse, or help in tracing and rectifying faults in an existing structure. If you are completely new to greenhouse gardening, read the book in its entirety *before buying*. You should then be able to form a clearer idea of a design that will best suit your purpose, and the type of greenhouse growing you wish to pursue.

Certain manufacturers of greenhouses have been in business for very many years, and they have developed a reputation for reliability and good workmanship through their long establishment and service. I strongly advise readers to patronize these suppliers, because their designs and materials of construction have withstood the 'test of time' – vital for all *permanent* buildings. Such firms are always researching and looking for reliable improvements. If anything worthwhile is developed or discovered, they will present it to the public after testing. I mention this because, in recent years, owing to the 'boom' in greenhouse interest, various firms of doubtful repute and brief existence have been offering so-called 'modern' designs in a blaze of pseudo-scientific publicity, and at outrageous prices. Some of these designs are no more than 'gimmicks', reducible to nonsense by genuine scientific analysis and often incorporate materials that can only be very short lived. (See also, Greenhouse shape, p. 14.)

A greenhouse always looks forbiddingly bare and empty when first erected. The space soon disappears with amazing rapidity and you start to cry out for more room. Always buy a greenhouse as big as you can afford and accommodate, but do not forget heating costs. If you propose to heat, check on probable running costs in relation to size, to see what best suits your finances. For an unheated greenhouse a good size is most desirable. Heating costs need not be considered, and many plants suited show their best when given plenty of space. For any large greenhouse it is an advantage to have an aluminium alloy framework which needs practically no maintenance, thus saving money in the long run and a lot of awkward and time-consuming work.

More features that may be worth taking into account, depending on individual circumstances, are the following: an easy foundation system; decorative frame finish; patent glazing; built-in gutter; wide door to allow barrow access; sliding door; facility to add an extension; compartments; plenty of ventilators or facilities to add extra ones; low maintenance; strength of framework with facility to prevent ridge bar sag; minimum incorporation of plastic components in structures required to be permanent. (See details below.)

GLASS OR PLASTIC?

Clear plastics are *not* substitutes for glass, despite what some publicity may suggest. Although glass is a 'plastic' in the physical sense it is an *inorganic* one. What are generally termed 'plastics' are *organic* by nature, i.e. composed of carbon compounds. To the layman the important significance of this is that organic plastics are *inherently soft*, coming way down the hardness scale compared with glass. This means they are easily scratched and abraded by weathering and wind blown dust and grit, and then soon begin to collect grime and dirt which may become ingrained and difficult to remove. Many become brittle on exposure to much sunlight. Polythene is no-

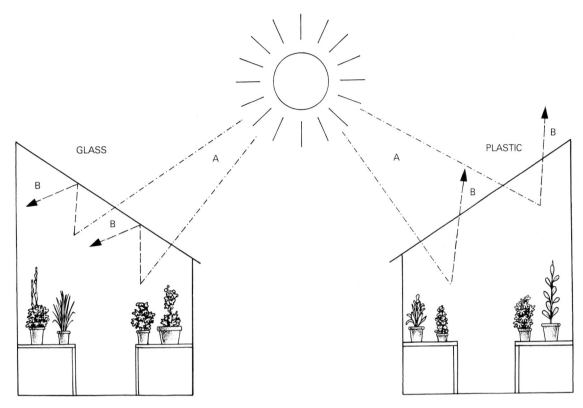

Fig. 1 Heat trap effect of glass
Glass is transparent to short wave radiation from the sun *A*, which is converted to longer wavelength heat radiation, *B* on striking the interior. Glass is less transparent to this and it is reflected back and trapped. In the case of plastics, much heat passes straight out again and the heat trapping effect is much less noticeable.

torious for quick deterioration on exposure to ultraviolet rays and special grades are now made to last longer (UV stabilized). Many plastics *warp or shrink with age, or may become opaque or turn yellowish*. Generally, in my opinion, the plastics are a very unwise choice for a greenhouse expected to be permanent and to last for many years like a glass one will. I write from bitter personal experience in this matter, having had plastics on test since they were first introduced to horticulture.

Another disadvantage with plastics is that they do not trap solar warmth or hold warmth generally so well as glass structures. Glass allows certain of the shorter wavelengths of the sun's radiation to pass through. These are converted into longer wavelengths we feel as warmth on striking the greenhouse interior. But the glass offers a resistance to the escape of this form of energy, acting like a 'one-way energy valve' (Fig. 1). For this reason early glass structures built on to dwellings, or used as garden rooms, were often called 'sun traps'. Solar energy collecting is therefore by no means a new idea – it has been the basic principle of the greenhouse since this form of gardening originated! Although some plastics do trap solar heat to some extent, the degree of trapping varying considerably according to the chemical nature of the plastic, none is as effective as glass. (See also Solar heating p. 34.)

From the aesthetic point of view, plastics also come way down the scale. None keep their sparkling clarity and brilliance – even if they had it in the first place – for a length of time comparable with glass. I have known glass panes in greenhouses over a hundred years' old to clean up almost as good as new, although it is true that poor quality glass can deteriorate through ageing over many years.

However, it should be understood that my strong criticism of plastics is directed to when they are used indiscriminately as glass substitutes. Plastic greenhouses have definite, and also unique, applications, although these are rarely brought to attention. This is a pity, since a proper understanding would allow the advantages of plastics to be exploited and avoid the disappointment invariably arising through misuse. (See Plastic greenhouses, p. 21, and the sections on Glazing systems, p. 16.)

GREENHOUSE SHAPE

In recent years there have been attempts to depart from the conventional greenhouse shapes (Fig. 2). Circular forms (six or more sides), not actually new and often employed for ornamental Victorian structures, domes, and some quite 'off-beat' designs are currently marketed. However, unless you want a green-house which must also function as an architectural feature, I recommend that you avoid the non-conventional; it is rather like trying to improve on the wheel!

The SPAN ROOF greenhouse, shaped like a simple barn or tent, is the most convenient to work in, and allows the best use of space usually right up close to the sides.

Glass is not completely transparent to light, about 10 to 20% of visible light being absorbed, the greater amount in the red region of the spectrum. The DUTCH LIGHT shape with sloping sides is an attempt to keep this light absorption to the minimum. The sun is low in the sky in winter and, by setting the glass sides as near to a right angle as possible to the direction of the sun's rays, the rays will have the least thickness of glass to travel through.

Fig. 2 Greenhouse shapes most practical for a home greenhouse.
(A) Generally useful is the 'barn' or span roof shape.
(B) The Dutch light shape is popular, but sides with a slope of more than about 10° can restrict headroom and working space.
(C) Lean-to. This can also be of Dutch light design.
(D) Circular or many-sided round house.
(E) Curvilinear or mansard shape becomes more practical with increasing width, and is then often fitted with double doors.
Shaded areas represent optional brick or timber walling which can be partial or complete around the greenhouse base as preferred.

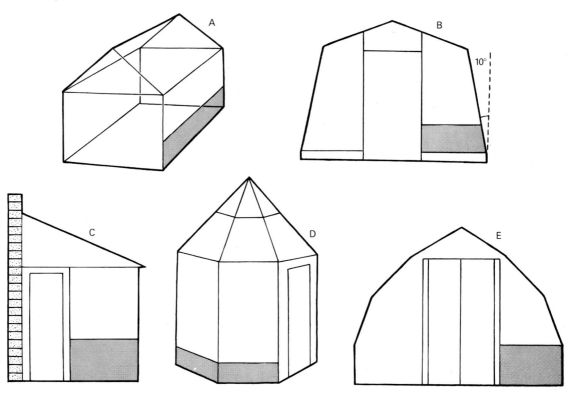

Plate 1 The author's lean-to greenhouse which is north facing. A wooden framed greenhouse is generally considered to be more pleasing to the eye than an aluminium structure, but is subject to maintenance problems.

The extra light so gained may be of some value to the professional grower where early crops are essential to profits. Where the home gardener is concerned, I am personally very doubtful whether sloping sides are of any noticeable advantage. Sometimes a greater stability may be achieved, worth consideration in very windy areas. Sides set at a very great angle can be a definite disadvantage owing to obstruction of head room and restriction of height for plant growth. The term 'Dutch light' has, in the past, much more involved associations with professional growing methods, employing portable and movable 'lights' (large framed panes of glass), but I am omitting a full account of these to save space for matters more important to the home gardener.

The LEAN-TO can have a vertical or sloped side, and is often an extremely useful structure. It can do all the jobs of a span roof house, but the rear wall against which the building is set is particularly useful for climbing plants. Placed against a dwelling with communicating door, it can become a conservatory (Plate 1), sun room, garden room, or even a kind of home extension and a place to sit in and relax – ideal for house plants!

The lean-to has several specialist applications such as fruit growing, and is also one of the most economical structures to heat. With a south-facing aspect, and against a substantial wall of brick or concrete, it becomes an extremely effective solar energy trap. Sometimes enough warmth will be held by the wall to keep the greenhouse frost free overnight.

However, too much sun is not always desirable, and a shaded lean-to will often make a good home for many of the popular ornamental plants from early spring onwards if it can be kept just frost free or, alternatively, if used for housing them for their display period only. (See also The conservatory, p. 184.)

TOTAL/PARTIAL GLAZING

The availability of the extent of glazing in the greenhouse structure is variable. It can be *total* as in the glass-to-ground house, or *partial* as in a greenhouse with base walls made from timber or brick and occasionally asbestos sheet. The base wall house is sometimes called a *plant house*, and is usually fitted with staging to about waist level. The plant house is mostly devoted to accommodating pot plants not demanding much height and placed on the staging. The understage area may also be

15

useful for shade loving plants, and it can be used for storing *clean* horticultural materials and tools.

The base walls of a plant house usually give good heat insulation, so that in some circumstances heating can be less costly than when more glass is involved, more especially when high temperatures are held in winter. However, on sunny open sites, base walls can obstruct the entry of sunlight, so there may be an appreciable loss of 'free' sun heat.

Base walls for a lean-to conservatory may give some degree of privacy if the structure is also used for living in, and the site is overlooked by neighbours. It is also possible to get greenhouse designs with a base wall along one side and glass-to-ground along the other.

For a general purpose greenhouse my personal preference is for the *totally glazed* type. Such a house is extremely versatile suiting all *popular* plants and crops. Conditions of good light are always worth having, since it is easy enough to shade artificially if necessary. In my experience, where plants are grown at relatively low winter temperatures from frost free to about 7°C (45°F) a totally glazed bright greenhouse results in healthier plants, of generally better quality than when light is more restricted, without an excessive extra expenditure in heating. (See also Double glazing, p. 34.)

It is now possible to obtain greenhouse designs with removable timber base panels. These structures can be quickly converted from base wall to glass-to-ground whenever required, making them even more versatile. A greenhouse with very dwarf walls, where it is set alongside a pathway or there is extensive cultivation in the greenhouse at ground level, may be useful to prevent accidental glass breakage. For most practical purposes it can be regarded as totally glazed.

FRAMEWORK AND GLAZING SYSTEMS

Aluminium alloy

The introduction of aluminium alloy has revolutionized greenhouse framework in recent years, although it has in fact been with us for over a century! It is now a well-tested material and ideal for horticultural use. It does not warp, corrode, rot, or become attacked by insects. It is extremely strong and lasts more than a lifetime with negligible deterioration. For people who do not like the harsh metallic appearance of 'raw' aluminium, various attractive decorative finishes, electro-deposited or stove enamelled, can now be obtained, white and green being popular colours. The alloy is lightweight and easy to transport, making it excellent material for DIY erection kits. The strength of the glazing bars means that they can be kept quite narrow and the maximum light is admitted.

Steel framework

Steel framework has some similar advantages but, even when galvanised or painted, is very prone to corrosion and rusting. It is also considerably heavier.

Timber framework

This has served as a traditional greenhouse building material since protected cultivation was first introduced. Provided a good quality timber is employed it can last well for many years. However, it is liable to rot, warp, and become damaged by wood-boring insects. Wooden houses must be well constructed, with adequate struts and braces, to avoid eventual sagging of the ridge bar and bulging of the eaves – very common faults.

However, the pleasing appearance of natural timber, such as teak (rather expensive) or the so-called 'red cedar' makes a wise choice where aesthetics are important and where a possible architectural clash with natural or period surroundings must be avoided. The so-called Western red cedar is now extremely popular, and ideal for the home greenhouse if you must have timber. It is very good looking, has excellent durability and is relatively inexpensive compared with teak. Do remember that all wood will need regular timber preservation treatment or painting to remain in good condition. For large structures this can be expensive, inconvenient, and time consuming. Always use proper proprietary timber treatment products which have been formulated for use where there are living plants – fumes from some products not so formulated can be toxic to plant life. *Never use creosote* in any circumstances.

A popular-sized cedar greenhouse, 1.93 m (6 ft 5 in) wide × 2.85 m (9 ft 6 in) long. Note the part boarding that allows tomatoes or other tall plants to be grown on one side and plants that like shade on the other side.

This heavyweight Dutch style cedar greenhouse cuts down light refraction to give plants as much light as possible. Size: 2.4 m (8 ft) wide × 3.8 m (12 ft 8 in) long.

A compact aluminium greenhouse which has excellent headroom and the wide, sliding door makes for easy access. Size: 2.55 m (8 ft 6 in) wide × 1.95 m (6 ft 6 in) long.

A larger aluminium greenhouse, 2.55 m (8 ft 6 in) wide × 3.75 m (12 ft 6 in) long, ideal for the serious amateur gardener.

1. **Making more geraniums** Take geranium (pelargonium) cuttings from a healthy mature plant. Use the shoot tips.

2. Take off the lower leaves and the scaly 'stipules' that grow below them. The two topmost leaves can remain.

3. Make a clean cut with a knife immediately below a leaf joint so that the cutting is 8–10 cm (3–4 in) long.

4. Insert the cuttings to half their depth around the edge of a pot of cutting compost. Kept moist but well ventilated they'll root in a few weeks.

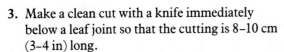

This heated propagator base is large enough to accommodate three individual seed trays.

This heated propagator has a moulded clear plastic top with adjustable air vents, specially designed to ensure that condensation is directed to the edges of the tray. The propagator is thermostatically controlled and provides even heat distribution.

Glazing systems

Nearly all modern prefabricated greenhouses employ various methods of patent glazing, using cushion strips and clips. The old linseed oil putty is rarely used except on some of the more traditional timber designs. If you do have to use putty for timber frames, it should be employed for bedding the glass only – do not run the putty on top of the glass as is done with domestic glazing. It is unnecessary, wasteful, and adds too much weight to the roof glazing bars.

Because of its tendency to go hard and crack with age, linseed oil putty has now been largely replaced with mastics. These should always be used for glazing metal framework. Mastic never sets really hard. It remains adhesive, yet pliable and allows the frame and glass to expand and contract with temperature changes. Thus leaking and cracking of the glass is less liable to occur.

In some timber Dutch light designs, the glass merely slides closely into slots in the glazing bars. Contary to what might be expected, rain rarely gets in, so putty is unnecessary.

EXTENSIONS AND COMPARTMENTS

It is not unusual for the keen greenhouse gardener to soon wish to expand activities. Some makes of greenhouse are designed with this in mind, and extra units can be bought as 'extras' and fitted easily at any time. That is, if you have remembered to leave space on the site.

Compartments, formed by fitting interior partitions with communicating doors, are also possible to fit extras and are supplied by some firms. By means of compartments you can have several different plant environments all under the same roof. For example, you can have a 'cold house' section at the entrance door end, giving access via a partition door to a central warm house, this leading on through another door to a cool, far-end compartment. Note that the warmest part should be the central section. Another idea involving compartments is to section off a small area of the greenhouse for heating in winter, leaving the rest empty until the spring rush and demand for more space, thus cutting your heating bill to the minimum. Simple temporary partitions can be made with thick polythene sheeting.

SPECIALIZED DESIGNS

Certain ornamental plants and food crops have become sufficiently important to warrant special greenhouse designs. This does not mean to say that the ordinary home grower will not get reasonably satisfying results by including these plants in the 'mixed' greenhouse. Specific ideal designs for such plants as orchids, alpines, carnations, and vines, are described in the appropriate places in this book.

A special greenhouse is not always vital. The totally glazed greenhouse is remarkably adaptable and can be used with excellent results for carnations, alpines, cacti and other succulents, various fruits, salad crops, and vines and the popular combination of tomatoes followed by chrysanthemums – all are light lovers. The plant house will give good results with orchids, exotic ferns and foliage, and most subjects preferring slight to heavy shade and moderate winter warmth.

A useful special design often overlooked is the shed-greenhouse combined. The shed section can make a very useful potting compartment and store for pots and greenhouse materials and equipment. There are two forms of structure: one with the greenhouse as a lean-to against the shed, and the other with the shed built on as an extension. Preferably there should be a door communicating with the greenhouse section in both cases.

PLASTIC GREENHOUSES

Greenhouses made from the more rigid plastics and longer lasting types, such as ICI Novolux, are the obvious choice where there are small children or risk of damage by vandals; the sound of crashing glass seems to attract from everywhere around! Easily portable and removable plastic houses, especially the polythene type, really come into their own when you wish to use the ground soil for growing; the structures can then be rotated with the crop. For a permanent greenhouse it is most unwise to use the ground soil for more than the first year. Commercial growers have found polythene tunnels, the plastic being stretched over metal looped frames, very useful for the more hardy crops needing little more than weather protection. Salad crops, many cut flowers and hardy pot plants can be grown well. For the home gardener, polythene tents tailor made to fit over a metal frame are supplied. In all cases make sure there is good ventilation and avoid maintaining wet and humid conditions. Condensation can be a great nuisance, because water droplets remain on the plastic and do not form a film as on a glass surface. The droplets cut light entry and should be tapped off at every opportunity. Structures with corrugated plastic roofs may constantly shower drips unless the roof is well sloped, the water droplets collecting along the bottoms of the corrugations.

Take great care when erecting to see that the plastic is well secured. Most designs are extremely vulnerable to wind damage, and I have known plastic houses to take off like balloons and disappear – an explanation for some UFO sightings?

Attention has already been brought to the non-permanent nature of plastic. When first introduced plastics were so cheap that frequent replacement made them practical. Nowadays they are not such a wise investment, so very careful thought should be given to their suitability before purchase.

BUILDING YOUR OWN GREENHOUSE

Nowadays it is doubtful whether it is worthwhile to build your own greenhouse, unless you want something out of the ordinary or to fit an awkward space or site. The leading manufacturers have the advantage of cheaper bulk buying of raw materials and mass production with specially designed machinery – making your own rarely works out cheaper, or an improvement on a bought, prefabricated house.

There are craftsmen firms who specialize in custom-made, fine quality greenhouses and conservatories, but the cost will understandably be high.

The rigid plastics could be very useful to the DIY enthusiast but, for reasons already given, should not be employed indiscriminately. They could, however, perhaps partially replace glass, particularly where a high degree of heat insulation is required. Several of the newer rigid plastics, such as 'Norplex' and 'Correx' have a double-walled cellular structure, rather like corrugated cardboard. This makes them excellent heat insulators. The very tough polycarbonate plastic is sold in similar form. Some of these cellular plastics are available in a range of colours. Generally it is unwise to use anything but *clear* near to where you are growing plants, but the neutral colours or opalescent forms could be employed where a high degree of shade is needed.

A problem with the cellular plastics is that water (condensation) and dirt can find its way in and can become almost impossible to remove. Special sealing tape is now available and should be used along the open edge before employing cut panels for 'glazing'. If you are making timber frameworks *never* treat the wood with creosote. This can severely stain or damage many plastics as well as being poisonous to plants. An ideal timber treatment in this case is 'Woody'. This is water based and can be obtained to give a red cedar or dark oak finish. It is completely non toxic to plants and does not produce poisonous vapours.

3 SITING AND ERECTION; FRAMES AS ACCESSORIES

RATES AND LEGALITIES

Before erecting a greenhouse, indeed before buying, it is wise to check whether there would be any objections. Also, it is a matter of courtesy to see neighbours, if it is to be put near a boundary. If the ground is rented, sometimes any structure erected could become the legal property of the landlord, so that it could not be taken away if you moved. If you are a freeholder, any deed of covenant could restrict building and should be consulted. In fact there is very rarely any objection to the average small home greenhouse. Rate assessment is also unlikely – unless the structure is to be built on to a dwelling as, for example, a lean-to conservatory. Greenhouses over 28.3 cu m (1000 cu ft) may be rateable, but buildings that can be regarded as 'portable', such as a kit form structure that can be taken down at any time, may not be. Your local authority is usually very helpful and will advise. When a rate is payable it is usually very modest

THE SITE

Because it can have a dramatic influence on the amount of light reaching the greenhouse, the site may have a corresponding effect on what you will be able to grow. In the home garden the choice of site is often limited, but always look for plenty of light. As already mentioned, it is easy enough to provide shade artificially when wanted, but light as powerful as daylight is a problem. If only a shaded place can be found, there is no need to despair since there are plenty of plants you can grow, but the choice will have to be adjusted to suit conditions. It is foolish to attempt growing the light lovers, many of which rate high in popularity. (See Choosing plants, p. 8.)

A site near the dwelling house can be a definite advantage. There is easier access which will encourage more attention during inclement weather, and it is simpler and cheaper to run services like natural gas, water, and electricity, which could all prove extremely helpful. It would also be easier to transport solid or liquid fuels.

At one time it was a common practice to hide away the greenhouse at the bottom of the garden. A well-constructed greenhouse need not be an eyesore – why not, when possible, make it a feature? In my own garden I have made two part of the 'landscape'. One, for example, used as a display house, is mounted on a raised area reached by stone steps and flanked by ornamental pots. The greenhouse flowers can be seen through the glass from outside and the general effect is quite decorative.

Situations to avoid are large trees in close vicinity that cast shade (particularly evergreens, which may exude gummy substances on to the glass, shed heavy cones or harbour diseases); hollow ground or the foot of slopes (which may get waterlogged or form frost pockets); and very windy and exposed places. However, in the last case, protection can be given by a suitable windbreak, such as a low wall, fence or hedge, placed at a distance to reduce the wind speed but not cast shade. High velocity, cold wind can cause a serious loss of warmth from the greenhouse.

Choosing a greenhouse in relation to its surroundings has been discussed. Where there are problems I have found *white* framework seems to blend almost anywhere, whether the home or garden is 'olde worlde' or 'futuristic modern'.

The ideal orientation for the conventional

rectangular greenhouse is, in my opinion, for the roof ridge to run east-west, or as near as possible. You then get maximum sunlight in winter and there is need to shade only the south side in summer. The south side is useful for such crops as tomatoes grown in low containers if this side can be kept glass to ground. The north side, fitted with staging, will accommodate all the favourite ornamentals.

FOUNDATIONS

The word 'foundation' often conjures up visions of laborious concrete mixing and heavy transportation, but for the average home greenhouse this is rarely necessary. However, it is *extremely wise* to take great care with the foundation. Movement or subsidence after erection can cause serious problems difficult to correct. Most greenhouse suppliers give full recommendations for the foundation most suited to the design and size – make sure you follow them. Some firms supply 'plinths' or 'curbing' as a base at little extra cost, and this is well worth having.

More recently introduced are designs to make the laying of foundations very much easier. These use 'ground anchors', which are strips of metal with widely flared ends. The framework of the greenhouse can be fully erected on firm flat level ground. At points along the base small holes are then dug and the ground anchors bolted on to the base so that one anchor, with the flared end at the bottom, is dipping into each hole. The holes are then filled with concrete. Only about one bucket of concrete should be needed for each hole. After the concrete has set, glazing can be carried out and the greenhouse completed (Fig. 3).

When a conventional concrete foundation is required, it can usually be made by digging a shallow trench along the outline of the greenhouse base, and pouring in a very fluid mix. This will find its own level, especially if lightly tamped or agitated immediately after pouring. Provided fresh cement is employed, there is no need to fear that a liquid mix will not set.

In all cases it is *vital* to use a spirit level for levelling the site, and again *frequently* during the framework construction. Also check all angles, verticals and horizontals, to get them as accurate as possible. Do not carry out erection on freshly dug or disturbed ground. Leave it to settle as long as possible and firm it well before commencing erection.

A brick base wall should always be given a proper concrete foundation and preferably also a damp course layer. The greenhouse suppliers always provide plans for any brickwork or concrete block construction needing to be done. Some people may have to get a professional builder to do this work, but for a small

Fig. 3 'Ground anchor' system of simple foundation.
The frame is completely erected on firmed, level soil. Holes about the size of a bucket are dug at intervals around the base *A*, ground anchors bolted on so that they dip centrally in the holes, and the holes then filled with concrete *B*.

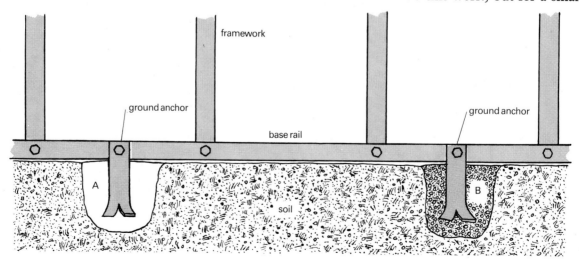

greenhouse it is often not beyond the capabilities of the DIY enthusiast. A useful tip is to coat the finished brick or concrete wall with a modern proprietary water repellent both inside and out. This maintains the clean new look of the wall and discourages slime and algae. It also keeps it dry, which means it has maximum heat insulation.

PUTTING UP THE FRAME

Most small greenhouses can be erected single handed, but the help from another person may be helpful and reduce erection time. The instructions given by suppliers often look formidable, and some still persist in using 'constructional engineering' terms to describe components. Fortunately the best firms usually also *number* each part making identification quite simple. Again the importance of frequent checking for correct angle and levels cannot be over emphasized.

When painting or any form of coating treatment is to be given to metal or timber, it should be done *before* the glass is put in. Red cedar houses are best given a coat of shellac varnish (knotting) before glazing if putty is to be used. This aids adhesion. Where glazing tacks are employed, use a type made from galvanised iron, or preferably brass. Ordinary iron nails or tacks eventually rust and stain the glass.

Raw (untreated) aluminium framework, and galvanised steel, can be painted with an undercoat and gloss paint if desired. Aluminium takes and holds paint well. However, painting will defeat the advantage of the no-maintenance property, since repainting will become necessary eventually.

GLAZING

The glass is usually cut to size when delivered. If you cannot use it immediately, store it out of the wet and where it cannot get soaked by rain. Wet panes stick together and can be quite difficult to separate. Choose dry weather for the glazing operation, and also avoid windy conditions. It is also best not to handle glass when it is very cold and the hands may become chilled.

Most greenhouse gardeners will find the practice of cutting glass useful at some time or other. Always use a steel wheel cutter obtainable from a builders' merchant – avoid 'fancy' devices. Place the glass, which should be clean, on several sheets of newspaper. Make sure the surface is absolutely flat. Measurement marks on the glass can be made with a chinagraph pencil. Oil the cutting wheel, and to guide it use a perfectly straight wooden batten held firmly. Also press firmly on the cutter and bring it towards you from the far end of the guide line. A harsh hissing sound should be heard if the wheel is making a deep scratch on the glass. Avoid going over the same line twice.

To break the glass along the scratch mark, turn it over. Then gently but firmly tap along the underneath of the scratch mark with the 'hammer' end of the glass cutter. A crack which follows the scratch mark will form and can be led along by tapping just in front. When the crack has traversed the entire length of the scratch, the glass should fall apart or can be gently pulled. This is a simple, accurate and easy way to divide glass, *without risk of accidents*. If a very narrow edge of glass has to be removed, such as is often necessary when a pane is just a tiny bit too large, lever it off with one of the notches to be found at the end of the glass cutter. Lever away from the scratched surface.

VENTILATORS, DOORS AND GUTTERS

Extra care should be taken to see that ventilators and doors fit snugly. There must be no gaps to admit uncontrollable draught. Plenty of ventilators are an advantage. You do not have to have them all open at once. If they are well distributed, you can open them according to wind direction and adjust ventilation to give good air change, but not admit gusts damaging to the greenhouse contents. I prefer to have roof vents as high up as possible and side vents low. Lightweight warm air passing out at the top will then draw the heavier, cool, fresh air in at the bottom, causing an efficient flow.

The most popular average size home greenhouse is about 2.5×3 m (8×10 ft) and this size should have at least two ventilators – one roof and one side. Larger houses should have ventilators in proportion. Two ventilators are best placed on opposite sides, but staggered so that air cannot merely pass straight through.

The conventional hinged vent with stay bar is still functional. For a greenhouse side adjacent to a pathway, the louvred vents, which do not open out so far, may be useful, but some tend to admit slight draught.

Sliding doors can be used as adjustable vents and need special care when fitting so that they slide easily and shut tightly. Take even more care in checking angles and levels. Some sliding doors are prone to let in draught, so ensure the design is a good-fitting one when buying.

Many greenhouses now have built-in gutters or guttering is supplied as an extra. A gutter helps to keep the soil around the greenhouse dry and prevent water seeping in. In winter this is a great advantage. Dry conditions will help to conserve warmth (wet soil being a good heat conductor), and the lower humidity will discourage moulds and mildews. Gutter water *must not* be used for watering plants in the greenhouse; this is important (see p. 50).

Frames as accessories

The frame as an important greenhouse adjunct should not be overlooked. Much greenhouse space is often wasted on plants that do not really need the height and could be grown for most of the time in frames. If frames are employed for propagation and growing-on, more of the greenhouse can be devoted to displaying plants when they are in their decorative stages, or for plants that really need the height. It is also cheaper to heat a frame, and frame space is invaluable for the many plants that have to have a dormant or resting period.

As far as design and construction materials are concerned, much of what has already been outlined for greenhouses also applies. Lites (lights), as the 'lids' of frames are called, should for the home gardener be reasonably lightweight and easy to handle. The 'roller frame', with its lites set on rails so that they

can be slid aside, is becoming more popular. Such a frame can be obtained from Alitex.

To help in the growing and temporary accommodation of greenhouse plants, shaded frames are usually more useful. It is therefore common to set them along the north side of an east-west orientated greenhouse. Sometimes it is possible to arrange that the greenhouse heating system also passes some heat to the frames, but soil warming cables are very effective and convenient where there is electricity. The cables can be used much as described for 'propagators' on p. 65.

For using in conjunction with the greenhouse, the bottom of a frame is best covered with plastic sheeting to prevent the entry of soil pests, then with clean shingle to hold moisture and keep the frame air humid when necessary.

FRAMES IN THE GREENHOUSE

The value of frames *inside* the greenhouse is often not realized, or overlooked. A frame can form a 'mini-environment' for plants with special requirements – thus enabling the range of plant types you can grow under one roof to be greatly varied and extended. It can be used for many forcing jobs; for growing numerous winter vegetables that don't demand much height; for producing the now popular seeds sprouts (p. 157), and for all kinds of propagation.

For these operations, the point of the frame is usually to provide a *small* area of elevated temperature which, with the internal site, is possible to maintain with little heat waste and therefore at low cost. In some cases, where the warmth demand is very low, the cost can be negligible.

If you can only afford to have a frost-free greenhouse, but wish to grow a few tropicals, a warmed frame is the answer. You could grow anything, provided it's naturally low growing. The possibilites include many exotic house plants, which you can also propagate, and flowers like the flamboyant cattleyas and other compact orchids. At much lower temperatures you can have a constant source of winter salads like beet, carrot, salad onion, and others (see Chapter 16).

4 INTERIORS AND FITTINGS

THE GREENHOUSE FLOOR

Where the ground soil of the home greenhouse is concerned, many beginners assume that it should be cultivated. This is usually successful for the first year or perhaps for two. If used for longer, the plants invariably deteriorate, some showing signs of distress sooner than others depending on the type.

There are several reasons for this; firstly, the importance of crop rotation has been ignored. Secondly, the soil under cover gets conditions very different from that in the open outdoors. Excess fertilizers and waste products produced by plants are not washed out by rains; the sterilizing effect of the sun's ultraviolet rays, which may deter undesirable fungi and bacteria, does not come into action (uv is absorbed by the glass), and there is an absence of many beneficial predators, including microorganisms, insects and even birds, that keep down plant enemies outside. Thirdly, even frost and freezing have their useful actions. The greenhouse soil therefore soon suffers from 'soil sickness' if intensely cultivated.

For this reason some people try changing the soil every year or so, or washing it out with lots of water. This is laborious and rarely satisfactory. Fresh soil will soon become contaminated if put in contact with infected surroundings. Soil sterilization can be carried out with some success (p. 100), but it is best not to use the ground soil at all after the first year. Vegetable crops, such as tomatoes, are particularly sensitive to soil sickness. All the plants, decorative or edible that the home gardener grows can be cultivated in containers or pots, using proper composts (p. 54).

If the greenhouse has been erected on soil, it should be levelled and firmed and strewn with clean shingle to give a neat pleasing appearance (Plate 2). A line of paving slabs can be run down the centre of the house, or alongside any staging installed, to give more comfort and firmness to the feet. A floor of this type will hold plenty of moisture – important in maintaining summer humidity – but not form puddles.

Sometimes a greenhouse has to be erected on paving, concrete, or even asphalt. This does not matter, but some holes should be knocked through to allow free drainage of any excess water that may be used in summer for damping down. It may also be useful to put down some duck boarding to walk on. (See also the conservatory, p. 184.)

STAGING AND SHELVING

In the older type home greenhouse, staging (Fig. 4) was often a permanent fixture and nearly always the slatted type. This may still be satisfactory for base wall greenhouses. With the now more popular glass-to-ground designs, staging can have two levels. Additional plants can often be grown at floor level as well, since plenty of light gets to them. It is also often convenient to have a more portable form of staging, and one that can be made more adaptable to give better localized conditions for the plants grown on its surface. For example, slatted staging or one with a surface of wire mesh is preferable in winter; it allows a free circulation of air around the plants and better distribution of warmth in heated houses. However, for summer it is usually better to have a solid surface that can be strewn with a moisture absorbing material – evaporation of the water has a cooling effect and maintains good air humidity. A slatted staging can, of course, be covered with plastic

Plate 2 Do not stand pots directly on the floor of a greenhouse if it's soil, gravel or shingle. Interpose pieces of plastic or other material to prevent roots passing through the drainage holes of the pots and into the floor. This is especially vital if a total weedkiller has been employed.

Fig. 4 Types of staging
(*A*) Stout wire mesh. (*B*) Slats – usually timber. (*C*) Shallow tray or plastic sheeting strewn with moisture retaining material. (*D*) Tier type or stepped staging useful for displaying plants.

sheeting for the summer. On this can be spread clean grit or coarse sand, but lightweight vermiculite or a mineral material like Hortag is often now preferred. Fine peat can be used too, and has the advantage that it can be replaced freshly each year, the old material being used in the garden for soil-texture improvement. Personally I prefer annual replacement of the covering material, since it often becomes messy and covered with slime or algae by the end of the autumn.

Modern portable staging is usually made up from aluminium angle and can sometimes be put together to give a variety of forms. Stepped or tiered staging can be useful for display of plants, and staging that can be easily taken down and stored may be useful when the greenhouse is used to accommodate a wide variety of plants over a comparatively short time.

When a slatted or open mesh staging is used for pot plants, and more are grown below, the top level is best covered with thin clear polythene sheet to prevent petals or shed foliage dropping on to plants underneath. Mesh drawn taut is now often employed instead of wooden slats. This should be made from wire or plastic covered wire. Plastic mesh

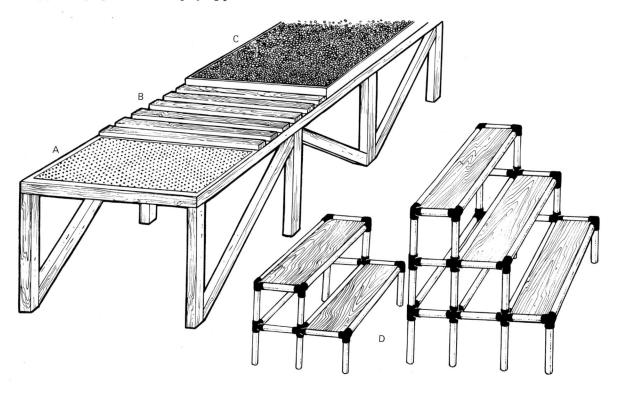

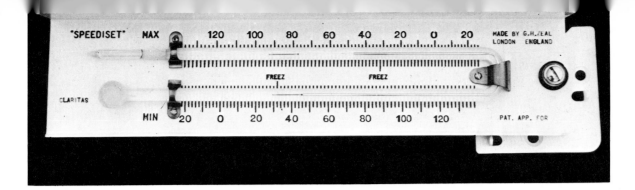

Plate 3 A maximum and minimum thermometer is an absolutely essential piece of equipment. There are a number of designs; the one illustrated is of a swivel type and the indicators are set by turning to a vertical position until they fall to the mercury level. The instrument is then returned to the horizontal. There is no need for magnets as in older designs.

should be avoided – it may become brittle with age and give way under the weight of the plant pots.

Shelving helps to make the most of greenhouse space and can also be useful for the display of plants. It can be constructed in much the same way as described for staging. As well as the conventional shelving fastened to the sides with brackets, sometimes it is suspended from the roof. In such cases be sure the roof is strong enough to take the weight. In all cases shelves should not be put up at random and without due thought to how much light they are likely to obstruct. (See also The potting bench, p. 61.)

THERMOMETERS AND HYGROMETERS

The thermometer, which should be the maximum and minimum type (Plate 3), is an *essential* piece of equipment and there *must* be one in every greenhouse, or section of one if there are compartments. Without this type of thermometer you cannot possibly ascertain how your greenhouse is performing under the influence of changing weather or assess the effectiveness of the heating system if there is one. There are several designs of maximum and minimum thermometer, but they all have indicators which can be set at the temperature of the moment. Any change will *move* the indicators, so that on your return during an absence you can immediately see at a glance

what the lowest and highest temperatures have been.

Sometimes soil thermometers can be useful. These are merely ordinary types with a protected bulb so that they can be thrust deeply into soil or compost. These are particularly useful for checking the temperatures of soil warming apparatus.

The frost forecast thermometer is really a kind of hygrometer (psychrometer) measuring humidity. This must be sited *outside* the greenhouse. The instrument is graduated to indicate when frost is likely. This warning can be very useful to allow time to cover plants or frames, or to check efficiency of heating.

A hygrometer is not really essential, but many beginners may find one useful. It gives a direct reading of atmospheric humidity and will indicate whether the greenhouse air is moist or dry. Most are graduated in units of relative humidity, the technicalities of which need not concern us here. The main point to remember is to aim at 'dry' or lower 'normal' in winter and at 'moist' during the seasons when active growth is being made (see also p. 48).

SUPPLY OF GAS, ELECTRICITY AND WATER

Nowadays natural gas is one of the fuels worth consideration for greenhouse heating since it is not toxic to plants to the extent of coal gas. Installation must be done by a professional contractor.

Whether you wish to use electricity for heating or not, a supply point in the greenhouse can prove invaluable. Many useful accessories such as automation systems, fans, propagators, soil warming, and lighting, need electricity. Again, proper wiring and electrical fittings are essential and the work should be carried out by someone fully acquainted with all safety precautions. Special electrical fittings designed for greenhouses are available.

A water supply is very desirable for two reasons. Mains water is clean and hygienic and, if it is on tap, it will stop the temptation to use gutter water or water that is stored until it becomes foul and stagnant. A mains pressure supply is also useful for operating various automatic or semi-automatic watering systems. A piped supply is always labour saving if the greenhouse is sited far from the dwelling, and avoids getting out the garden hose on frequent occasions for relatively few plants in the greenhouse.

The connection of a water supply is not beyond the capabilities of the average handyman now that alkathene tubing and plastic fittings make the job of plumbing so much easier. I have had alkathene piping on test for very many years, and can thoroughly recommend it; it does not burst when conditions are freezing, even when run above ground. However, any Water Board regulations must be adhered to, and it is wise to consult your local authority. An extra charge is usually made for each extra supply point.

AUTOMATION

At one time, those very many people who have to be away from home all day, or for long periods, were rarely able to get the best from a greenhouse – there were too many problems in the reasonable control of growing conditions, watering being a specially serious worry. A number of important maintenance chores can now be very accurately controlled by automatic methods, so automation has been instrumental in bringing greenhouse gardening within the scope of many more millions of people.

Temperature
Temperature has been automatically controllable by thermostat for a long time and all heating systems should, if possible, be checked for reasonably accurate thermostatic control. The cost of running heating can be very greatly influenced by the relative efficiency of the thermostat. Cheap fuels that cannot be accurately controlled may work out considerably more expensive than those that can. For example, electricity is popularly thought of as expensive, yet it can be the most accurately

thermostatically controlled of all and there need be no waste (see p. 41 and Chapter 5).

Ventilation
This can be very easily and well achieved by electric fans blowing air out of the greenhouse and controlled by thermostat. *Special models* are made for the purpose and to deal with volumes of air to suit all greenhouse sizes. For the home greenhouse only one fan is usually needed. This is best set at the far end high up in the apex. Suppliers always give full instructions and recommendations.

Where there is no electricity, excellent ventilator operation can be obtained by fitting a thermal expansion piston device. This takes the form of a piston containing a special compound, that gives a good expansion with rise in temperature and subsequent contraction on cooling. This movement controls a piston connected to levers operating the ventilator. This is another device I have had on test since it was introduced, and can recommend it with confidence. Full fitting and temperature adjustment instructions are supplied by the various makers, but each device will usually only operate one ventilator. The cost of equipping the many ventilators of a large greenhouse would be high, and it would probably be better to employ an electric fan in this case.

Watering
Much attention has been paid to automatic watering and there are now numerous systems on the market. However, some are, in my opinion, too complicated and 'fiddly' to be reliably practical, and some are very badly designed and will inevitably fail after they have been in operation for some time. My advice here is to patronize a well-established and reputable firm when buying equipment for automatic watering (see Appendix).

The capillary sand-bench watering system was first introduced by the National Institute of Agricultural Engineering, and has been popular for many years. It is still used, but the sand is being replaced by more lightweight materials and recently by capillary matting. The basic principle of capillary watering is that water will rise against gravity through any porous substance – like liquid goes through a wick. If a bed of sand or similarly absorbent material, or matting, is kept constantly moist, and pots are stood on it so that the compost in them comes into close contact via the drainage holes, the moisture will rise up into the pots (Plate 4). As the plants use up the water, it is automatically replenished provided the base material is kept moist. This can be done also by wicks, dipping into a water reservoir maintained at constant level by a suitable float valve, and other methods described here.

By far the most convenient capillary system for the home greenhouse is matting. This is a synthetic fibre material very much like thick felt in appearance. It will absorb and hold a remarkable amount of water. A simple set-up I have employed with success, is to place the matting on the staging, on top of a layer of polythene sheet, and allow it to overlap the front edge at intervals to dip into plastic guttering fastened just below the front of the staging (Fig. 5). This gutter is kept at constant water level by a small constant level valve obtainable for such purposes. The staging must be flat and level, and the matting can be cut to fit with an ordinary pair of scissors. A supply of water from the mains, or from a tank

Plate 4 Plants on a capillary sand bench in the author's greenhouse. Note that the staging has been first covered with sheet polythene. Instead of sand, capillary matting is now often used.

Fig. 5 Automatic watering with capillary matting.
(*A*) Staging must be flat and level and covered with plastic sheet (polythene) if slated or of open type. (*B*) Matting cut to size with scissors and lapped over edge of staging so that it dips into a plastic gutter (*C*). The gutter is connected to a constant level valve by tubing (*D*). (*E*) Side view of arrangement. (*F*) Plastic pots with large drainage holes must be used.

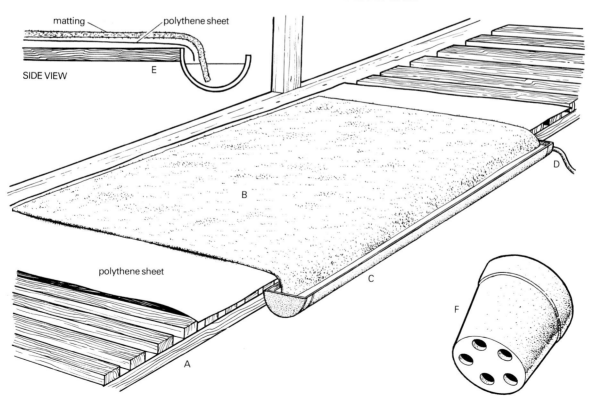

matting   polythene sheet

SIDE VIEW   E

polythene sheet

B

C

D

A

F

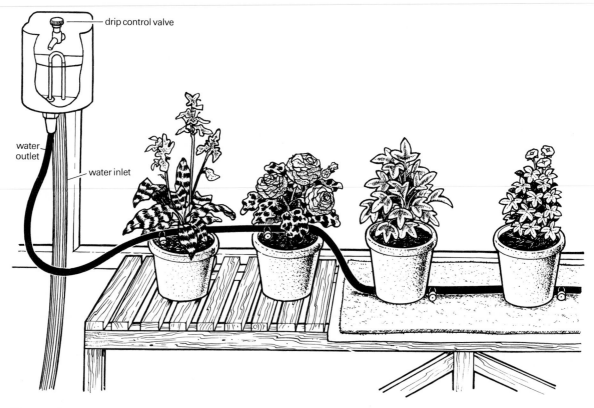

drip control valve

water outlet

water inlet

Fig. 6 Siphon system of automatic watering. A small tank is fitted with a drip valve and a siphon. The frequency of filling and hence siphoning is manually adjusted initially by means of the drip valve to suit the conditions. The system can be used to keep capillary matting damp if desired, as well as for trickle irrigation.

filled when necessary from a hose, can be used to keep the gutter topped up. To make plastic guttering watertight, Araldite or a similar adhesive can be employed, and the water supply tubing sealed in with the same material.

The pots used on a capillary system must be plastic and have a good drainage hole area. The pots must not be crocked, but some coarse peat can be put at the bottom if the compost tends to fall through. An unfortunate problem with the capillary system is that plant roots often grow through the drainage holes and into the capillary material, even into matting. This can be a nuisance when moving the pots, but the same thing can happen when pots are stood for any length of time on any absorbent material holding moisture whether automatically controlled or not.

Watering by means of a form of trickle irrigation avoids the problem of 'rooting through' if the pots are stood on a non-porous surface. The water is delivered to each pot via a nozzle, sometimes adjustable, the amount or frequency of the water being controlled by an 'electronic' or porous block 'leaf' or photoelectrically as described below. An early semi-automatic method was to connect the trickle pipeline to a small reservoir via a siphon (Fig. 6). The rate at which the reservoir fills is controlled by a drip feed manually, and hence the frequency of siphoning. This method needs some time for testing to get the frequency of watering right, but this frequency will remain relatively constant regardless of the greenhouse conditions and changes in water requirements. Fully automatic control is therefore preferable. Trickle irrigation methods are, in any case, in my opinion, rather inconvenient if you have lots of pots. In fact, they are hardly suited to watering the entire contents of a greenhouse. For a row of special plants, such as tomatoes, cucumbers, or chrysanthemums, the method becomes more practical.

To sense the need for watering and to control its supply automatically, according to

Plate 5 The photograph shows a small mist propagation unit which also illustrates some principles of automatic electronic irrigation and watering. In the centre can be seen the misting jet controlled by an electromagnetic valve in the water supply to the jet (lower right of picture). The valve is operated by the 'electronic leaf' to be seen standing slightly to the left of the misting jet.

the requirements of plants, two devices have been in use for some time. The first was the 'electronic leaf'. The sensor depends on the conductivity of a film of water between two contacts. When this film dries up, the micro-current ceases and this activates a relay operating a water valve passing water to the delivery system (Plate 5). Similar devices, not needing electricity and depending on the evaporation of moisture from a porous block, can do the same sort of job. Unfortunately these devices are liable to interference from the lime deposited by hard water and also from slimes and algae. They must be cleaned and checked regularly.

More recently the photoelectric method has overcome this problem. The sensor in this case is a photocell and the water flow is controlled according to the light conditions, which is a measure of the sun's energy, and hence the evaporation rate and the rate of plant photosynthesis. I have had this system on test from the experimental stages and have found it excellent. All these sensor-controlled devices can operate a wide range of water delivery systems: capillary, nozzles, or misting jets for overhead irrigation. They usually activate a water valve controlled by an electromagnet. Overhead watering is not generally recommended, since flowers can be damaged if kept constantly wet. Misting is useful for automatic humidity control, if the jets are sited away from plants, and invaluable for mist propagation (p. 70).

5 HEATING – EQUIPMENT AND HEAT CONSERVATION

SOLAR HEATING

In recent years there has been much publicity given to solar heating. A serious effort to harness the sun's energy is long overdue, but where the greenhouse is concerned there is much muddled thinking – the glass greenhouse has been a highly effective heat trap since it was first introduced. During sunny weather the problem is more involved with *keeping down* temperature rather than trapping warmth. If the sun's heat could be simply stored for use when it is not shining and overnight, this would definitely be of great use. So far, where the home gardener is in mind, a convenient means of storing heat has not been developed. In commercial experiments, heat insulated tanks of water have been employed, but the equipment is all very bulky and lacks practical elegance for scaling down. So-called 'solar greenhouses' so far offered to the home gardeners have really been little more than designs to trap more *short term* sun heat, which could be more nuisance than it is worth.

A lean-to set against a substantial brick or concrete wall and facing south, is already a fairly effective heat trap. The wall absorbs warmth during the day and radiates it at night. A well-filled greenhouse will also store useful warmth. Substantial staging, the floor, the compost in pots or containers, and anything like stored, clean clay pots or bins or compost, will take up day warmth and give it out over night. If there is space to spare, a row of concrete blocks set to face the sun along the south side of a greenhouse will also act as storage heaters. They are even more effective if painted with matt black emulsion.

The greenhouse design once called 'the pit' could well be revived. This is part sunken and can be used like a dwarf wall greenhouse. The surrounding soil holds warmth and also acts as effective heat insulator. This type of house was often used for high temperature plants and propagation. If you want a bulk supply of soil to make a rock garden or elevated mini-landscape, the pit is still practical. After digging out and bricking up the sides, a dwarf wall type frame, which can be bought ready made, can merely be set in position. Erection is little different from putting a framework on a brick dwarf wall, except that a few steps down will have to be built at the door end of the greenhouse.

DOUBLE GLAZING

There is also a great deal of misunderstanding about double glazing. The fact that it will cut an enormous amount of heat loss is indisputable. Unfortunately, in my own experience, it is impractical for the greenhouse. Unless sealed-unit glass panes (hermetically sealed to enclose specially dried air) – which are very expensive – are employed in the construction, there is invariably trouble from condensation. Once water gets between the panes, algae and slimes follow in due course. It is also remarkable how dirt and insects find a way in. This means that all the interior glass panelling has to be taken down for cleaning at intervals, no convenient matter when the house is full of plants. A double glazed greenhouse was marketed many years ago and the idea is not *new*; it did not prove successful. Bearing in mind the extra expense of glass and the problem of its cleaning, it is usually simpler and more convenient to get the 'double glazing' effect by using plastic film. This can also be put up and taken down with less risk of disaster. Moreover, it is questionable whether for a greenhouse *permanent* double glazing is an advantage anyway.

LINING A GREENHOUSE

The heat insulation effect of double glazing is due to the poor heat conductivity of air – it is important that the air is *static*, and not changing or moving by convection. A layer of air about 2–2.5 cm (¾–1 in) is an ideal insulator. Less does not give such sufficient insulation. With more, there is risk of air movement due to convection – moving air will accelerate heat loss. An air layer can be trapped around the sides of the greenhouse by using plastic film; it does not have to be glass. Originally *thin clear polythene* was employed, and this is *still* for a variety of reasons *the most efficient*. Many of the fancy lining materials now marketed, such as so-called 'thermal screens' are far too opaque. If the light reaching plants is seriously reduced, warmer conditions can be a disadvantage. Indeed, before lining a greenhouse the possible winter light demands should be given careful thought. It may be a better investment to pay for more heat rather than cut light and have a batch of sickly plants as a result.

Lining with plastic nearly always brings problems with condensation which collects on plastic surfaces as droplets. This reduces light entry still further. It can be very excessive where interior, non-flued heaters are used which burn gas or paraffin – both produce water vapour on combustion. Lining really comes into its own where electrical heating is employed, particularly fan heating. In such cases ventilation can often be cut entirely during severe cold spells with enormous saving of heat, and fuel bills. When there is electrical heating there is also less trouble from condensation. However, in all cases ventilators should be lined separately so that they can be opened when necessary, and condensation should be tapped off the plastic at every opportunity. Timber frames can be lined by simple drawing pin fastening. With metal frames, small pieces of wooden batten can be glued on at intervals to take the pins. There are now numerous fixing systems made available by the suppliers of lining materials, but I repeat: thin clear polythene is still the best, and heat loss can be cut by about 40%.

IS ARTIFICIAL HEATING WORTHWHILE?

Although a lot can be done with an unheated greenhouse, just a little artificial warmth – even to keep out frost – enormously widens the range of plants that can be grown. The benefit may well be only pleasure rather than a high financial return in the value of the plants grown, but the cost of the warmth need not be excessive, no more than many domestic and personal luxuries commonplace today. Moreover, the possibilities of the greenhouse in the production of winter salads and other foods are worth exploring for health and aesthetic reasons, apart from their money value. In some cases a considerable saving can be made – in the production of bedding plants and house plants, as examples. A little artificial warmth will allow full exploitation of this aspect.

To maintain *high* temperatures does become costly. For this reason I have devoted most of this book to plants with less exacting temperature requirements. There are, however, some very desirable, warmth-loving plants not beyond the scope of the home greenhouse if a little individual consideration is given. I have brought this to the reader's attention where necessary.

COMMON SENSE HEAT CONSERVATION

A few simple precautions can have a dramatic effect on what you need to spend on heating. It is extremely important not to have the artificial heating system raising the temperature higher than is absolutely necessary for the plants' safety. A few unnecessary degrees in excess will waste an enormous amount of heat.

Draughts must not be allowed. Just a small chink in the structure, letting in a gust of icy air, can completely counteract any benefit from a heater.

Windbreaks have already been mentioned. Lagging of base walls or sides may also be useful if serious heat loss must be checked, but any material used must always be prevented from soaking up water and so losing its effectiveness. Remember that warm air rises. This means that if you wish to line a greenhouse only partially, the roof is the most useful place to seal. Heaters that give out a localized current of warm air that rises to the area of roof immediately above, can also waste heat owing to overheating at that point. This area is therefore another good place to site some lining.

The positioning of heaters generally should be given thought. They should always be placed to get maximum distribution of the heat evolved. Pipes or tubular electric heaters are much more effective if well distributed around the house, not all banked together in one place as so often seen. Gas and paraffin heaters should ideally have some attachment to improve distribution of the hot air and prevent it rising straight up above the heater to the greenhouse roof. Fan heaters present few problems, but the best site is usually at the far end from the door with the blast of warm air directed towards it.

To save heating costs, some people prefer to shut down the greenhouse for the mid-winter months, bringing the heating system into operation only from late winter to spring. This is the period when there is usually much plant activity and much sowing, propagating, and starting of plants into growth, to be done. At this time, the sun's warmth will be increasing, and will give a lot of free supplement to the artificial warmth. Although this shutdown method means a certain limitation to what can be grown during mid-winter, it may be a useful practice for people who live in very cold winter areas.

The importance of always looking out for a heating system that can be accurately controlled by thermostat has already been emphasized.

The advantages of a bright open site for the greenhouse has already been brought to attention. Plenty of sunlight in winter will greatly reduce the need for artificial heating. Even a little sunshine can elevate the temperature to a very comfortable level, although it may be well below freezing outside. The importance of keeping the exterior glass clean in winter can

be appreciated. As well as letting maximum light in, clean bright shiny glass also helps conserve interior warmth. Remember your school physics – dark rough surfaces are good radiators, smooth bright ones are poor radiators.

HEATER-OUTPUT REQUIREMENTS

Heating equipment must have a heat output to balance that lost by the greenhouse when the interior temperature is at the minimum required by the plants and the temperature outside is at the lowest expected. The loss can be calculated approximately, by taking into account the heat conductivity of the materials of construction, their area, and the temperatures involved.

To save you the complications and time of calculation, I have worked out heat losses for a wide range of greenhouse sizes (Table 1), which also cover the most popular and practical range of temperatures for the home greenhouse.

The heat loss is measured in terms of BTU/h (British Thermal Units per hour) or Watts (W) for electrical measurement. (1000 W approximately equals 3412 BTU/h.)

The figures in the table are for glass-to-ground greenhouses and assume a lowest possible outside temperature of minus 7°C(20°F) or 12 degrees of frost. For dwarf-wall or boarded-base, and lean-to, structures, the figures are lower, but it is wise to always err on the side of slight over-rating. With a thermostatically controlled heating system there is no fear of waste. The figures in the table can therefore be taken as a rough guide for most types of structure.

Heaters with unknown heat output should not be bought or installed – unless they are small types for emergency use. Permanent heating systems should not be considered or selected until the heat requirement of the greenhouse is known and the right heat output for the heating equipment can be certain. Nowadays most reputable suppliers of greenhouse heaters or heating systems will state definitely the heat output of their various designs (but see also Table 1, p. 41).

A colourful display of assorted pot plants. Note the achimenes and pendulous begonias, also displayed in hanging pots to add extra interest.

Abutilon hybrid. Very easy and quick flowering from seed. The hybrid illustrated is a new one I am growing called 'Bella'. It is more compact and free flowering; note that the flowers 'look you in the face', rather than droop, as in most other varieties.

Ipomea 'Heavenly Blue' is a favourite variety for its glorious vivid blue colour, and an easy annual climber from seed.

Cineraria 'Spring Glory' forms dwarf compact plants, fine for 13-cm (5-in) pots, and flowers for 8–10 weeks with a wide range of vibrant colours.

Coleus (Solenostemon). A group of varieties sown by the author in March, and photographed in summer. Bottom left, in small pots is a new variety, 'Scarlet Poncho', with low spreading habit and especially useful for hanging baskets.

Impatiens 'Super Elfin' is a compact large flowered Busy Lizzie for pots and has brilliant colours.

Exacum affine 'Starlight Fragrance'. This variety has not lost its sweet scent, as is the case with some other varieties bred for larger flowers.

TABLE 1. HEATING EQUIPMENT HEAT OUTPUT REQUIREMENT (approximate)

| *Size* | | 2°C (35°F) | | 4°C (40°F) | | 7°C (45°F) | | 10°C (50°F) | |
m	(ft)	BTU/h	Watts	BTU/h	Watts	BTU/h	Watts	BTU/h	Watts
1.5×1.8	(5×6)	3000	900	4000	1200	5000	1500	6000	1800
1.8×1.8	(6×6)	3600	1000	4800	1400	6000	1800	7000	2100
1.8×2.4	(6×8)	4200	1200	5700	1700	7100	2000	8600	2500
1.8×3.0	(6×10)	5200	1500	7000	2000	8750	2500	10000	2900
1.8×4.2	(6×14)	6200	1800	8400	2500	10500	3000	12500	3700
2.4×2.4	(8×8)	5200	1500	7000	2000	8750	2500	10400	3000
2.4×3.0	(8×10)	5800	1700	7800	2300	9750	2900	11700	3400
2.4×3.6	(8×12)	6600	1900	8800	2600	11000	3200	13200	3900
2.4×4.2	(8×14)	7000	2000	9300	2700	11600	3400	14000	4200
3.0×3.0	(10×10)	7300	2100	9800	2900	12200	3500	14600	4300
3.0×4.5	(10×15)	9700	2800	12900	3800	16100	4700	19200	5600
3.0×6.0	(10×20)	11800	3500	15800	4700	19700	5800	23600	6900

ASSESSING HEATING COSTS

A rough estimate of heating cost may be useful in helping to make a decision about heating a greenhouse. Table 1 gives the heater rating for the size of greenhouse and temperatures in question so, with a knowledge of the current price of the relevant fuel, it is usually a simple matter to work out a very approximate cost, knowing the heat output of various fuels, which is as follows:

Electricity	3 412 BTU/unit
Paraffin	157 000 BTU/gal
Fuel oil	165 000 BTU/gal
Solid fuels	12 000–14 000 BTU/lb
Natural gas	100 000 BTU/therm
Liquid propane/ butane	21 500 BTU/lb

Once you have determined the amount of heat you need per hour for your greenhouse and know the price of your proposed fuel per unit, gallon, pound, or therm, an approximate idea of running cost can be obtained. Remember to take into account that the heat will be on only for a limited time of the year. The variable winter climate will also make a considerable difference, depending on geographical area. It should also be borne in mind that some fuels cannot be used so efficiently as others, and their theoretical heat output may not be obtainable. For example, in 'boiler' systems, a lot of heat is wasted up the flue, but with electricity there may be little or no waste. The apparent differences in fuel costs do not, therefore, reflect the actual differences with complete accuracy.

ELECTRICAL HEATING

In my opinion this is the most efficient and desirable form of heating for the average home greenhouse. It has an ill-deserved reputation for being expensive. This is mostly due to unsuitable equipment being used. With proper thermostatic control, and the right choice of heater, there need be no waste of heat. Moreover, there is *no atmospheric contamination* and plants in electrically heated houses are usually in excellent health by the end of the winter. Ventilation can be cut to the absolute minimum during severe cold spells without harming the plants, and this also leads to a great saving in the amount of electricity used – all these factors should be taken into account. Lining the greenhouse with polythene film becomes much more useful for electrically heated houses owing to less need for ventilation and non-contamination of the air. This will further cut costs by about 40%. There is usually less condensation too.

The fan heater is ideal, but be sure to buy one in which the fan and heat are *both* controlled by the thermostat – a continuously running fan can waste heat by constantly stirring the air around the cold sides of the structure, unless the greenhouse is lined.

Convection heaters also give good heat circulation, and heating tubes, usually rated at about 60 W per 30 cm (12 in) run, will also spread warmth about if well distributed around the greenhouse, but not too close to the sides. Soil-warming cables are valuable for specific applications such as winter salads, warming benches, bedding plant production, and frames, all of which are described in the appropriate sections of the book.

PARAFFIN AND GAS HEATING

Both contaminate the greenhouse atmosphere when burnt in non-flued interior heaters. Both must have air for efficient combustion, and a little constant ventilation must be allowed. This can usually be in the form of a small orifice low down and another high up in the greenhouse side, stuffed loosely with glass wool to stop wind blowing through. The normal vents must always be opened to give free ventilation whenever the weather permits and the heaters are not in operation. Both fuels produce a lot of water vapour on combustion and may make the air extremely humid – not desirable in winter – hence the importance of ventilation when possible. Sometimes natural gas heaters have been known to evolve oxides of nitrogen, which are toxic to plants. Both fuels also produce carbon dioxide, of course, but in the home greenhouse this never reaches a significant concentration to affect plant growth.

Gas can be more efficiently controlled by thermostat than paraffin. In the latter case, heaters with a form of thermostatic control that I have had on test have been quite unsatisfactory.

The paraffin wick heater can still give useful service, more especially if someone is around to adjust the wick with weather temperature changes. The 'blue flame' type is the most efficient. It burns the fuel with greater efficiency and produces less fumes. When buying a wick heater be sure that it is designed for greenhouse use and has a satisfactory heat output – demand to know this in terms of BTU/h. Always follow the supplier's running and maintenance instructions strictly.

When buying a wick heater look for a copper oil reservoir, stainless steel chimney, and good heat distribution. Some of the wick heaters used to be fitted with humidity troughs, quite undesirable and unnecessary. These troughs should *not* be filled with water. The paraffin produces more water vapour than wanted on combustion.

Do not allow the wick to become wet, as could happen if the heater is left in the greenhouse over summer. It's a good idea to dry wicks by leaving in the hot sun if necessary, and then keeping them in a dry place until needed. Never use anything but best quality domestic paraffin, and always keep the lamp free from spilled oil and be sure the wick is regularly trimmed. Attention to these matters will avoid trouble from fumes. Certain plants, such as schizanthus and tomato seedlings, may be prone to fume damage. Plants usually show it by browning around the leaf edges. If this is seen, give more ventilation and check heater efficiency and operation. A small paraffin heater should always be kept ready for emergencies and heating failures, whatever type of heating system is installed.

HOT-WATER PIPE HEATING

This is the earliest method and can now use solid fuel, fuel oil, paraffin or gas. Oil, which lends itself to easy storage and trouble-free operation, is the most practical. The most common for the home greenhouse is solid fuel and paraffin. In my opinion, and for technical reasons, pipe heating is most suited to the higher temperature greenhouses. Pipes hold a lot of heat and at low temperatures do not respond promptly to thermostatic control. At high temperatures there is better response. The modern 'boilers' are great improvements on the old, and can usually be installed and in operation within a day or so. There is a better degree of thermostatic control and with solid fuel types stoking is no longer a tedious chore. Aluminium alloy has usually replaced the old, heavy, easily corrodable cast iron. If pipe heating is to be considered there should be full consultation with a supplier and full details of the greenhouse to be heated should be submitted for their recommendations. The length of piping needed to distribute the heat from a boiler is also important; the makers of equipment will advise on this.

I would not recommend electric immersion

heaters for hot water pipes. This method in my experience is too costly.

OTHER HEATING METHODS

Bottled gas is now being used to fuel natural gas heaters where a piped supply is impractical. However, this form of heating is probably the most expensive of all. The larger the bottle, the cheaper the gas becomes, but the bottles are heavy and carrying them about may become a problem.

Boilers for heating water pipes can be fuelled by wood and by waste lubricating oil. I am doubtful about the practicability of wood as a fuel in this case, since it burns far too quickly. Waste oil may vary in composition and this method needs further time for assessment.

COLD SPELL EMERGENCY

The weather is always breaking records and there may well be periods when temperatures fall well below what might be expected. Short these may be, but perhaps long enough to cause serious plant damage if no emergency measures are taken to give some protection.

A useful instrument for predicting the possibility of frost is the frost forecast thermometer. A small greenhouse, and certainly frames, can often be simply protected by covering with old discarded, *dry* textile material, such as old blankets. However, any covering that cuts out light must be removed for the daylight hours or employed only during a special emergency.

A small paraffin heater is valuable for helping out in an emergency. However do not use domestic paraffin heaters of the 'catalytic' type, or car sump heaters with restricted air reaching the flame. Both are liable to give off fumes which could cause slight plant damage if used for long periods. In a crisis, a few hurricane lamps may avert disaster if not turned up too high. Bottled gas heaters may be useful too.

Covering plants with newspaper during a cold spell is an old ideal that works, and may hold in just enough warmth to save them. The modern clear bubble plastics are a great improvement and their clarity means they can be left over the plants longer. Always remember to restrict watering to the absolute minimum during exceptionally cold conditions.

PART II
TECHNIQUES AND PROPAGATION
6 CULTURAL ROUTINE

CLEANLINESS

In my opinion there is nothing mystic about the quality of being 'greenfingered'. Where greenhouse gardening is concerned, it is an approach to working that embraces clean and tidy habits, attention to detail, and application of common sense. To remember the motto 'do it now' also helps – procrastination can lead to unnecessary work, waste of time, and often disappointment.

Attention is drawn to the importance of sterilization of the greenhouse structure, clean water, clean pots and utensils, and sterilized composts. I strongly advise readers to bear the advice given always in mind. It is wise to make a routine inspection of the greenhouse each day if possible, looking for any signs indicating that plants may not be happy. Any problem found should be dealt with immediately. As a daily routine any faded flowers or foliage should be removed from plants or from the staging or floor if fallen. Such plant material must not be left to decay. Sickly plants are best cleared from the greenhouse if the cause of their ill health is not immediately obvious. Keep the interior clean generally and do not let weeds accumulate in, or around, the greenhouse. For glass cleaning agents see Appendix.

Never use the greenhouse to store garden tools, junk, or oddments, and particularly dirty pots and seed trays. Clean pots and equipment necessary for the day-to-day running of the greenhouse can be kept inside with advantage, provided this is done in moderation. A clutter will provide excellent hiding places for pests and diseases and make routine cleanliness and tidiness more difficult. Many pests can transfer diseases from weeds and unhealthy plants; hence the importance of prompt disposal of both sources of trouble.

CHOOSING PLANTS, BUYING, AND STOCKING THE GREENHOUSE

It is always wise to grow your own plants if possible, and much useful information on this subject will be found in Chapter 8. Seed is now an especially good source of plants. As well as all the favourites, the leading seedsmen offer novelties each year. There are also specialist seedsmen that make available an exciting range of rare and unusual plant seed imported from countries all over the world. Seed is also the cheapest way to acquire plants.

When buying plants, best quality is extremely important. Always look out for a specialist nursery if there is one, for example, for subjects like alpines, chrysanthemums, orchids, carnations, bulbs and other storage organs, nerines, achimines, tropical plants, fruit or vines, and the like. The Appendix lists some useful addresses. Most nurseries send out their plants as rooted cuttings where appropriate. This is really the best way to buy. Young plants usually soon acclimatize to the conditions of *your* greenhouse – mature plants may not react well to sudden change, and they are usually more expensive to buy and transport anyway.

In recent years many seedsmen have been supplying seedlings of popular favourites in special pre-sown growing kits in the case of some of the seeds more difficult to germinate, or as chitted seed, which is seed already in the process of germination and especially prepared by the supplier. Such services may be of interest to the absolute beginner, and to those who want to take short cuts.

In the case of storage organs and bulbs, it is particularly desirable to buy carefully. It is not unusual for the names and identity of these to get mixed up, when they are purchased from garden shops, chain stores and the like. Never buy anything spongy or soft – it may well be rotting – or affected by moulds or mildews.

The choice of plants for your greenhouse must be made with common sense. It will have to depend on its *minimum winter temperature* and light conditions, and of course what kind of greenhouse you want. A very common mistake made by complete beginners is to fill the greenhouse with anything that comes along or takes their fancy. Such a varied collection may last well enough for a few months – perhaps during the spring to summer – but with the approach of more adverse temperatures and the lapse of time, many of the plants begin to look sickly. It is important to make sure the plants you choose all like similar environmental conditions, and that these are the conditions you can provide. You cannot expect a mixture of plants like shade lovers, sun lovers, cacti, alpines, plants from tropical rain forests, semi-aquatics, and dry region subjects, to get on together in the same greenhouse. Yet, if you look at the collection that some beginners start with, it contains just such a mixture.

PLANNING AND ORGANIZATION

The importance of deciding exactly what you want your greenhouse to do, and how you propose to use it, has already been covered. However, if a little care and thought is taken over the positions in the greenhouse you choose for plants, moderate variations in their environmental individual preferences can be provided to some extent. For example, under the staging or under climbers or tall growing shrubby plants is an ideal place for many shade lovers. A part of the greenhouse can perhaps be shaded specially for them if necessary, plants liking lots of light being put where it is unshaded. Plants sensitive to chill or draught, should be sited at the rear of the greenhouse and away from doors or vents. Those preferring plenty of air, and liable to mildews where the air is stagnant, can be found places where air is frequently entering. Many plants like a localized humid atmosphere, and this can be

often provided as a 'micro-climate' by grouping plants of the same or similar type, or by standing them in moist peat, shingle, or capillary matting.

A single greenhouse can be used for practically year round growing of a wide variety of subjects if the plants are properly chosen and the routine is planned; even some of the 'specialist' plants can be often fitted in the schedule. Typical examples are chrysanthemums and cymbidium orchids which have environmental requirements much the same as many other popular subjects.

To illustrate a plan to make the most of an ordinary, relatively small home greenhouse the following is a typical example. Assuming it can be kept frost free, some useful winter salads can be grown, and many plants that may be dormant or just 'ticking over' stored safely for restarting into growth in early spring. Early in the year climbing French beans can make a rewarding crop. These will yield early and can be cleared away for tomato planting to give fruit from summer to autumn and perhaps even into winter if the weather is favourable.

From about late winter to early spring, you can start raising bedding plants and plants for later display in the greenhouse. Melons, cucumbers, sweet peppers, and aubergines, can be started from seed too. All will grow quite happily together in the same greenhouse if suitably placed and trained as described under the individual headings in this book. Nearly all the popular flowering and foliage pot plants will do well in company with the fruit and vegetables suggested.

The ornamentals usually like a position on or under staging run opposite the vegetables and tomatoes which should be set along the south side of an east-west orientated greenhouse if possible. If a minimum of about 5–7°C (40–45°F) can be maintained in winter, cymbidiums should give an impressive display from late winter to spring. In autumn, late chrysanthemums, grown outside in summer, can be moved into the greenhouse to give another wonderful display of colour, or yield cut blooms, until well into winter.

There are many large shrubby plants like citrus, neriums, and callistemons, that can be put outside the greenhouse in summer to make more room inside. They can be returned for

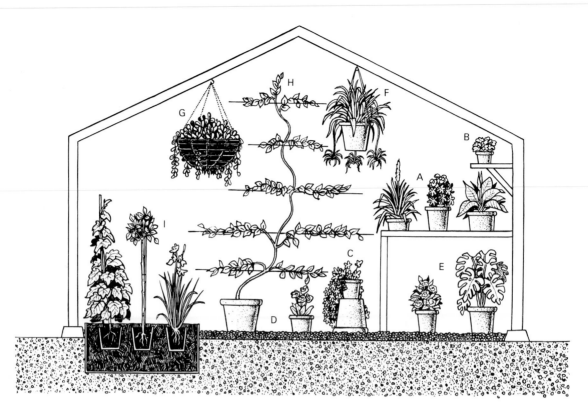

Fig. 7 Ways to display plants.
There are many attractive ways to display plants according to their habit, and a professional 'look' will be obtained if these are fully exploited.

(*A*) On staging. (*B*) On shelves. (*C*) On inverted pots, for trailers. (*D*) On floor level. (*E*) Under staging for shade lovers. (*F*) In hanging containers – pots. (*G*) In hanging containers – baskets. (*H*) Along wires – climbers. (*I*) In sunken troughs with pots plunged in peat to give border effect.

winter protection well before the first frosts are expected. Frames can also be used to take over many greenhouse propagation jobs not requiring much height – they can play a very useful role in organizing and planning. For notes on displaying ornamental plants, see The conservatory, p. 184.

TRAINING PLANTS, SUPPORTING, EXPLOITING NATURAL HABIT

Chapter 20 deals with these subjects in more detail, with the artistic aspects in mind. There are few plants that grow in our artificial greenhouse environment that do not benefit from some degree of training (Fig. 7). Sometimes it is absolutely essential to get satisfactory results, e.g. the de-shooting of tomatoes.

In the case of very many pot plants 'stopping' is often an extremely important operation. This is merely the snipping off of the growing tip of a shoot. It encourages further shoots to grow from below and hence induces shorter, neater, more bushy growth, and a compact shape, usually most desirable for plants grown in pots. Often, stopping is also necessary to get plenty of flowers or perhaps fruits, and recommendations are given throughout this book where appropriate.

Training plants as standards, on a supporting stem of suitable length, like the garden standard rose, was a practice extensively employed by Victorian greenhouse gardeners (Fig. 8). It could well be revived and experimented with for many pot subjects, since it is now hardly ever used for anything but the fuchsia. You can start from a seedling, or from a rooted cutting (as in the case of the fuchsia), depending on the plant in question. To form the stem you merely grow on, potting on as necessary, but removing all *side shoots* that may form – leaves must not be removed until the stem and head growing is completed. When the stem is at the required height, the growing tip is 'stopped' by snipping off. This should encourage a number of shoots to start growing from just below. These can be further stopped if necessary, until a nice bushy head has developed. When this stage is reached, the leaves can be carefully stripped from the supporting stem.

The process of growing a standard may take more than a year. It is usually best to begin in early spring. Depending on the nature of the

plant, a moderate winter warmth may have to be maintained to prevent dormancy. Some plants – including the fuchsia – may tend to die back in winter unless given a temperature just sufficient to keep them growing very slightly. A die-back may mean that all the initial work of growing the stem is ruined. Although the roots may still be alive, they will probably resume growth from the base in spring.

It is usually necessary to provide a strong support such as a cane or stake and tie the stem to this as it lengthens. It is vital not to get any kinks or bends. Leaves are the 'lungs' of a plant, and satisfactory growth will not be obtained if they are removed before there is plenty to take their place on the ultimately formed 'head'. As well as fuchsias, many shrubby plants like callistemons, perennial daturas and abutilons, lend themselves well to standard training, and pelargoniums and marguerites were also once very popular. For some woody plants grafting, in a similar manner to standard rose production, can also be employed.

In many respects the training and supporting of greenhouse plants, their pruning, fruit thinning, disbudding, and the like, follows

Fig. 8 Growing a standard.
(1) Choose strong unbranching seedlings or rooted cuttings.
(2) Cleanly remove any side growth or growth from the roots that may develop, but *not* leaves from the main stem.
(3) When the desired height is reached snip off the growing tip at the top.
(4) Allow a bushy head to develop by further stopping the shoots that form at the top if necessary.
(5) Stem leaves can be removed when the 'head' has fully formed. Most standards will need support with a stout cane.

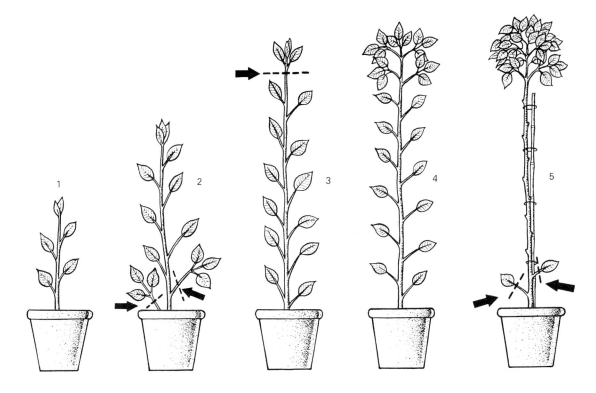

much the same methods and rules as for outdoor plants. Any special techniques are brought to attention in this book where the plants are discussed. For supporting plants under glass, bamboos or split canes are used according to the size or weight of the plant material to be sustained (Fig. 9), but always use clean or sterilized supports. Bamboos, in particular, are likely to harbour pests like earwigs in their hollow centres. String, which should preferably be of the rough textured type for better non-slip grip, should also be replaced fairly frequently. Where climbers are trained on the walls of lean-to structures, they can be secured to wires fastened a few inches from the wall or on plastic covered wire mesh. Mesh or trellis made entirely from plastic is best avoided. With time it is liable to go brittle, and it may disintegrate suddenly with devastating effect if it is supporting a large mature plant. Rough walls should be preferably cement rendered to give a smooth surface, where pests and diseases cannot lurk, and then given a coat of white emulsion paint.

The natural habit of a plant – bushy, climbing, trailing, short or tall – should always be borne in mind when choosing plants for a greenhouse. Varieties or cultivars of plants can also vary in habit quite considerably as well as species. For example, if you have only a very small greenhouse, there are now seed strains and varieties of popular plants that are very dwarf and compact in habit. In such a case, obviously vigorous fast climbers, and perhaps perennial climbers, should be ruled out, but short term fast growers or annuals may well be a practical proposition.

By choosing plants with a wide variety of habit the interest of the greenhouse is greatly increased and you can achieve a much more professional effect.

HUMIDITY

The humidity of the air refers to the amount of water vapour it contains – the technicalities need not concern us here – and this has a very marked effect on plant growth and welfare. The subject has already been discussed in Chapter 4, since the humidity can be greatly influenced by how the greenhouse is fitted out.

To understand the effect of humidity on

Fig. 9 Fan of canes for climbers in pots. For large climbers use a heavy clay pot for greater stability.

plants it is as well to remember that plants are constantly passing out water vapour from their leaves. This process ensures a flow of sap through the plant and the take up of moisture, with its soluble nutrients, by the roots. This loss of water is called 'transpiration' and, curiously enough, it tends to be carried out very wastefully by plants if they get the opportunity. However, the higher the amount of water vapour already in the air, the slower transpiration can take place, and vice versa. When plants are making active growth, and conditions are warm and bright – favourable to photosynthesis – plants are very liable to flag and droop if the air is dry, since the roots are unable to take in enough water to make up that lost by transpiration.

Many of our popular greenhouse plants, coming from temperate moist climates, also seem to prefer a moderate humidity like that of their natural environment. The problem of inadequate humidity is one often encountered in the growing of house plants, where a very moist atmosphere in the home is rare and undesirable. Many house plants will, in fact, revel in the moist air of the greenhouse.

To keep up humidity, the routine of 'damping down' is an important one to be carried out from late spring to early autumn. The warmer and brighter the weather the more important and the more frequent damping down should become. All you do is to make sure the staging and the floor of the greenhouse is kept nicely damp. This can be done by applying water with a water can rose or sprayer. If there is automatic watering, it can usually be adapted to also keep, say, the surface of the staging moist. Some systems can be made to spray part of the floor with a mist at appropriate intervals, and this is extremely effective.

The advantage of covering the floor and staging with a moisture-retaining material has already been mentioned. Unfortunately, where there is moisture and light you tend to get slimes and algae forming. Although not in themselves directly harmful, they may encourage pests and, in any case, look unpleasant and unsightly; for prevention and control, see Chapter 11.

The general aim should be to achieve a reasonably high humidity in summer, or during warm bright periods, but the minimum atmospheric water content in the winter and when plants are dormant. When the temperature is low, light is poor, and the air tending to be stagnant due to restricted ventilation, moulds and mildews will run riot. For this reason, in winter it is wise to do any watering that is necessary by hand, and to cease damping down. Staging and floor should be kept quite dry. Generally in winter watering should be kept to the absolute minimum.

Further advantages of damping down in summer are that it creates a cooling effect as the water evaporates, and reduces the necessity for frequent root watering as the air becomes more humid and suppresses transpiration. Although the water can be thrown about freely, do be careful where there are flowers in bloom – they can be damaged or rotted by water saturation. Plants can also be damaged if wetted when exposed to bright sunlight. Droplets of water act as tiny lenses and focus the light to cause small scalded spots, like a 'burning glass'.

WATERING AND FEEDING

I have deliberately put these two subjects together because they are both related and the same rules often apply. Plants cannot eat their nutrients – they have to *drink*! Apart from gases absorbed from the air through their leaves and sometimes via the roots, all their nutrients have to be in the form of a solution. This means watering can have a considerable effect on nutrient uptake, and obviously dry plants are liable to be starved. However, it is generally agreed that the greatest cause of failure in pot plants is overwatering. This often leads to poor aeration of the compost and roots, which in turn leads to proliferation of undesirable micro-organisms that multiply rapidly in the absence of air, and thus to subsequent rotting of the roots. Giving excess water to the extent that water streams from the drainage holes of the pot, also carries away soluble nutrients, like nitrate and potassium salts in particular, resulting in poor growth and yellowing foliage.

When plants are actively growing the ideal is to aim at nicely *moist* compost. It is important to distinguish between wet and waterlogged, and dry desiccated compost. Most of the modern peat-based composts should never be allowed to become really dry in the latter sense – if they do, they become very difficult to re-wet. Water may just roll off or run down between the shrunken compost ball and the pot sides; it may not penetrate to the roots unless a good and prolonged soaking by immersion is given. In normal circumstances plants should not be soaked or stood in water.

When plants are not making active growth, are growing only slowly, or are dormant in winter, watering should be done sparingly, if at all. Cold conditions mean extra special care, since plants wet at the roots are more liable to sustain damage both from freezing – wet compost conducts heat away quickly – and from rotting.

The plant type, time of year, temperature and light conditions, and the plant's vigour, all greatly affect the amount of water needed; you cannot give fixed definite doses as many

Plate 6 Beginners may find an electronic moisture meter useful; the sensor probe is inserted into the compost and so cannot be seen in the photograph.

beginners imagine. You must use common sense. In bright warm conditions plants need the most water, so that the best time to water is in the morning. A simple way to check whether a plant needs water is to lift the pot, in the case of small ones – its weight will soon tell you whether the compost is wet or not after a little experience. An old check used for clay pots, and still effective, is to tap them with a cotton reel forced on to the end of a cane to make a 'sounding hammer'. A hollow sound is emitted from dry pots, and a dull thud from wet ones. A simple method I often use is merely to feel the compost by carefully inserting one's little finger under the surface. However, with experience and practice you often get to know when water is needed by the plants' appearance. A very *slight* flagging is a good indication, but this must never be allowed to regularly occur or become severe.

In summer it is often necessary to keep a careful watch on watering needs, since during a hot day water may have to be applied several times, particularly in the case of vigorous plants like fruiting tomatoes and cucumbers. It is very important to try to avoid rapid changes between wet and dry conditions.

Often useful as a modern aid to moisture content checking are the electronic moisture meters now available, which work on the principle of conductivity. provided they are used carefully and as instructed, they can prove very helpful – especially to beginners. I particularly recommend the JMA design which is also supplied with a reference book relating meter readings to the moisture requirements of a wide range of plant types (see Plate 6 and Appendix).

Dirty water must never be used for watering – this includes water collected from roofs and stored in butts. Such water may be a 'soup' of pests, diseases, slimes and algae. It is also inadvisable to use it for damping down. Remember that you are, I hope, taking the trouble to use sterilized composts, so that contaminated water will soon render them useless. If a supply of soft lime-free water is needed for any special plants, it is best to put out clean bowls soon after rain has commenced, and to store the water collected in sealed containers. However, I am inclined to think that the need for lime-free water is sometimes exaggerated, and have used quite hard mains water, even for orchids, with no apparent ill effects. This laxity does not apply to cases where it is especially recommended to omit lime from a potting compost.

For applying water in the greenhouse a can

with a long narrow spout is desirable so that it will reach pots at the rear of staging. For a large greenhouse, a hose reel can be fixed to a supply tap and water applied with a lever-operated watering lance. A large reservoir pressure sprayer is valuable as an additional aid. It can be used to mist over plants in summer and to water seed trays and seedlings – a fine mist is very penetrating and will not disturb them. The sprayer should be reserved entirely for water if possible, although it could also be used for *harmless* pesticides if necessary and if washed out afterwards. Always water thoroughly but avoid so much that excess streams from the pot.

Plants prefer to be fed little (in weak concentration) but often, and the remarks about insufficiency and excess of water similarly apply. When plants need the most water, they also generally can make the most use of nutrient. Nowadays numerous balanced plant foods are on the market specially designed for pot plants and containing the basic nutrients as well as trace elements. These should be used according to the makers' instructions and make feeding quite a simple business. The composts recommended in Chapter 7 already have adequate nutrients added to ensure a good start. Feeding is not usually necessary until the plants are growing well and have been in their pots for about eight weeks or so. Often the time to begin feeding is when flower buds are just beginning to form. The need for food may also be shown by growing tips of shoots losing a healthy green colour and becoming weak.

For general purposes, I personally prefer the application of *liquid* feeds – soluble mixtures or solution concentrates dissolved in the recommended amount of water. However, for plants long established in borders or large pots and when potting-on is no longer practical, 'top dressing' is often carried out. This entails removing the upper layers of compost, trying not to disturb roots if present, and replacing with fresh. A modification is to incorporate a balanced fertilizer concentrate, such as Phostrogen, in the top layers of compost. Subsequent watering will carry the fertilizer down to the roots. Special slow-dissolving tableted preparations are also made for this purpose.

The best time for top dressing is spring.

Crude animal manures should not be used in the greenhouse. They are smelly and un-hygienic and can introduce all manner of pests and diseases. The specially prepared sterilized, dried forms are all right, although these may emit a slight odour when they become moist.

Foliar feeding is the application of special *suitable* feeds by drench or sprayer. Foliar feeds are formulated so that the nutrients are absorbed via the leaves; not all plant feeds are suitable, so the labels must be checked. Some foliar feeds contain special ingredients such as vitamins and hormones to aid growth. Most plants respond well and rapidly to foliar feedings, particularly epiphytic types that are found in nature growing in moss or plant debris that collects in rocks or in tree branches above ground level. Specific recommendations are given later, where necessary.

Winter feeding of any kind should always be cautious, and only those plants making some winter growth in a frost-free greenhouse or slightly warm conditions need to be fed, e.g. cinerarias, calceolarias, primulas, and winter salads. Even then the requirement is usually very modest, and there will usually be enough nutrient in the compost to keep such plants happy. From late winter onwards, and when plants are seen to be forming buds, feeding should be dramatically increased to keep up with the fast spurt of growth that usually then occurs. Dormant and resting plants should not be fed at all; as they come into growth the plants should be fed with increasing frequency, as they are also gradually increasingly watered.

SHADING

The importance of shading is often not fully appreciated, especially by beginners. An un-shaded and perhaps unventilated greenhouse on a hot sunny day can become literally an oven and the entire contents can be scorched to death in a matter of hours during the summer months. Both the high intensity of full sunlight and the considerable heat trapped by the glass can cause damage. Blinds have long been used as protection and it is customary to fix them outside the roof, preferably on rails a few inches above the glass so that absorbed heat is not transferred to the glass by conduction. (Opinions differ on this matter.) Such blinds are best made from timber slats, bamboo, aluminium strip, or some similar substantial wind and weatherproof material. Flimsy materials like plastic sheeting, hessian, and synthetic fibre textiles, are sometimes employed, but are prone to tear or blow away in a high wind! For this reason interior blinds are now frequently advocated, but they are far less efficient. Once the sun's rays have passed through the glass they are inevitably converted to heat radiation which is trapped by the glass.

Because well-made blinds are expensive and usually have to be custom made, it has long been a practice to coat the glass with a shading paint. Until recently, this has been far from satisfactory and some of the older preparations could damage framework. Many were so difficult to wipe off at the end of the year that the efforts of the gardener to effect removal has resulted in nasty accidents in the form of cuts and lacerations when glass has given way. Moreover, the extraordinary common practice of using green coloured paints has often meant that the greenhouse becomes *hotter than if left unshaded*!

In all cases green, or any colours apart from white, should *not* be used for shading. Green in fact means that a great deal of the sun's energy is being absorbed – plants are green for the same reason, the energy being used for photosynthesis. A green-shaded greenhouse actually gets hotter, and the darker the colour the hotter it will get. White, on the other hand, reflects much of the sun's heat and light, a fact known in hot sunny countries for centuries! White also gives a better rendering of plant colour inside the greenhouse. Where green is employed it often looks as though the plants are growing in an underwater cavern!

In recent years shading paint has been revolutionized by the introduction of the 'electrostatic' type sold under the name of Coolglass. This is, of course, brilliant white giving an excellent cooling effect, but it is unique in that the particles adhere to the glass by some kind of electrostatic attraction, like tiny magnets. This shading can be brushed (Fig. 10) or sprayed on the glass after suitable dilution of the concentrate, to give any desired intensity of shade, from very slight to very

Fig. 10 Home-made brush for applying shading. This simple brush with home-made handle allows access to the roof without using ladders and steps. If the electrostatic shading Coolglass is employed, it will also *remove* it in the dry state.

heavy according to needs. It dries almost immediately, but thereafter even torrential rain will not wash it off, yet it can be instantly removed by friction, such as wiping lightly with a dry duster. It can therefore be used much like a blind and put on, or taken off, according to weather conditions. For the average home greenhouse, application to the roof can be made with a soft broom without the need for ladders. Removal can be done similarly by wiping off with a duster wound around the broom head.

VENTILATION

Ventilators and their use have already been discussed. It should be appreciated that plants also 'breathe' and the air is a vital source of nutrient. Carbon dioxide is vital and is well known, but other gas exchanges also occur. A good air circulation is always desirable. In winter it will help reduce moulds and mildews by making it difficult for the spores to settle. When the temperature is low, it has been found that moving the air with a fan works well enough – there is no need to let cold air in from outside. In summer a good air exchange will help reduce temperature directly and by hastening the evaporation of water applied by damping down. However, as in most things, moderation is the keyword, and ventilation must always be adjusted to give the optimum effect – it must not be confused with un-wanted and uncontrollable draught or with devastating gusts when vents are forgotten and left open during an adverse change of weather.

GENERAL TEMPERATURE CONTROL

It is essential to adjust temperature according to the plants' needs over the entire year. In winter it is often easier to do, because if you have thermostatic controlled heating it is done automatically very efficiently. In summer, the control has to be done largely by you, by manipulating vents, shading, and damping down. In summer it is rarely wise to let temperatures rise above 27–30°C (81–86°F). Even tropical plants will not want higher than this, and many of the ordinary popular favourites may well begin to show displeasure at higher levels. For example, the proper ripening of tomatoes can be seriously im-paired.

The greenhouse may be too cold in winter for a number of desirable plants that will grow there happily from spring to autumn. These can often be taken into the home and used as winter house plants.

THE GREENHOUSE DURING ABSENCE

A very common and important problem is that a home greenhouse has to be left unattended most of the day whilst the owner is at business, and for longer periods during holidays. Obviously automation solves much of the difficulty in such cases, even if only semi-automatic systems are employed. Watering is of course the most important, but if any automatic watering method is used make sure that it is operating effectively and efficiently before leaving the greenhouse for a long period.

Shading is also extremely important, and if the greenhouse is to be left for a prolonged time a fairly heavy coating of Coolglass is best applied if the period is during summer. Some ventilation must be left too, but not too much or the greenhouse is liable to dry out very quickly and there could also be wind entry damage. A really thorough damping-down should be given and it is an advantage to have a shingle covered earth floor which can be very well soaked.

Before leaving for a prolonged absence, cut off any flowers or advanced fruit so that they do not fade and rot. Make sure all watering is done and any urgent potting-on, but be cautious about feeding which may only en-courage faster growth and mean a greater water demand. Covering plants with clear polythene bags or sheeting often keeps them in excellent moist condition for a long time, but unhealthy plants should not be covered, since they may rot or grow fungi. If possible it is always wise to get a friend or neighbour to take over for a long absence.

7 COMPOSTS, POTS AND POTTING

SEED AND POTTING COMPOSTS

For greenhouse growing, and raising plants in pots or containers, ordinary garden soil must never be used – that is, if you want reliable, good results! For certain types of mass production growing, of specific crops or flowers, say, for cutting, the ground soil is employed by some people, mostly by professional nurserymen who have special equipment for sterilization such as steam pipes. For the average home greenhouse I would personally advise not using the ground soil after the first year. The matter is discussed in Chapters 7 and 11.

The word 'compost' in greenhouse gardening, and container growing under cover, refers to specially prepared mixtures to give ideal conditions for root development or germination of seeds. Three vital factors are taken into account: the best texture, freedom from pests and diseases including weed seeds, and an ideal balance of plant nutrients which will be made available for a reasonable time. Garden compost. so valuable to the outdoor gardener, *must not* be employed in the greenhouse or for pots. It is too pest ridden.

In the early days the making of composts was often considered something of an art and innumerable different mixtures were suggested – often these were reminiscent of the witches' brew in Macbeth! Results were extremely hit or miss. After years of research, composts were put on a scientific basis by W. J. C. Lawrence, of the John Innes Horticultural Institution, and the formulae were published in 1938. The composts are now quite famous and they pointed the way to further research leading to the development of the many proprietary composts we have today.

Most of the modern composts try to avoid the use of the specially prepared loam important to the J.I. composts. Loam selection, treatment, *and sterilization*, is not a job that can be undertaken without care and patience. Modern composts are mostly based on selected peat, peat/grit mixes, or peat with the incorporation of other inert mineral material like vermiculite or perlite. The nutrient content is of course very carefully scientifically balanced and very special ingredients are employed. The proprietary composts usually give excellent results and are extremely convenient to use straight from the bag. For this reason hardly anyone now makes their own John Innes composts, today's ready-made composts being such a good buy. I still prefer the J.I. formulae for plants needing to be grown with perfection and for long-term plants.

When purchasing John Innes compost look out for the seal of the John Innes Manufacturers' Association. As I have pointed out, the making of the composts needs strict attention to detail and J.I. composts recently came into disrepute – mixtures were being sold which had no right to be given the honourable name. If you buy a compost with the J.I.M.A. seal of approval you can be sure the product meets the original John Innes' specifications. Because so few people now make their own J.I. composts, I will omit the lengthy details here; the formulae are, however, given in the Appendix.

DIY peat or peat/grit mixes have now become much simpler because the fertilizers are sold ready-mixed in the right proportions under proprietary names. This is often *a cheaper way to obtain a larger amount of compost* when compared with the 'complete' proprietary products in final cost (see Appendix).

Readers wishing to make their own j.i. compost are referred to the original publications of W. J. C. Lawrence and J. Newell where full details on the use of the compost will also be found. There are several grades of potting compost according to the amount of fertilizer added. For nearly all the plants described in this book, and generally, the No. 2 potting compost should be employed. Other recommendations will be given where appropriate. No. 3 usually being preferred for very vigorous growers, and No. 1 for plants that are less so.

USING SEED AND POTTING COMPOSTS

The difference between seed and potting composts is that the former has a finer texture and a different balance of nutrients designed to promote germination and initial seedling growth. However, seedlings should not be left in the seedling compost for longer than necessary. Personally, I find that seeds that are large enough to handle easily can be sown directly in a potting compost, and sometimes they can be sown individually in small pots and left to grow on, thus avoiding pricking out.

Seed and potting composts are usually sold in sealed plastic bags and in a nicely moist condition. They should on no account be wet and waterlogged, and should *not* be accepted if in this condition. During use keep the composts in the bags and close the bags carefully after use, to *keep out pests and disease organisms*. Alternatively store in clean small plastic *lidded* dustbins. Try to avoid keeping composts for longer than about four months if possible, and keep them in a *moist* condition during storage. Always see that the composts are moist before use. Addition of water if necessary is best done with a sprayer delivering a fine mist, stirring and turning over the compost with a clean trowel.

When mixing your own compost, make sure the surface on which the job is done *is clean*. It is easier to mix relatively small bulks of compost at a time (Plates 7 and 8), say on the potting bench. A small surface can be instantly sterilized by swabbing over with 'meths', wiping off any excess with a clean cloth, and

allowing to dry thoroughly for a few minutes. Thorough mixing of ingredients is always essential. Needless to say, any ingredients used for DIY mix must also be thoroughly clean. 'Washed grit' as it is known, a gritty coarse sand sold by builders' merchants, is used in a peat/grit mix. Do not use fine or clayey sand. Washed grit is usually fairly clean and weed free unless it has been stored in the open. If a source of clean material cannot be found, it is better to use a peat vermiculite mixture, or better, a peat/perlite mixture. The two are similar, but vermiculite can sometimes be a little alkaline which could be a disadvantage (see below and Appendix).

The application of fertilizers and feeding plants in relation to potting composts was discussed earlier. For the j.i. composts a special j.i. feed was developed, but the ordinary proprietary balanced general feeds are quite satisfactory. The j.i. composts tend to retain fertilizers longer than the all peat or peat/grit formulations, so plants do not usually need to be fed so soon after potting, when these composts are used.

Seed or potting compost *must never be used twice*. However, old compost from discarded plants can be broken up and used for terrace pots, tubs, or window boxes and the like *outdoors*. For such purposes I usually incorporate some good garden soil and add a suitable quantity of a balanced proprietary fertilizer.

SPECIAL COMPOSTS

The j.i. and modern standard potting composts can be used for a remarkably wide range of plants. The few exceptions are brought to attention where appropriate in this book. The most common special requirement is for an acid compost – that is, a pH below about 6.4, but not lower than about 5.5. Many plants that naturally grow in peaty, heathland and woodland soils deficient in lime, often grow poorly and develop leaf yellowing or poor flower colour if given a compost with higher pH. The pH of normal potting compost is usually from about 6.4 to 6.5, which is only very slightly acid, pH 7.0 being neutral, and this suits most of the ordinary plants grown. A typical case where a much lower pH is of paramount

Plate 7   It is essential to thoroughly mix the ingredients when you make your own potting or seed composts. This can be better achieved by preparing small quantities at a time on the potting bench.

Plate 8   To get your composts nicely *moist* use a sprayer to apply water as a penetrating mist. The same method is also best for watering-in seeds and irrigating tiny seedlings.

importance, and well known to gardeners, is the hydrangea where the performance of the whole plant is affected. Other cases are brought to the reader's attention where necessary.

A special J.I. acid compost has been formulated which incorporate flowers of sulphur (see Appendix). However, once again ready-made mixtures are sold by many garden shops and centres, and usually supplied under the name 'ericaceous composts' since they are also commonly used for heathers.

Unless there is good reason or special recommendation, never add extra ingredients to the standard composts.

GROWBAGS AND GROWBOARDS

This is a modern way to grow plants and is fast becoming very popular. Specially prepared compost is supplied by various famous horticultural firms and packed in plastic sack-size bags. These are placed flat on the greenhouse floor and holes cut in the upper side to take the plants. Although these bags can be used for flowers, they are mostly useful for edible crops like tomatoes, cucumbers, melons, or sweet peppers. Full instructions for use of the bags are printed on them. A recent introduction is the 'growboard'. This is a plastic bag packed with compressed dehydrated compost, and consequently extremely light in weight to carry or transport. The compost is 'reconstituted' on the site by merely adding the prescribed amount of water according to the printed instructions. I prefer to leave the compost at least overnight to ensure complete absorption of the water before planting. Both the 'boards' and bags give excellent results and can of course be used even if the greenhouse has a concrete floor.

POTS AND CONTAINERS

The plastic flower pot is an instance where the material has been put to advantageous use. Plastic pots are very easy to clean, and sterilize if necessary, and since their common use the general health of plants has benefited (Plate 9). Their light weight makes storage convenient, but can be a disadvantage; peat compost has little weight too, so that a compost of this type in a plastic pot may give minimum stability to a large plant, and pots may easily get tipped over. A tall and possibly 'top heavy' plant, such as a standard, may be safer in a heavy clay pot, or a plastic pot of slightly larger size than necessary weighted with clean pebbles.

Clay pots are still useful, particularly for plants that like well aerated roots and the extra weight mentioned. However, they must be well cleaned before use. This is best done by soaking in water overnight, and then scrubbing. Since clay pots are porous, care must be taken when sterilizing them to make sure all fumes and vapours of the agent used have evaporated before potting.

Plastic pots, being non-porous, hold water better than clay. Plants need less frequent watering, but if you have been used to using clay care must be taken not to over water. Apart from this, plants seem to be just as happy whichever type of pot you use.

Plastic pots are not indestructible. They often become brittle with age. Large pots full of compost are liable to split when picked up, especially if they have been left out in the sun for any length of time. Powerful light is the usual cause of the brittleness developing. This, by the way, can happen to many other kinds of plastic equipment such as sprayers. For pots intended to be stood outdoors for long periods and exposed to full sunlight, it is wiser to choose a more durable material like clay, cement, or timber. See also 'liner pots', p. 10.

Garishly coloured pots are best avoided in the greenhouse. The conventional terracotta colour is fine, and black, white, grey and neutral colours are also suitable.

Disposable pots are sometimes useful; they are made from polythene bitumenized cardboard or a fibre preparation. There are also 'peat pots' or fibre pots, usually employed for bedding plants. These are intended to be left in place around the root ball and planted with the plant. The idea is that the roots remain undisturbed and the pot material soon rots down after planting, allowing the roots free access to the soil. Unfortunately, in my experience, this does not always work. I have dug up plants that looked unhappy, only to find that the pots have not rotted and the roots have been seriously restricted. If you use these

Plate 9 Plastic pots stay very clean and hygenic in use, but may become brittle and split with age and exposure to sunlight.

pots, it is vital to see that the peat pot is moist at planting-out time and that the soil is kept nicely moist for some time after planting out.

Compressed compost blocks are sometimes used for a similar reason, for which purpose a special proprietary 'blocking compost' is employed. Pots are then dispensed with altogether. However, when growing the plants in these blocks initially, do not place them so that they touch or roots may pass from one block to another – this means inevitable damage when separating them for planting and their object is defeated. It would have been better to have used ordinary flowerpots!

POT SIZE

Choosing the best size of pot or container for the stage of development of a particular plant is important, and demands common sense! An *unnecessarily* large pot is undesirable. By keeping the pot size to the minimum and potting-on when necessary, the compost is kept 'sweet' and fresh. For some plants a relatively small pot is essential. Most annuals flower better if their roots are restricted, and some climbers also perform better. The latter tend to make excessive rampant growth if given a free root run and an excess of rich compost.

On the other hand, plants known to be quick vigorous growers, particularly if they are to bear large bloom or fruit, must have a container of reasonable size from an early stage. Remember too, that small containers will dry out much more quickly than large ones. This can be a serious disadvantage when a greenhouse has to be left unattended all day. For vigorous crops, like tomatoes and cucumbers, I recommend that the home greenhouse owner errs on the side of choosing larger rather than small containers (see Chapter 16). Recommendations as to pot size for various plants are given where appropriate throughout the book.

For plants in their final decorative stage, a pot size in proportion to the plant should be chosen to give the proper aesthetic balance; a tiny plant in an enormous pot will look ridiculous, for example. For many short or low growing plants, the type of pot known as the 'half pot' is worth considering. This is also sometimes called 'alpine pot', since it is ideal for 'rock' plants, being half the depth of the normal flowerpot.

HANGING CONTAINERS

Many pendent and trailing plants are seen at their best when grown in hanging containers, and some very striking and beautiful effects can be achieved. This can give a display greenhouse a very 'professional' look. Most plastic pots can be easily drilled around the rim and wired for hanging (Fig. 11). The pots will often become hidden from view as the plants grow. Baskets are well known, and some modern plastic types are designed with a drip prevention saucer below. Wire baskets are usually moss lined, but it is a good idea to place on top of the moss some thin polythene sheeting, slit for drainage, and to fill up with compost on top of this. Quick drying out, to which hanging containers are prone, will then be prevented.

Hanging containers can be very heavy after watering – do make sure the greenhouse roof will take the weight!

Fig. 11 A simple way to hang a flower pot.
Holes for hanging can often be made in the rim of a plastic pot with a piece of hot wire held in pliers.

POTTING

All pots must be clean before use, and clay pots should have been well soaked in clean water. Dry clay pots will absorb water from the compost and may tend to adhere to the root ball so that the pots do not slip off easily when potting-on.

All pots must be well drained. It is customary to place a few pieces of broken pot (crocks) over the holes (Fig. 12) if the latter are large, to prevent compost falling through. Instead of crocks, which can be pieces of plastic or clay pot, a few clean pebbles can be used; these will give extra weight and stability.

However, if the pots are to be stood on a capillary watering bench, crocks must *not* be used. A fibrous tuft of peat can be employed if necessary. For capillary watering, plastic pots only should be used, and these should preferably have several moderate sized drainage holes.

When potting fast-developing plants into relatively small pots, I usually find crocking unnecessary. Very often initial potting of small seedlings can be avoided by planting into standard seed trays and well spacing them.

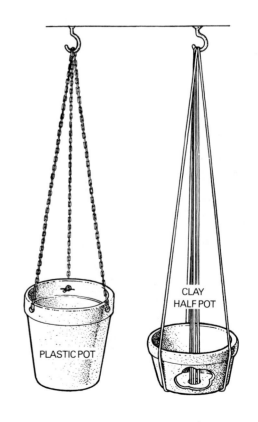

PLASTIC POT

CLAY HALF POT

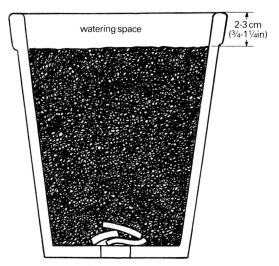

Fig. 12   Correctly filled flowerpot.
The pieces of broken pot over the drainage holes are called 'crocks' but clean pebbles can be used. Perforated zinc discs are also sometimes used. Note the space left between compost surface and top of pot. This acts as a reservoir for water and also helps in assessing how much water is given.

Fig. 13   Principle of potting-on.
(*A*) Plant to be moved on. (*B*) New pot providing space for fresh potting compost for the roots to grow into.

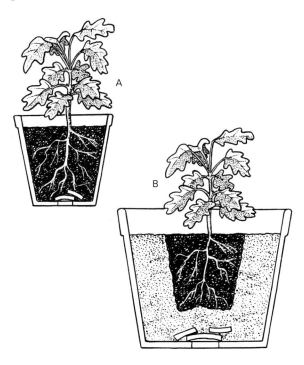

This avoids the use of lots of tiny pots, which also tend to dry out rapidly. When the seedlings are of moderate size, they can be transferred from the trays to 8-cm (3-in) pots or larger according to their nature.

There is no need to ram modern composts into the pot firmly. A good sharp tap on the bench to settle the compost around the roots of the positioned plant is adequate, or sometimes a *gentle* firming with the fingers. Do not set the plants too deeply so that the compost comes way up the stem; this can sometimes encourage stems to rot. It is very important to leave a space of about 2.5 cm (1 in) – more or less according to the size of the pot – from the compost surface to the pot rim. This is the *watering space* and acts as a reservoir for the water when applying water (Fig. 12). It is valuable in assessing how much water is given, and often, if this space is filled, it affords a useful measure of the quantity of water that will be taken up by the compost in the pot. Hence never fill a pot right up to the rim with compost; water will often just pour off and it is impossible to judge how much is being absorbed.

Compost should always be nicely *moist* when potting, but *not* soaking wet. It should be damp enough to 'pour' from a small hand trowel into the pot without sticking.

POTTING-ON

This term refers to the move of a plant from a smaller pot to a larger one (Fig. 13). The point of potting-on is to ensure that the compost around the roots is always as fresh as possible with the optimum balance of nutrients. Although it may seem tedious to pot-on through several pot sizes, the difference it makes to the quality of a plant is quite dramatic. As a general rule the size of the pot to which the move is made should give about another 2.5 cm (1 in) of compost around the roots, but judgement must be made acording to the type of plant and stage of growth, as well as its vigour. The art of potting-on is only learnt after some experience.

When to pot-on is usually fairly easy to ascertain by tapping the plant out of its pot. If the roots are seen to be very advanced and encircling the inside of the pot, the plant is *pot*

Plate 10 A plant removed from its pot and showing a mass of roots crying out for more room. It is clearly 'pot bound' and demands potting-on.

Plate 11 Plants that have been grown in clay pots for a time may need an extra sharp tap on the pot rim to effect removal. A *small* hammer is useful if employed with care.

Fig. 14 Removing a plant from a pot.
If possible pass the plant stem or base between the fingers as shown. Tapping the inverted pot rim on the edge of the potting bench or other suitable object often helps to dislodge the root ball which should come away cleanly. It is usually best to make sure that the compost is moist before this operation.

bound (Plate 10). A move on is indicated. Potting-on is usually done as plants are resuming growth and need more root space. It is also a routine practice at intervals after raising plants from seed or cuttings.

To remove a plant from its pot, let the base pass between the fingers of one hand placed palm down over the flower pot. Invert the whole and tap the rim of the pot with a small hammer (Plate 11) or on the edge of the bench – the pot should then easily pull away if lifted with the other hand (Fig. 14). When potting-on, it sometimes helps to use a piece of stick or thin batten (called a 'potting stick') to

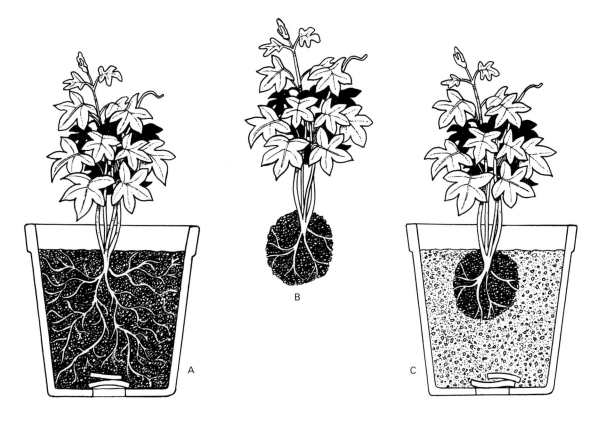

Fig. 15 Repotting.
(*A*) Plant to be repotted. (*B*) Plant removed from pot and with the root ball well reduced in size. (*C*) Plant potted into same size pot with fresh compost.

ease the compost down in the space between the root ball and the pot sides, but as already mentioned the compost should not be rammed.

Obviously there is a limit to the potting-on that can be done in the case of plants that are perennial and may reach an appreciable size. Such plants may have to end up in, say 30-cm (12-in) pots or small tubs. It may then be possible to *repot* (see next section) or further feeding may be done by 'top dressing' (p. 51). For most popular pot plants about three potting-on operations are usually required. For example, 8 cm to 13 cm to a final 15 or 18 cm (3 in to 5 in to 6 or 7 in). The instruction 'pot-on as required' means that this type of potting-on is advisable as the plants become pot bound.

REPOTTING

When it is no longer possible or desirable to pot-on, and also in the case of certain rather old, established plants after they are coming out of a dormant period, repotting is advisable (Fig. 15). This entails removal of some of the old root ball to reduce its size, and potting back into the *same sized pot* with fresh compost. Obviously this entails some root damage, but often it is done to plants that make roots very easily and the old ones may well have deteriorated anyway. Typical examples of popular plants that can be repotted each year are pelargoniums and fuchsias; other examples will be mentioned in this book where appropriate.

THE POTTING BENCH OR SHED

Early greenhouses often had a potting shed attached – you can still get designs with this innovation. In a shed you can keep all the tools and equipment associated with the greenhouse, and probably the garden equipment

three-sided tray made from thin sheet
aluminium or zinc

Fig. 16 Home-made potting bench.
On the bench is shown a small brush, such as an
old clothes brush, which is useful for keeping the
surface brushed free from compost after working
and clear for other jobs. For details of other items,
see text.

too, but easy access to the greenhouse is essential. Most home greenhouses do not have the luxury of a special shed but it is easy enough to make yourself a portable potting bench (Fig. 16). I use a simple three-sided tray made from sheet aluminium. You can get aluminium or zinc sheeting from most builders' merchants. It is easy to bend and can be cut with a pair of tin snippers or an old pair of stout household scissors. Make the tray a fair size so that you can mix composts if necessary, and it can be custom-made to fit a section of the staging. A comfortable space and hygienic surface to carry out all the operations of seed sowing, potting and tending to plants, is an important convenience to help the smooth and efficient running of the greenhouse.

To keep the potting bench clean and clear from compost, that will inevitably either be spread or spilt over the surface from time to time, have a small soft brush at hand, such as an old clothes brush (Fig. 16). The bench can then be used for a succession of different operations without getting everything unduly messy!

If, during summer, you have little need for a potting bench, a lightweight one, made as I have described, can be stored out of the way somewhere until required, leaving the staging free for normal use or display of plants.

A shed, frost free – as is likely if it's attached to a greenhouse – is ideal for winter storage of *dormant* plants that *don't need light*. Typical examples are storage organs packed as described for overwintering on p. 92, or plants that can be left dry in their pots.

8 PROPAGATION

MAKING A START

A new greenhouse always looks horribly bare but it is surprising how all beginners soon cry out for more space. Important advice for making a start has already been given in Chapter 7, but information given in this chapter will also be extremely helpful – with a propagator in operation there are so many exciting possibilities.

For the beginner, friends can be a very useful source of stock. Most friends will be only too pleased to pass on cuttings or other material from which new plants can be easily propagated. However, do remember to accept only absolutely healthy vegetation. A certain discernment should also be given to acceptance; some plants which are rather too common or too prolific will, of course, provide an abundance of material for propagation! It also helps to be able to identify the species or variety, and you can be more certain about this when buying from a reputable nursery.

PROPAGATORS

Equipment for efficient propagation is an invaluable, if not essential, asset to any greenhouse. It is an extremely wise investment too, since raising your own plants saves an enormous amount of money. Aesthetically, it is also extremely satisfying.

The starting of plants into growth from seed, cuttings or storage organs usually demands extra warmth and higher moisture and humidity conditions. To achieve this some form of enclosed area that can be warmed has to be organized.

A number of greenhouse accessory firms market excellent propagating cases. The best are electrically heated and thermostatically controlled (Plate 12). If you propose to purchase one of these, it is very wise to go for the largest you can afford or accommodate. A large case can be used to house small plants, and seedlings in pots or trays, for which the extra warmth can sometimes be very useful in giving a good start. A sizeable propagating case may also be employed as a miniature warm greenhouse, since the heating cost is usually quite minor, and some designs have fitted shelves to take extra pots. Good features of design to look for when buying are: variable thermostat so that temperature can be easily changed, a neon pilot light showing when the heating is on, useful when adjusting the thermostat, and a high maximum temperature.

Remember that for germinating certain seeds of tropical plants a temperature of about 27°C (81°F) is required. After germination the temperature can usually be dropped dramatically. Remember too, that the temperature attained by a propagator will depend on the temperature of the surroundings. If it is to be operated in a cold greenhouse, it must have an adequate heat source to reach the degree of warmth required. With thermostatic control, there is no need to fear that heat will be wasted.

Where there is no possibility of electricity, paraffin heated propagators may have to be considered, but these obviously do need careful manual control and attention. In essence a propagator merely consists of a base of sand kept warm and moist to give good humidity above, and a covered case to retain the warmth and moisture, but to let in a moderate amount of light. A simple, paraffin lamp-heated propagator is therefore easy to improvise (Fig. 17). Where there is pipe heating in the greenhouse,

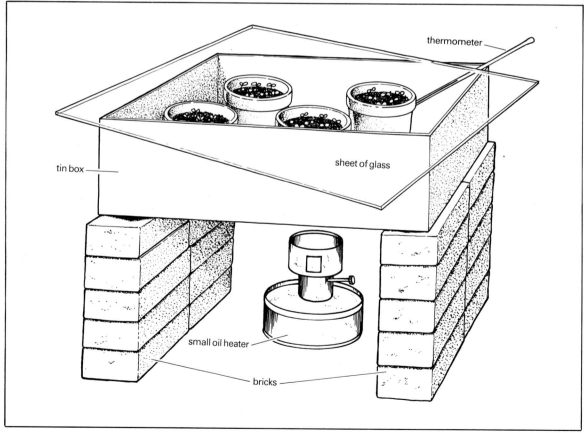

Plate 12 (*Left, above*) A well-designed, small electric propagator sold for the home greenhouse. The temperature can be varied and the control is thermostatic.

Fig. 17 (*Left, below*) Home-made propagator. All that's needed is a tin box, some bricks, and a small oil heater. It is important to check temperatures maintained *before* putting in plants, so that adjustments can be made.

an area of the staging above may also be utilized (Fig. 18).

Excellent propagators can be DIY constructed with soil-warming cables. An example is illustrated in Fig. 19; this is based on equipment I have built in my own propagating house. A good rod-type thermostat is essential, and I find that the warming cable needs to be run so that it gives about 15 W per 0.093 sq m (15 W per sq ft). The warming cable should be covered with just sufficient sand to protect it from damage by changing containers stood upon it. Do not cover with peat – this becomes a very poor heat conductor when dry and may cause the cable to overheat and burn out. Some people do put a layer of peat or

vermiculite on the sand layer and immerse the propagating trays or pots in this. However, in a covered case I have found it unnecessary and indeed a disadvantage. The less bulk of material around the cables, the more accurate is the thermostatic control because there is less heat-holding capacity.

Warming cables that operate direct from the mains or from a low-voltage transformer can be bought. The latter are safer for ground work where there is a possibility of damage by tools. The former are the most convenient for case or bench warming. They are usually rated at 75, 150, 300 and 600 W, and two or more can be used if necessary. For the average greenhouse propagation, a 120 to 150 W cable

Fig. 18 Propagation on the staging.
(*A*) Slatted staging. (*B*) Corrugated iron or metal sheeting (zinc or aluminium are easier to cut). (*C*) Layer of moist peat. (*D*) Oil heater or hot water pipes. With an oil heater, temperature can be adjusted by altering height of bricks (*E*). (*F*) Plant containers plunged in the peat layer can be covered with cloches, plastic covers, or any suitable clear transparent material.

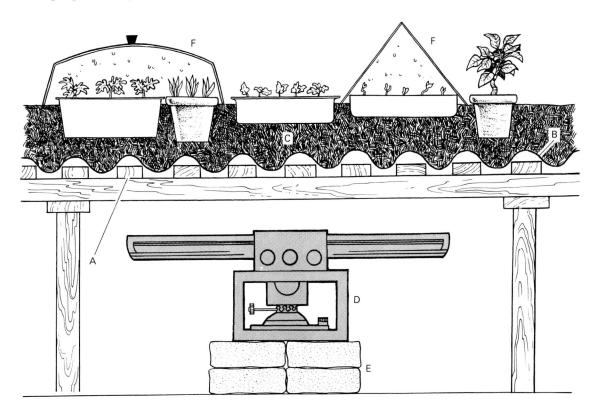

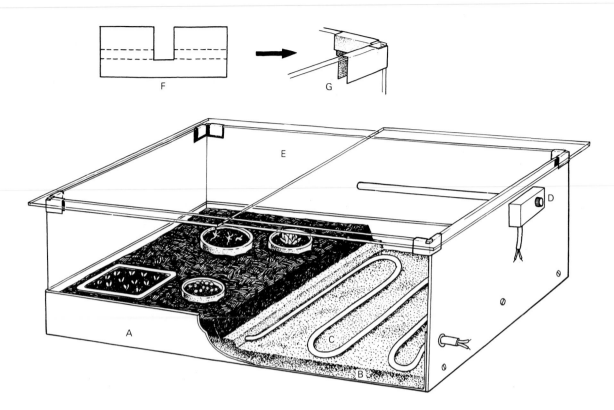

Fig. 19 Propagator as constructed by the author. (A) Large tray made from sheet aluminium. (B) Sand layer immersing electric warming cable (C) which is covered with moist peat, or a layer of more sand according to type of propagation to be performed. (D) Accurate thermostat is a wise fitment, but can be optional if fairly constant attention can be given. (E) Casing made from glass panes held together with clips made from aluminium or zinc sheet, cut and bent as shown (F & G). For seed germination the peat plunge can usually be omitted.

will heat a space 1.5 m × 60 cm (5 × 2 ft). When putting down the cables do not allow any lengths to touch each other; the spacing must be as even as possible. Full instructions are usually given by the manufacturers.

USING A PROPAGATOR

Keep the base sand nicely moist at all times. Never site a propagator in direct sunlight – the temperature may be seriously increased to levels that can damage or even kill plants and seeds. Do not operate the propagator at unnecessarily high temperatures. For most of the ordinary bedding and greenhouse plant seeds, a *maximum* of about 18°C (64°F) is adequate, and most cuttings will root well at about 21°C (70°F). Excessive temperatures for ordinary hardy or half-hardy plant seeds can spoil the seedlings by causing etiolation (spindly, forced weak growth) or even inhibit germination.

By planning and timing sowings and propagation the propagator can usually be kept productive over a long period, one tray of propagation material being put in as another is taken out ready for pricking out or potting. The busiest time is usually from late winter to spring. From then until autumn, use of a propagator is rarely necessary, there being adequate natural summer warmth for any propagation jobs that arise.

GENERAL PROPAGATION RULES

Unhealthy plants must never be used as a source of propagation material. This rule especially applies to *diseased* plants, since some troubles can be passed on and such plants become a menace of infection to others. A special watch must be kept for virus diseases, and plants that show deformity, stunting, mottling of foliage, or undesirable, abnormal flower colour, must on no account be propagated. It is also unwise to propagate *anything that is not up to standard*. The whole point of propagation is to reproduce desirable characteristics.

PROPAGATION FROM SEED

Because of its importance this subject is dealt with fully in the next chapter. Nowadays F_1 hybrid seed has attracted much attention – justifiably so! Plants from this source are usually superior, easier to manage, often more cold and disease resistant, and far more vigorous generally. F_1 seed is produced by experts and by careful crossing of the parent plants. It is consequently more expensive, but an excellent investment. Do not attempt to save the seed from F_1 hybrids, or other hybrids in most cases; it will not bread true to type.

However, seed from pure species can be saved in many instances. If you wish to save seed, it is a good idea to remove most of the flowers or fruits to divert the plant's energy to developing a few. Make sure the seed is ripe before collecting.

SOFTWOOD CUTTINGS

The practice of takings cuttings is fairly well known and documented in most books on general gardening. In the greenhouse cuttings can be taken almost the year around except from plants that are dormant. The ideal time, however, is when plants are just into their active period of growth, and spring is consequently usually a busy time. Some important cuttings can also be taken in early autumn.

The technique of taking cuttings is shown in Fig. 20. Always select *small* vigorous shoots, usually a finger length is adequate. The lower leaves should be pulled away from the stem and a clean cut made just below where the leaves joined. The sharper the blade used to cut off this piece of stem the better. A razor blade or a surgeon's scalpel is a useful tool. A blunt blade may cause bruising of the tissue,

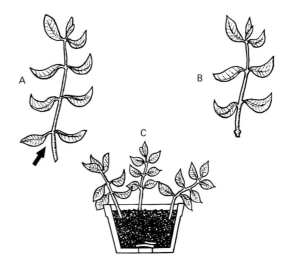

Fig. 20 Softwood cuttings.
(*A*) Piece of plant selected; leaves to be removed arrowed. (*B*) Lower leaves removed and clean cut made immediately below the nodes left by the removed leaves. (*C*) Cuttings inserted in cutting compost.

which may lead to rotting instead of rooting.

The ease and speed of rooting varies considerably from subject to subject. Sometimes rooting is hastened by using a hormone preparation in which the stem of the cutting is dipped. However, this technique does not seem to help those cuttings taken from plants known to be very difficult to root. The presence of flowers or buds in all cases should be avoided, since these tend to inhibit root formation.

Nearly all the cuttings taken from the greenhouse plants are *softwood* type – from soft or immature growth or shoots. *Semi-hardwood* cuttings are taken from more mature shoots especially from shrubby plants. *Hardwood* cuttings come from decidedly woody shrubs and trees, and are usually taken when these are dormant. Both semi-hardwood and hardwood cuttings are not often taken from greenhouse plants proper, but they may be taken from outdoor subjects and rooted in the greenhouse. Both types are, in general, more difficult to root than softwood cuttings, and hormone rooting powders may be beneficial here. Some cuttings from greenhouse plants root with

Plate 13 To slit the veins of leaves for propagation use a *very sharp* penknife, razor blade, or surgeon's scalpel sold by most artists' equipment shops. In this illustration a *Begonia rex* leaf is being prepared.

little compost can be put at the bag's bottom and the cutting pushed down into it. This method has the advantage that rooting can be seen through the polythene when it has taken place. In *all* cases, the cutting compost *must not be allowed to dry out at any time.* Where a lot of propagation from cuttings is proposed, the method of mist propagation is worth consideration (see below).

LEAF CUTTINGS

This is very useful for many important greenhouse plants, but it is not a method applicable to *all* plants. Numerous recommendations will be found in the plant sections of this book.

There are several ways leaf cuttings can be taken and prepared. A simple technique is to carefully detach a leaf from the main stem and to slit the veins on the *underside* of the leaf with a sharp blade, such as a penknife or scalpel as shown in Plate 13. The leaf is then placed slits down on the surface of a cutting compost in a shallow tray and covered with glass or plastic to retain moisture (Fig. 21A). After a time in a warm propagator, roots will grow from where the slits were made and tiny new plants will develop which can be separated and potted.

Another useful method is to cut the leaf into small triangular sections (Fig. 21B), with a leaf vein at the apex of each triangle. This point is then inserted into the cutting compost and treated as above.

Sometimes a small leaf will root if it is merely detached and inserted into compost so that the leaf stalk is covered. Long sword-shaped leaves can also be cut up into cross-sections (Fig. 21C) and rooted if they are pressed upright into the compost.

great ease, even when merely placed in a jar of water. For example, nerium, tradescantias, zebrina and many other trailing plants, and even some fuchsias.

When taken and prepared the cuttings are inserted in a *cutting compost.* This is usually merely a mixture of equal parts of peat and grit, but perlite (Appendix) is often used on its own giving excellent results. Some growers add fertilizers, but I have not found this necessary provided the cuttings are potted up as soon as adequate roots have formed. The cutting compost can be contained in pots or seed trays, but there is no doubt that rooting often occurs much more quickly and readily when the cuttings are inserted *around the edge of a pot.*

Rooting is accelerated by warmth at the base, popularly called 'bottom heat' and a high humidity to prevent rapid loss of moisture from the leaves. The containers of cuttings are therefore put in the propagator case. Cuttings taken in summer can often be covered with a transparent polythene bag. Alternatively, a

DIVISION

Clump-forming perennial pot plants can be very easily propagated by simple division of the roots when they are about to start into growth – usually early spring is the best time. If the roots are very entwined and matted, it is often better to divide by cutting through with a very sharp blade. This is less likely to bruise root tissue which may then instigate rotting. Divide when the roots are slightly moist – not wet – and water very carefully after repotting

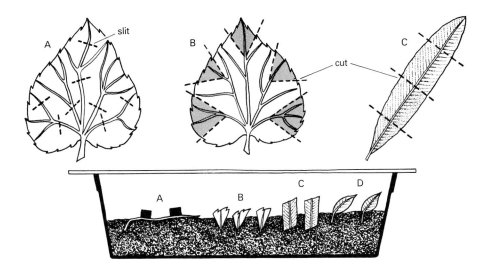

Fig. 21 Types of leaf cutting.
(*A*) Leaf with undersurface veins cut cleanly preferably with razor blade and placed cuts down on cutting compost. A few small pieces of pot or pebbles help to keep the leaf flat to the compost surface. (*B*) Triangular sections cut from leaf and set in the compost. There should be a cut leaf vein at each immersed triangle. (*C*) Some long narrow leaves can be cut into sections as shown. (*D*) Simple leaf cuttings, a short length of the leaf stalk being allowed to remain.

and until the plants are making active growth. Tuberous plants can be multiplied by cutting up the tubers also with a sharp blade. This should be done *after* the tubers have started into growth and shoots are clearly seen. Each segment you cut should have a healthy growing shoot. It helps to dust the cut surfaces of the tubers with powdered charcoal, which reduces loss of sap and keeps out disease organisms.

OFFSETS

A number of greenhouse bulbs produce tiny bulblets around the side when reaching maturity. These can be detached (Plate 14) and potted individually at repotting time; such small bulbs may take several years' growing on before flowering. Some rhizomes and tubers reproduce themselves during the growing season, and can be tipped out of the pots and separated for individual potting at potting time. Special cases are brought to attention in the plant chapters of the book.

SIMPLE LAYERING

This is sometimes useful for trailers and climbers (Fig. 22). A length of stem from the plant is brought down so that a section of stem passes just below the surface of compost in another pot. It often helps rooting if a leaf is detached carefully at this point, or a shallow slit is made in the stem, but not enough to cut it completely through. When roots have

Plate 14 Many bulbous plants form offsets (baby bulbs) around their base as they grow and reach maturity. These can be separated at repotting time and potted individually for propagation.

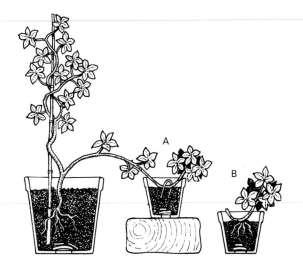

Fig. 22 Propagation by layering.
(*A*) A length of stem of the 'mother' plant is fastened down in another small pot with a piece of bent wire or other suitable means. It may hasten rooting if a slit is made in the stem at this point, where it is held just below compost level, and rooting hormone applied. When the stem is well rooted in can be severed from the parent (*B*).

Fig. 23 Air layering.
(*A*) Plant from which lower leaves have fallen. (*B*) Slit cut in stem in upward direction. (*C*) Wedge of peat or moss, dusted with hormone powder. (*D*) Thin transparent polythene. (*E*) Tie. (*F*) The enclosed polythene 'chamber' filled with peat.

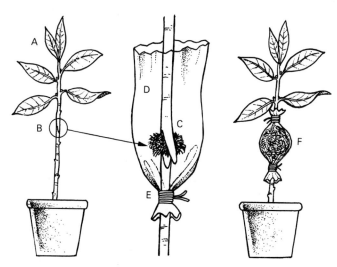

formed, the shoot can be severed from the parent plant and grown on.

AIR LAYERING

This is not often employed, but may be useful for plants that have become leggy or lost lower leaves. It is probably most commonly used for *Ficus elastica*, the popular rubber plant. A slit is made in the stem where the new roots are required to form, and a small wad of peat dusted with hormone powder inserted. A moist larger wad of peat and moss is then bound around with some clear polythene and tied in position. In warmth roots should eventually form and can be seen through the polythene. The stem can then be cut off just below the new roots and potted (Fig. 23).

For air layering to be quick and successful moderate warmth is usually necessary, so it is best done, in the home greenhouse, from early summer onwards when there is adequate natural warmth. Plants suitable for this technique are usually far too large to fit a propagator.

MIST PROPAGATION

This is an extremely successful method of rooting cuttings of all types. The apparatus consists of a means to keep the cuttings misted with water at intervals, controlled automatically, so that they are always coated with moisture. Bottom warmth is provided with warming cables. It is possible to set up your own equipment using one of the automatic watering methods involving the 'electronic leaf' or similar device, described on p. 33. However, for the home greenhouse gardener, small complete units are supplied, with full instructions, by greenhouse accessory firms (see Appendix). Although extensively employed by commercial growers, mist propagation (Plate 5, p. 33) is usually only adopted by the more enthusiastic home gardener.

9   GROWING PLANTS FROM SEED

SOWING TECHNIQUE

Sow seed as soon as possible after receiving it, and do not leave packets in the heat and humidity of a greenhouse. Seed sowing tools are shown in Fig. 24. (See also relevant details in Chapters 7 and 8.)

To make handling of small seed easier, it is sometimes 'pelleted' by coating with an inert substance. Personally, I prefer not to use pelleted seed, since I find germination can be unreliable – special attention must be given to keeping the seed nicely moist after sowing.

Fig. 24   Seed 'management' tools.
(*A*) Small home-made sieve (see text) for riddling seed compost if necessary. (*B*) Small piece of bent metal sheet for smoothing and levelling compost surface. (*C*) Pair of long and easy-to-handle, finely tipped tweezers for seed sowing – also very useful for pricking out. (*D*) Many people prefer this pricking-out tool made by cutting a 'V' notch in a piece of stiff plastic or sheet metal.

The germination of some large seed can be hastened by removing a tiny sliver of the coating with a razor blade and/or soaking overnight in tepid water before sowing. Large seed can be sown individually in small pots or spaced with the fingers in seed trays. All seed should be sown thinly to facilitate pricking out of the seedlings. Small seed – but not too small – can be handled with a pair of finely tipped tweezers when spacing. Much finer seed is best carefully tapped out of the packet with a forefinger whilst moving the packet over the compost surface (Plate 15).

Always use a proper seed compost in a nicely *moist* condition. Plastic seed trays are sold by most garden shops and are easy to keep clean – cleanliness is essential. For most seeds a depth of compost from about 2.5–4 cm (1–1½ in) is adequate. A proper seed compost should be of a suitable texture for most seeds, but if it appear too coarse, it can be passed through a sieve (Plate 16); one that has 8

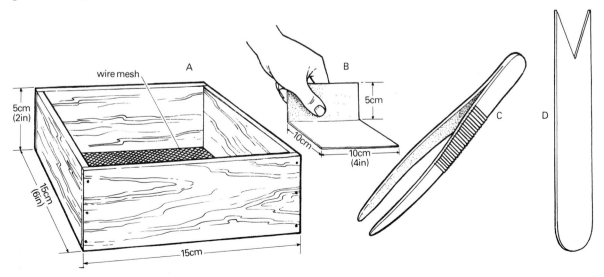

Plate 15 (*Above*) With a little practice many seeds can be sown direct from the packet by tapping with the forefinger as shown. Keep your eye on where the seeds are falling – not on the packet – to ensure even distribution. Always sow thinly.

Plate 16 (*Below*) Using a home-made 8-mesh sieve to riddle seed compost, if necessary, for sowing very fine seed. This is usually more likely to be required when you make up your own mixes.

meshes per inch is ideal. A small piece of stainless steel gauze is suitable. Tap down the compost and level before sowing. *Do not cover very fine seed.* It is customary to cover larger seed with about its own diameter of compost. No seed should be sown too deeply, since this can impede germination. To help even sowing, very fine seed can be first mixed with a little clean fine sand.

There is often no need to sow all the seeds in a packet. Some can be reserved in case of accidental failure. Sowing in batches at intervals of a week or so – staggered sowing – is also often useful in keeping up flowering or cropping. You will have plants reaching maturity over a longer period.

Water-in the seeds after sowing with clean water using a fine mist delivered from a sprayer. Cover the seed trays with clean white paper and then with clear glass or plastic to keep in moisture (Fig. 25), and place in the propagator. Certain seed, such as the following examples, germinate better if exposed to some light. These should also not be covered with compost regardless of size, but just lightly pressed into the compost surface:

Anthurium spp.	*Gramineae* (grasses)
Bellis perennis	Iris spp.
Bromeliads	Lettuce
Cacti and other	*Lobelia cardinalis*
succulents	Mimulus spp.
Calceolarias	Nicotiana
Crossandra spp.	Petunias
Ficus spp.	Philodendron spp.
Gesneriacae spp.	Saintpaulias
Gloxinias	Streptocarpus

GERMINATION AND AFTERCARE

The seed trays must not be allowed to dry out whilst germination is taking place, as this may cause complete germination failure. Conversely, the compost must not be soaked since this will cause 'suffocation' of the seed which needs *air* for the germination process. Make sure the germination temperature is suited to the subjects. As soon as germination is seen to be under way, remove covering from the trays to give full light, but *not* direct sunlight.

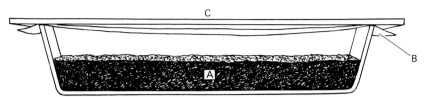

Fig. 25 Preparing a seed pan or tray.
(*A*) Seed compost. (*B*) Sheet of white paper. (*C*) Sheet of glass, *over* the paper.

Prick out as soon as possible (Plate 17), i.e. when the seedlings can be lifted without damage. I use a finely tipped pair of tweezers for this purpose; for larger seedlings a 'v' notched piece of wood or plastic 'lolly' stick are equally useful. Transfer the seedlings to a recommended potting compost in small pots or seed trays depending on the nature of the plants. After germination most seedlings are quite happy in a much lower temperature, but sometimes it is a good idea to return the potted seedlings of extra tender subjects to the propagator for a while until established.

To avert the risk of damping-off it is also a wise precaution to water-in seedlings of all kinds with Cheshunt compound. Good light is essential to seedlings or they will become drawn and pale in colour, but they should be introduced to full sun, when this is necessary, gradually. See also Bedding plants p. 8.

Plate 17 Pricking out should be done as soon as seedlings can be safely lifted without too much damage. For tiny seedlings I prefer to use finely tipped tweezers (Fig. 24), but for larger seedlings, as illustrated, a strip of thin metal, plastic or wood, can be employed if preferred.

Colourful Home Greenhouse Plants from Seed: Selected List

The variety names recommended in the list are important – try to obtain them when possible. At the end of the list, Table 2 gives brief details of more easily grown and interesting plants that can be grown from seed.

ANNUALS (HARDY GARDEN FORMS)

Many of the modern varieties of hardy annuals and half-hardy types used for outdoor bedding make excellent pot plants. Choose dwarf compact types and F_1 hybrids if available. The hardier forms can be sown in autumn and grown on over winter in just frost-free conditions for extra early flowering. Often sowings can be made both in spring and in autumn. Generally a final 13-cm (5-in) pot is suitable for flowering. Certain annuals are outstanding for pots in the greenhouse and have been singled out for special mention in the following pages.

ABUTILON HYBRIDS

Although shrubby perennials, these plants often tend to become untidy and straggly with age. They can be flowered as annuals and, if desired, kept for a year or so, since they frequently flower well into winter in frost-free conditions. The foliage is maple-like, and the flowers showy and attractive. They are beautifully veined, and cup-shaped, with rich colours and shades of pink, red, orange, and yellow and striking central clusters of yellow stamens.

A fine new introduction to look out for is 'Bella'. This has a very much more compact habit, growing little over 60 cm (2 ft) in height. Another important improvement is that the flowers face towards you, instead of drooping as in most other hybrids.

The plants can be stopped in the seedling stage to induce a more bushy development, but this may delay flowering by some weeks. If preferred plants can be allowed to grow up as a single stem, if some height is needed for

example for a staging display. Young plants can be grown in 13-cm (5-in) pots for some time but, if to be grown-on, will need potting-on to 18-cm (7-in) pots at least. Seed germinates readily at about 16°C (61°F).

ARDISIA

A. crispa was once very popular, but nowadays is rarely seen – it deserves a return to favour. It is a shrubby species but, in pots, grows to form the shape of a miniature tree. The leaves are fleshy and evergreen with slightly 'toothed' edges (crenulated). These leaves harbour nitrogen fixation bacteria – such as one finds on roots of the pea family – so the plant is partly self-feeding and high nitrogen fertilizers should be avoided. During summer there are masses of small pinkish to red, or white flowers, sweetly fragrant although they are not showy. The main attraction is the show of bright red berries that follow. These last well into the winter and over Christmas.

A disadvantage is that from seed, which is the best way to grow good sturdy plants, it takes at least two years to develop a fully decorative specimen. To grow on the young plants a winter minimum of about 7°C (45°F) is essential, preferably a few degrees higher. Once a plant has formed berries, keep the conditions cool so that they are retained in good condition as long as possible.

If a mature plant becomes too tall, cut it back after watering has been reduced. For a while after, sap will ooze from the cuts. When this ceases, watering should be resumed and plenty of new stems should quickly arise. Mature plants are also best re-potted into the same size pots, rather than potted-on. Seed, now readily available, germinates easily at about 20°C (68°F). Sow during spring.

ASCLEPIAS

An old favourite shrubby tender perennial, which most people prefer to grow as a half-hardy annual, is *A. curassavica*. This is quick flowering from seed sown in early spring. The flowers are extremely attractive, being borne in umbels. Each floret has petals in an unusual shade of coral-red and a contrasting golden yellow centre. Recently a new hybrid, 'Butterflies' which is claimed to be hardy, has been introduced. This is more compact making a very neat pot plant, and comes in a wide range of subtle colours, including orange, pink, gold and scarlet shades.

A species that's entirely different is *A. physocarpa*. Some botanists now call this *Gomphocarpus fruticosus*. It grows tall and shrubby and bears masses of white to cream flowers in summer. However, the attraction is the strange large maroon tinted green inflated seed pods that follow. These can be cut and used for floral art work if desired. The shape of the pods inspired the popular name of 'Swan Plant'. Both these asclepias are extremely easy from seed sown in the usual manner.

BEGONIA

Fibrous-rooted bedding begonias make splendid neat pot plants. There are very many named varieties from which to choose, in mixed or separate colours. Those with bronzy coloured foliage are often especially attractive. A few hybrids are obtainable that do not set seed and thus flower continuously for an extra long time. 'Pink Avalanche' is a newcomer of this type.

Some tuberous kinds, such as 'Double Fiesta' can be grown from seed, sown early in the year, to give fine blooms from summer onwards. All begonia seed is extremely fine and must be sown with care. Most flower well in final 13-cm (5-in) pots. For foliage begonias, see p. 129; for tuberous rooted begonias, see p. 93, and for pendulous begonias, see p. 140.

BROWALLIA

B. speciosa is an old favourite greenhouse flower once prized for its blue or white blooms borne in winter in a warm greenhouse, or in the home as a house plant. However, by sowing in late winter in a warm propagator, plants giving a good show from autumn onwards can be obtained. The older varieties grow about 60 cm (2 ft) in height, and need a final 13-cm (5-in) pot. The young plants should also be stopped to encourage branching. Recently new 'Troll' browallias have been introduced. These are very dwarf, being less than half the normal height. They do not

need stopping, and should be grouped, say, three seedlings to each pot.

B. viscosa is not so well known, yet it is an extremely pretty blue and white annual very easy to grow, as several seedlings to each 13-cm (5-in) pot. Height is about 30 cm (12 in) and a few thin canes may be needed for support. Flowers late summer onwards from spring sowing.

CALCEOLARIA

This is a very popular and important greenhouse plant giving masses of beautiful pouch blooms in a very wide range of glorious colours from winter to early summer, depending on sowing time and variety. Only conditions well free from frost are needed to grow them. The clusters of inflated blooms are also usually speckled or spotted in red/yellow colours presenting an exotic and 'tropical' appearance, yet excellent results can be obtained in the average home greenhouse.

Seed is best sown from late spring to early summer. The giant flowered types with enormous blooms borne on plants about 45 cm (18 in) tall are most impressive, but are usually much later flowering than the multiflora kinds, which are dwarf and compact and have masses of smaller flowers. The multiflora F_1 hybrids are often very fast to mature, and make useful Chrismas present plants. Two varieties such as these are 'Glorious Formula' and 'Jewel Cluster'. Two giants for flower shows are 'Monarch Mixture' and 'Perfection'. A newcomer is 'Anytime Mixed' which has red to spotted bright yellow pouches. This is exceptionally early and fast to bloom. It can be sown at about Christmas time for spring colour, and in succession to give a very long period of pleasure.

The giant flowered types need potting-on to 13-cm (5-in) pots or larger. The multifloras are usually suited to about 10-cm (4-in) pots. When growing on during the summer and autumn, *cool* shaded conditions are essential. Frames shaded with white Coolglass often make convenient accommodation. Keep a careful watch for aphids and take care not to damage the foliage which is rather brittle. During winter, ventilate whenever weather temperature permits.

Calceolaria rugosa 'Sunshine' is a recently introduced F_1 hybrid replacing the original species at one time propagated from cuttings for summer bedding. This new hybrid makes a fine compact pot plant easily raised from seed sown late winter to early spring. It makes a good subject for the frost-free greenhouse, often flowering well into winter and remaining nicely evergreen.

CAMPANULA

Probably the most eye-catching greenhouse campanula is *C. pyramidalis* the chimney campanula which reaches about 1.5 m (5 ft) in height in a final 25-cm (10-in) pot, which will take three plants. The flowers are blue or white and the plants become smothered from top to blottom. Sow in spring, pot-on as required, overwintering in a frost-free frame or greenhouse. From spring onwards the plants grow tall very quickly and need transferring to the greenhouse, if previously kept in frames. The flowers appear in summer. (See also p. 140.)

CAPSICUM and SOLANUM

These are different species of the same family but need similar treatment, and sometimes they are confused in seed catalogues. Both have very attractive showy berries. In capsicums the fruits are usually elongated, and in solanum they are more spherical. However, both, and solanum in particular, are notorious in the remarkable variation in forms they can produce. Note that solanum berries can be poisonous.

Solanums were at one time best sown in late winter if needed for display the following Christmas; the winter cherry is a popular common name. However, modern varieties may well form berries too soon if sown early, and experience by practical trial is the only certain way to arrive at the best sowing time. Capsicums nearly always form berries sooner and more easily, and can be sown in spring. They will often give berries from late summer onwards. To get a good set of berries on solanum, stand the plants outdoors whilst in flower so that insects can polinate. Numerous named varieties with berries of different shape, and colours including purple, yellow, orange, and red, will be found described in the seed catalogues. Solanums are prone to suffer from magnesium deficiency causing yellowing foliage. Water with Epsom salt solution (about 2%) from time to time. For all types use final 13-cm (5-in) pots.

CATHARANTHUS (Vinca)

The delightful *C. rosea* is commonly called Madagascar periwinkle. It forms a very sturdy, neat, shrubby, pot plant with very glossy foliage, and rarely exceeds 30 cm (1 ft) in height. From seed it will flower in a few months. These are usually either rose-pink or white with a carmine 'eye'. They are typically of 'periwinkle' shape, freely produced and very attractive. There are a few named forms, 'Little Pinky' being of particular merit.

Since the young plants do not like cold, it's best not to sow before early spring. Germinate the seed at about 21°C (70°F). Avoid subsequent chill and keep the plant humid and shaded over summer. Best flowering usually occurs on second year plants, but the plants cannot be saved over winter unless a moderate temperature is maintained. It's worth taking a few plants into the home where they will often survive in a warm room and can be returned to the greenhouse in spring. Plants may often come through the winter at relatively low temperatures if kept on the dry side. They may lose foliage and become tatty but recover with the return of warmth.

CELOSIA

C. argentea pyramidalis (Prince of Wales' feathers) with silky plumes, and *C. a. cristata* (cockscomb) with strange velvety 'combs', both with a range of lovely colours, make excellent pot plants. Indeed they are usually seen at their best when protected from the wet and weather. Sow in spring and pot-on to final 13-cm (5-in) pots. There are many named varieties from which to choose and are often listed in seed catalogues as 'plumosa' and 'cristata'. An outstanding fine new *C. plumosa* is 'Apricot Brandy' with extra large long plumes of glowing yellow-orange colour. One of the finest *C. cristata* varieties giving a wide assortment of colours is 'Jewel Box'. Both varieties are especially suited for pot work.

CINERARIA (SENECIO CRUENTUS)

This is of similar merit to calceolaria and the two are often grown together, then giving a most dazzling display. Cinerarias have masses of daisy-like flowers in both pastel and deep vivid colours. There are also some rich blues and purples, not found in calceolaria and so making an excellent complementary contrast. In some varieties the flowers also have striking white zones, and there are also both giant flowered and small multiflora types. In modern varieties the habit is sturdy and compact making the plants ideal for gifts. The giant exhibition types are, however, much more easily damaged and are not easily transported. The culture and sowing is much the same as outlined under calceolaria.

Of the many named varieties to be found in the seed catalogues, 'Spring Glory' is one of the best for general purposes and is very early flowering. Although dwarf it has remarkably large flowers. A new splendid multiflora is 'Merry-go-round' which ultimately forms a 'dome' of dainty blooms and includes both rich and pastel colour shades. A giant to impress in the conservatory or in flower shows is 'Single Superb', which also includes a good proportion of flowers zoned with striking white circles. Cinerarias are very attractive to aphids, so keep vigilant watch. It is best to spray with a systemic as a preventive.

COLEUS

This is probably the most colourful of all foliage plants and certainly the easiest to raise from seed. Among the very many named varieties can be found every possible colour and colour combination imaginable, and there are now numerous different leaf shapes too. In the home greenhouse coleus is best regarded as an annual, although it is a tropical perennial in congenial warmth, and can also be propagated from cuttings, as any special named cultivars require if colour and form are to be exactly reproduced. From a spring sowing, fine plants will be obtained quickly for summer to autumn display. Ensuing colder conditions cause

Plate 18   Transferring coleus seedlings from seed trays to small pots for growing on, after the colours have developed to enable selection of the finest.

deterioration and the plants can then be discarded.

Prick out seedlings into seed trays and grow on until the colours can be seen developing; early on the leaves may look uninteresting. The best colours can then be isolated and potted (Plate 18); discard any not up to standard. Pot-on to 13-cm (5-in) pots or slightly less according to vigour and size of the variety. Any flower spikes that form are usually best removed at an early stage to direct the plants' energy to forming foliage. Some modern varieties have less tendency to produce flower spikes.

Generally useful is the F_1 hybrid 'Carefree'. It has a wonderful colour range with unusual bright hues and contrasts, as well as sturdy compact habit. Another new variety is 'Sabre' which has unusual elongated foliage. Both these need the minimum of attention and no pinching out or stopping, being naturally dwarf and bushy. With generous treatment and potting-on to large pots, some varieties, such as 'Red Velvet', can be grown to a considerable height for conservatories or flower shows. There are also fancy varieties with frilled or lace-edge foliage which make an attractive contrast and semi-trailers for baskets. 'Mosaic' is a very new ultra dwarf.

CUPHEA

The best cuphea for the home greenhouse is *C. ignea*, the Mexican cigar plant. Sow late winter to early spring and pot-on to 13-cm (5-in) pots. The plant forms a low neat compact little shrub soon smothering itself with masses of small white- and black-tipped, crimson, tubular flowers. It is very fast flowering indeed, usually blooming when little more than a seedling.

CYCLAMEN

From an autumn sowing fine specimens can be grown in about 14 months. Numerous named varieties will be found described in the seed catalogues, including giant flowered and miniature types, and some notable for scent or specially attractive foliage too.

Sow by placing seed on the compost surface and then covering with a layer of fine moist peat about twice the diameter of the seed in thickness. Germinate at 18°C (64°F), keep as steady as possible. Germination may be erratic, but prick out each seedling as soon as possible when it has formed two leaves. Transfer to individual small pots and return to the propagator until growth is vigorous. Then transfer to about 13°C (55°F), held steady if possible. By spring plants should be ready for final 13-cm (5-in) pots, and should be grown on in summer in shady cold frames. In autumn, take the plants into a greenhouse and treat as described on p. 94. At this time, any flower buds that may appear too soon can be removed to conserve the plant's resources for a later show around Christmas time.

Of the numerous fancy types recently introduced, an F_1 hybrid double-flowered type has been given much attention – personally I do not find it attractive, preferring the graceful beauty of the single or frilled varieties. For general use the variety 'Triumph' will be found very pleasing and reasonably easy. A fine new F_1 hybrid is 'Firmament', now popular with commercial growers, and it has some specially rich red and pink shades as well as pure white.

DATURA

Perhaps the most popular and easily grown is the annual *D. metel* 'Fastuosa', with creamy-white purple flushed trumpet flowers which fill the greenhouse with a lily-like scent. There are forms with other colours, often wrongly named, including a fine golden yellow. One of the loveliest shrubby forms, needing plenty of space to display itself, is *D. arborea*, also powerfully scented. This has white 'trumpets' which may be born the first year of sowing if this is done early. *D. sanguinea* is another shrubby beauty with pendant orange-red trumpets, usually borne in the second year from seed. This species makes a splendid plant for a small conservatory, and grows to about 1 m (3¼ ft). It survives outdoors in *mild* areas. *D. suaveolens* is similar with white pendant flowers, but grows tall and needs lots of space.

Seed of all these species germinates well in congenial warmth – about 20°C (68°F) or a few degrees higher. The perennial species need at least 7°C (45°F) over winter if they are to be saved without risk. The flowers are usually very shortlived – one to two days – but there are always plenty of buds waiting to open and the flowering period is quite reasonable. Most daturas are *poisonous* – the seed particularly so!

EXACUM

Exacum affine is an old favourite with tiny, pretty blue flowers having golden yellow anthers. A special feature is a delightful fragrance which in some varieties has been lost in attempting to breed forms with larger flowers. Fortunately in the variety 'Starlight Fragrance' the sweet scent has been retained. Sow late winter and pot-on to 10-cm (4-in) pots, several seedlings to each. Final height is about 23 cm (9 in). Exacums like moderate warmth, humidity, and shade. Protect seedlings from chill.

GLOXINIA (Sinningia)

At one time gloxinias were not particularly easy to grow from seed, but with the introduction of F_1 hybrids the culture has been made a simple matter. Sow preferably at the beginning of the year in a propagator at about 21°C

(70°F) and do not cover the seed with compost; just press it into the surface. Retain the seed trays in the propagator until the seedlings are large enough to handle, and prick out into small pots which should also be kept in the propagator for a while. Pot-on as required to final 13-cm (5-in) pots. The plants like warmth, moderate humidity, and shade. Plants grown from seed as described should flower the following late summer to autumn. After flowering the corms can be dried and saved as described on p. 92. The saved corms should give better plants in their second year. The F_1 hybrids may have slightly smaller flowers than others from seed and from named cultivars grown from corms, but they are extremely beautiful and free flowering.

HELIOTROPIUM

H. peruvianum, popularly called cherry pie, is another old favourite of the conservatory. It has bold flattish heads of deep blue to purplish flowers with a characteristic and captivating fragrance. A well known variety is 'Marine' with dark blue flowers. Sow late winter and pot-on to 13-cm (5-in) pots, one plant per pot. Flowers should appear from late spring to autumn depending on the time of sowing. In a slightly warm greenhouse, plants will survive the winter, but should be cut back to encourage new growth in spring.

HIBISCUS

There are a number of exquisite exotic hibiscus for the greenhouse, but for the home greenhouse the F_1 hybrids are the best proposition and easier to grow. There are two remarkable hybrids: 'Southern Belle' and the very new 'Rio Carnival'. The former has incredibly large flowers the size of dinner plates and grows to about 1.5 m (5 ft). The latter also has gigantic flowers but the plants are far more compact and a better proposition for the small greenhouse. Sow as early as possible in the year and pot-on to about 23-cm (9-in) pots. Growth is very fast once the seedlings are established and flowers appear from summer onwards. The flowers are short lived, like most hibiscus, but there are always plenty of buds waiting to open.

IMPATIENS

The busy Lizzie is one of the most popular of all flowering pot plants and, in fact, is far better grown from seed. There are now an enormous number of named varieties listed in the seed catalogues and most make fine pot plants. The best are those with a dwarf spreading habit, and again the F_1 hybrids should be given preference. Recently some very fine strains have been introduced giving a wide range of exceptionally beautiful and unusual colours. An example is 'Futura' also with larger flowers than usual and a great abundance of them, but it is not so dwarf as some varieties and can be used in hanging baskets as well as in pots. 'Blitz' has huge dazzling scarlet blooms. The varieties with white contrasting 'stars' or stripes are very striking too, e.g. the F_1 hybrid 'Gem Bicolor'. One of the best varieties for general use is 'Grand Prix' with neat habit, large flowers and an excellent mixture of lovely colours.

An exciting new 1983 introduction is a *double* flowered form – the first of its kind – 'Rosette'. Twenty-five per cent of the flowers are fully double, the remainder semi-double, in a wide and lovely colour range. For pots only.

In a warm greenhouse, Impatiens can be sown at almost any time. The easiest way is to start in late winter or early spring, potting-on to final 13-cm (5-in) pots, but the seedlings often start to produce flowers before this stage. The plants can be further propagated from cuttings if you get any special colours you wish to reproduce exactly. However, starting from seed usually gives far more vigorous and more floriferous plants.

LANTANA

Considering the ease with which lantanas can be grown – and the distinctive charm of the flowers – they should be better known and seen more often. Best for the ordinary greenhouse and for pots, are the modern dwarf hybrids of *Lantana camara* which grow to a height of only about 90 cm (3 ft) at the most, usually flowering well and easily the first year from seed. They are of shrubby habit and can be saved as perennials when the winter minimum is about 7°C (45°F). If you do this, cut back the plants in spring to preserve a compact form and to encourage new flowering shoots. Saved plants may also need potting-on then, but first year plants flower well in 13-cm (5-in) pots.

Flowers are very like verbena of the same family, and there is a range of pleasing colours. An interesting and unusual feature, not often reported, is that the flowers often *change colour* as they age, passing through at least three distinct shades, each bright and attractive. Thus it often appears that three different plants are being grown together. Seed germinates easily at about 20°C (68°F). Plants can also be used for summer beds and borders outdoors.

LOBELIA

The exotic lobelia to grow in the greenhouse is *L. tenuior*. This is a very large flowered species with glorious, rich blue blooms in profusion. Sow late winter to early spring and transfer several seedlings to half pots, with twiggy sticks for support, or hanging baskets. Flowering is from early summer onwards, but this species does not like chill. (See also p. 141.)

NEMESIA

Nothing could be easier to grow than the well known nemesia, yet so colourful. Choose the large flowered dwarf compact varieties such as 'Carnival' and grow several seedlings to each 13-cm (5-in) pot or more in proportion to the container size. Sowings can be staggered from late winter onwards. Be sure to give excellent light conditions or the plants will become weak and straggly. High temperature must also be avoided. An unusual and delightful variety is 'Fire King'. This has a selection of brilliant, rich red colours, but is nicely dwarf and compact; it should be much better known.

PELARGONIUMS

Regal, ivy-leaf 'geraniums'* and named cultivars of zonal pelargoniums must still be bought as rooted cuttings. The recent introduction of F_1 hybrid zonal pelargonium seed has, however, revolutionized the growing of these plants. Really superb specimens can be obtained in a matter of months from a late winter to early spring sowing. The flowers are absolutely beautiful and come in an extraordinary wide range of colours, some quite new to pelargoniums, There are also varieties with excellent leaf 'zones' and markings. The plants are easy to manage, strong and vigorous, and ideal for the home grower to raise.

Seed is still rather expensive, but germination is usually almost one hundred percent at about 18°C (64°F). Some fine names to note are 'Carefree', 'Sprinter', 'Smash Hit', 'Ringo', 'Bright Eyes' (red with white 'eye'), 'Orange Punch', 'Picasso' (unusual cerise colour), and the very new 'Startel' (quilled petals like the 'cactus' flowered pelargonium). Many more will be found listed and described in current seed catalogues. These pelargoniums are now so easy from seed, it is doubtful whether it is worth saving them over winter in a heated greenhouse. However, they can of course be further propagated from cuttings, if you wish to save any specially desirable colour or form.

New in 1983 is 'Red Fountain'. This is the first hybrid pendulous variety to be grown from seed. It has vivid vermilion flowers and attractive zoned foliage.

PHLOX

P. drummondii is another extremely easy plant to grow from seed that can create a wonderland of exciting colour. It can be autumn sown and grown-on over winter in frost-free conditions for early spring flowers. A late winter sowing, preferably with further sowings in succession, will provide plants for colour from summer to autumn. Put three to four seedlings to each 13-cm (5-in) pot or in proportion. It is important to choose varieties that grow no more than about 15 cm (6 in) in height or the plants may become untidy. No stopping is necessary. 'Beauty' and 'Cecily' are two ideal varieties for pots. The range of colours is wide and many of the flowers have pretty contrasting 'eyes'.

---

* It should be noted that many catalogues still incorrectly name pelargoniums as 'geraniums'.

Hibiscus 'Southern Belle'. One of my favourite flowers for impressing friends – the blooms are the size of large dinner plates! Easily raised from seed; the plant illustrated is growing in a 23-cm (9-in) pot.

Hibiscus rosa-sinensis, another form of this delightful greenhouse shrub. The flowers can measure up to 8 inches across.

Primrose 'Jewel Box' has an exciting colour range and is an ideal pot plant for unheated conditions.

Schizanthus 'Star Parade'. This extremely dwarf sturdy variety is superb for growing as a quick, free-flowering annual, but is not recommended for autum sowing.

Salpiglossis 'Splash' with exotic-looking flowers, three plants per 13-cm (5-in) pot in the author's greenhouse. Plants illustrated were spring sown and are flowering in summer.

Statice suworowii in the author's greenhouse. The flower spikes can be cut and preserved by drying, but it's a fine pot plant.

Lagerstroemia indica deserves to be better known. Plant shown, from the author's greenhouse where it's perennial, is in 13-cm (5-in) pot. Easy from seed and flowers first year.

Daffodil 'Red Devon'. The variety is splendid for outdoors, but also makes a wonderful show grouped in pots. The 'cup' is a very unusually rich red giving striking contrast with the golden yellow perianth. Splendid for a cold or frost-free greenhouse or conservatory.

POLYANTHUS and PRIMROSE

Both are exquisite pot plants yielding all the beautiful colours of the rainbow. They are especially valuable where little or no artificial heat can be maintained. The polyanthus is well known, and may fine named varieties will be found in seed catalogues. Yet again, F_1 hybrids are usually superior for vigour and flower quality, and two very fine ones are 'Spring Promise' and 'Jumbo'.

The primrose – in its modern multicoloured form – is not so well known, but it is an ideal pot plant being very compact. All the polyanthus colours are now represented. A particularly fine F_1 hybrid is 'Colour Magic', and another popular F_1 is 'Ernst Benary Show Mixture' which also lends itself to gentle forcing for extra early bloom. Both polyanthus and the primroses often have a delightful fragrance which is more noticeable under glass.

Sow late winter to early spring, germinating at *no higher* than about 16°C (61°F). High temperatures may spoil germination. Prick out into seed trays and grow-on in shady cold frames until large enough for transfer to final 13-cm (5-in) pots. Grow-on over winter preferably in just frost-free conditions; again high temperatures are undesirable. Flowering in the greenhouse occurs from late winter to late spring. Watch out for red spider and aphids.

PRIMULA

Several species are greenhouse favourites flowering from early winter to late spring. Sow during late spring. Do not cover the seed – just press it into the surface – and make sure the seed is fresh and from a reliable source. The seed germinates best if exposed to some light. When pricking out and potting do not plant too deeply; this may instigate rotting. Do not use composts known to be excessively alkaline – often better results will be obtained in an acid compost. If the mains water is excessively hard, water with *clean* rainwater (not, however, collected from roofs). Final pots of from 10–13 cm (4–5 in) are suitable. Both for germination of the seed and subsequent culture of the plants, only cool conditions are necessary and desirable.

P. sinensis, Chinese primula, is the earliest

to flower from late winter onwards. The variety 'Dazzler' is an old favourite with low compact habit and brilliant orange flowers. *P. obconica* can be obtained in numerous varieties with a range of colours, and it is remarkable for flowering almost the year round when once grown to maturity. The flowers are borne on short stems and clustered as a 'head', and are produced very freely indeed. *P. malacoides*, fairy primula, is extremely dainty and also available in a number of delightful colours. The flowers are borne on the stem in whorls, one above the other, but are not so long lasting as the previous species. *P. kewensis* is an odd one out in this group, in being yellow flowered.

It is important to note that both *P. sinensis* and *P. obconica* can cause a severe skin irritation if a person is allergic to them. Should this occur it is best to avoid growing them. The other species are non-allergenic so far as I know. Two new 1983 recommended easy varieties are *P. malacoides* 'Bright Eyes' with large 'eyed' flowers, and *P. kewensis* 'Yellow Perfection' ideal for a cold greenhouse. Both are unlikely to be allergenic.

PUNICA

P. granatum nana is the *dwarf* pomegranate. It forms a splendid neat little bushy pot plant growing to little more than about 45 cm (1½ ft) in height, and it will flower and bear fruit the same year of sowing if this is done early. The foliage is tiny and dainty, and in proportion to the plant – a kind of 'bonsai' effect! The fruit, too is small and exactly like a minature pomegranate in colour and shape, about the size of a small marble (inedible). The flowers, which have brilliant red papery petals are, however, surprisingly large and showy.

The seed germinates readily at about 20°C (68°F), and the plants can be grown-on in 13-cm (5-in) pots for the first year. They can be over-wintered in a frost-free greenhouse and trimmed back in early spring just before new growth is about to be made, to keep them neat.

ROSA

For some years *R. polyantha nana* (miniature

roses) have attracted much attention – but it is not often realized that it's fun to try them from seed. Admittedly you are unlikely to get plants as fine as the named types, but there is a chance. You might even get one worth naming! Growing roses from seed may seem impractical but, in this case, you will get *flowering* plants only a matter of months after sowing. Good seed strains are available from the leading seedsmen. Sow in early spring at about 16°C (60°F). Germination is often erratic. Much of the seed should germinate within about 3 weeks, but some may take over a month. Prick out seedlings to 5 cm (2½ in) pots. Only one further potting-on to about 10-cm (4-in) pots will be necessary. Flowering begins in summer and continues as with normal roses.

It must be realized that miniature roses are *hardy*. The plants must not be coddled. They should be given a *bright airy* and well ventilated position if kept in a greenhouse or conservatory. They will object to very hot, humid and stuffy conditions. Winter accommodation can be in a greenhouse just free from frost. The plants must be rested, but not allowed to completely dry out. Prune cautiously as for named minatures. From a batch of seedlings it is wise to keep only the best for growing-on. Any not up to standard can be discarded.

SAINTPAULIA

F_1 hybrid African violets are easy to grow from seed with the aid of a warm propagator. Two popular ones are 'Blue Fairy Tale' and 'Pink Fairy Tale' and a variety with variegated foliage, 'Fondant Creams', is also worth trying, but not so easy in my experience. From early sowings, plants flowering late summer to autumn can be obtained. Give final 10-cm (4-in) pots. Plants can be transferred to the home for winter as they may not survive in a cool greenhouse.

SALPIGLOSSIS

This is a real beauty, with masses of trumpet flowers borne freely over a long period and in the richest imaginable colours enhanced by gold veining. The variety 'Splash' is *the* one to

grow, being an F_1 hybrid and standing out from all others. From late winter to spring sowing, preferably staggered, a wonder of colour can be achieved very quickly and lasting from summer to autumn. Sowing can also be made in autumn if the plants can be grown-on in frost-free conditions. You then get very early flowering in spring. Winter-grown plants should be stopped several times if necessary to keep them well branched and low growing. Plants grown from early in the year sowings, should be stopped only once when the seedlings are about the length of your finger. A final 13-cm (5-in) pot is usually suitable, but winter grown plants may need slightly larger. The plants reach about 60 cm (2 ft) in height and will need a short cane for support.

SCHIZANTHUS

A similar merit to above, but with masses of dainty butterfly flowers in a great range of colours and markings. The 'ferny' foliage is also extremely graceful. Sowings can be made as for *Salpiglossis* and similar culture is necessary. However, plants grown *as annuals* should be allowed to grow naturally and not stopped; three varieties for this purpose are outstanding and important: 'Hit Parade', 'Star Parade' and 'Sweet Lips'. All are notably dwarf and compact and ideal for pots. 'Sweet Lips' comprises all the exciting red colours with contrasting white markings found in *Schizanthus*. The other two are splendid mixtures.

For overwintering the giant flowered types are recommended: 'Suttons Giant' and 'Pansy Flowered'. These must be stopped frequently whilst growing (Plate 19). They grow to about 1 m (3¼ ft) in height. Culture is not so easy, but they are really spectacular when in flower. As for *Salpiglossis*, bright airy conditions are essential, and only cool temperatures are necessary.

SPARMANNIA

In mild areas the shrubby *S. africana* is hardy outdoors. It is easy to raise from seed, But may not flower well, if at all, until the second year, during which time it can be overwintered in a frost-free greenhouse. It reaches a height of about 90 cm (3 ft). The foliage is somewhat heart-shaped, but of no special interest. The flowers are white with a structure rather like St. John's wort. There is a conspicuous central cluster of showy golden stamens. These stamens are sensitive and, if touched, spring forwards and then backwards.

Germination is easy at about 20°C (68°F) and plants can be grown-on to final 18-cm (7-in) pots for flowering. It is not unusual for plants to shed foliage or deteriorate in winter chill, but they can be cut back just before new growth in early spring. Generally, a bright airy position should be found. Mature plants saved over several years may form a sizeable shrub, and can be used for conservatory decoration.

STATICE (Limonium)

S. suworowii does not seem to be well known although having the common name of pink pokers. It is easy, unusual, and quite delightful, with long fluffy pink erect catkin-like flowers rising from a neat rosette of foliage. From late winter sowings, fine plants flowering from summer onwards will be obtained. Give final 13-cm (5-in) pots.

TETRANEMA

T. roseum (*T. mexicana*) is a dainty minature and not well known, but it is very easy to grow as an annual. It can be perennial in *warm* conditions. The foliage forms a rosette above which the flower stems arise to about 10 cm (4 in). The stems bear clusters of tubular purple flowers which some people liken to foxglove, hence the popular name Mexican foxglove. The plants will flower well in only 7.5–10-cm (3–4-in) pots. Flowering continues from summer to autumn. The plants can often be saved as house plants over winter if given a warm window sill in the home.

Give about 20°C (68°F) for germination and retain the seedlings in the propagator for a while until established in their small pots.

TORENIA

T. fournieri, wishbone flower, is a neat grower also sometimes used around the edge of baskets. The flowers are of unusual structure, small but very pretty in two-tone blue and yellow making an attractive contrast. Best

Plate 19 *Schizanthus* of the giant flowered type for growing-on over winter at the stage when the first stopping should be made (arrows) to induce branching growth. Further stopping may be necessary.

sown early spring and planted several seedlings to each pot with a few twiggy sticks for support if needed. This species likes moderate humidity, shade and absence of chill, but usually grows well in a greenhouse.

TRACHELIUM

T. caeruleum is another plant that tends to get forgotten, yet it is attractive and something 'different' to add interest to the greenhouse. It can also be used as a cut flower to add distinction to floral arrangements. It is, however, a fairly neat pot plant growing to about 90 cm (3 ft) maximum. The flowers form large corymbs made up of vast numbers of tiny pale mauve florets with protruding styles. When viewed from a distance, this produces a 'bluish haze' effect. The foliage is small and the corymbs are borne on stout stems.

The plant is easy to grow as an annual, provided it is sown early. It can also be treated as a biennial if sown in summer and overwintered at about 7°C (45°F). In both cases a final pot size of about 13 cm (5 in) is adequate.

This species should be given plenty of light when developing, and over winter, to keep it compact, but it needs shading from direct sun during summer. It prefers good ventilation and not too much humidity. Lack of attention to these requirements may lead to leaf yellowing and shedding.

TABLE 2.   MORE INTERESTING PLANTS FROM SEED

Plant	Characteristics and cultural hints
Allamanda nerifolia	A shrubby pot plant with large yellow flowers, but needs winter minimum of at least 10°C (50°F).
Amaranthus	Many foliage types make excellent pot plants, e.g. 'Illumination' and 'Joseph's Coat', a change from coleus!
Anigozanthus	Various species (Australian) have strange flowers. Popularly called kangaroo paw.
Aristolochia	Various species. Climbers with very strange pitcher-like flowers, exotically veined and marked. Called Dutchman's pipe.
Browallia viscosa	This species is not well known. It bears masses of dainty blue flowers with white centres. Should be seen more often.
Bunfelsia calycina	A beautiful subject, often sold as a house plant, with flowers that change from purple-blue to white as they age. Needs winter minimum of about 10°C (50°F).
Caesalpina gilliesii	Called bird of paradise flower, not to be confused with *Strelitzia*. Shrubby with mimosa-like foliage, and showy yellow flowers with red protruding stamen clusters. A beautiful plant for a large frost-free conservatory.
Coccoloba uvifera	Bronze-green, glossy-leaved foliage plant that withstands some neglect.
Cyphomandra betacea	Tree tomato. This can be grown for its tomato-like fruits, usually formed the second year from seed. These, however, are often very seedy and not of the quality of those naturally grown. Also needs moderate winter warmth.
Dracaena draco	Easy tropical-looking foliage plant with narrow strap-shaped leaves with reddish margins. Can be used for sub-tropical bedding effects.
Eucnide bartonioides (*Microsperma*)	Good annual pot plant. Large golden flowers with showy clusters of stamens.
Ixora hybrids	Fine foliage plants with showy flowers in various colours. Seed may take a long time to germinate.
Jatropha podagrica	Strange foliage plant with large shiny leaves and swollen club-like stem.
Lagerstroemia indica	Choose dwarf hybrids These make bushy compact plants with small dainty foliage. The flowers are freely produced first year from seed, mostly shades of pink and red. They have a curious 'wheel-like' structure. Plants are perennial, but deciduous. Highly recommended – should be better known. Practically hardy.
Leea coccinea	Shrubby evergreen foliage. Large long lasting eye-catching red berries.
Maurandya (several species)	Usually described as climbers, but they make excellent trailers. Dainty foliage, and pinkish, purplish, or reddish tubular flowers.
Nertera granadensis	Forms mat of beady orange berries. Grow in half-pots or pans of seed compost. Germination is slow.
Rhoeo discolor (*R. spathacea*)	Erect foliage, green above, purple below. Strange purple bracts with white central flower – popularly called Moses-in-the-cradle.
Solanum	Ornamental egg plant. Several forms make unusual pot plants with variously coloured egg-like fruits (inedible).
Tweedia caerulea	Sprays of blue starry flowers and grey-green foliage. Give 13-cm (5-in) pot. Very easy.

10 GROWING PLANTS FROM STORAGE ORGANS

GENERAL PROCEDURE AND TECHNIQUE

The unattractive name 'storage organ' is nevertheless an apt one. It refers to bulbs, corms, tubers, rhizomes, and the like, all of which store in their tissues the foods needed to give the plant a good start in life. It is not possible to give details of the subtle differences between these organs here, but true bulbs can be singled out for special mention. A bulb forms its flower inside in an 'embryo' form during its growth and development. If bulbs are to flower well, it is the treatment they receive during foliage development that is the most important; it is then a new embryonic flower, to be produced the following year, is being formed. In the case of *all* storage organs the period of foliage development is important – in all cases nutrients are then being passed down for storage. In the case of the bulb, it should be obvious that, to ensure flowering, a reasonable size is important. Undersized bulbs may not have reached flowering, and may have to be grown on for a longer time. More general advice on purchase of storage organs is given on p. 44.

Table 3 shows a good selection of bulbs for pot cultivation. Descriptions of some of the lesser known bulbs listed will be found in specialist bulb catalogues (see Appendix). With the exception of *Crinum*, plant several bulbs to each pot.

There are two different types of organs: spring flowering which are pretty hardy, and half-hardy or tender types usually flowering from summer to autumn. The hardy bulbs must all be given hardy treatment, since unnecessarily high temperatures can inhibit flowering. After potting the containers should

TABLE 3. BEAUTIFUL BULBS FOR POTS

Name	Plant	Flowering time
Acidanthera	Late spring	Summer
Allium	Autumn	Spring
Babiana	Autumn	Spring
Brodiaea	Autumn	Summer
Bulbocodium	Autumn	Spring
Calochortus	Spring	Summer
Camassia	Autumn	Summer
Chionodoxa	Autumn	Spring
Chlidanthus	Spring	Summer
*Crinum**	Spring	Summer/Autumn
Crocosmia	Spring	Summer/Autumn
Crocus	Autumn	Winter/Spring
Eranthis	Autumn	Spring
Erythronium	Autumn	Spring
Fritillaria	Autumn	Spring
Galanthus (snowdrop)	Autumn	Winter/Spring
Galtonia	Spring	Summer
Habranthus	Spring	Summer
Hermodactylus	Autumn	Spring
Hyacinth	Autumn	Winter/Spring

*Pot singly in large pots.

TABLE 3 (cont).

Name	Plant	Flowering time
Iris (Bulbous)	Autumn	Spring/Summer
Ixia	Autumn	Spring
Ixiolirion	Autumn	Spring/Summer
Lapeyrousia	Spring	Summer
Leucocoryne	Autumn	Spring
Leucojum	Autumn	Winter/Spring
Lycoris	Spring	Summer/Aut.
Muscari	Autumn	Spring
Narcissus (*daffodil etc*)	Autumn	Winter/Spring
Oxalis	Autumn	Spring/Summer
Puschkinia	Autumn	Spring
Ranunculus	Early spring	Summer/Aut.
Scilla	Autumn	Spring
Sternbergia	Autumn	Next Autumn
Tecophilea	Autumn	Spring
Tulip	Autumn	Spring
Zephyranthes	Early spring	Autumn

be plunged (Plates 20 and 21) in a plunge bed *outside* the greenhouse (Fig. 26). The cold plunge is essential to prevent top growth *before* a good root system has formed.

SPRING FLOWERING BULBS

The best time for potting and plunging spring flowering bulbs is in autumn. Some, but not all, can be gently forced once a good root system has formed. Suitable bulbs for forcing are given special symbols or description in the bulb catalogues – do remember to look out for this. To check the root system and readiness for forcing, do not be afraid to carefully tap the bulbs out of their pots.

It usually takes *about eight weeks* for bulbs in the plunge *to form a reasonable root system and to be ready for removal*, either to force or to grow-on in the greenhouse. After removal always introduce to full light gradually over a week or so. Afterwards, good light is essential to sturdy growth and proper leaf colour. When

Fig. 26   The plunge bed.
A raised box or a pit can be used. (*A*) Cover to keep off rain and prevent waterlogging when the plunge is used for bulbs. (*B*) Layer of coarse gravel to ensure drainage. The right-hand section shows how the plunge can be used for plants that have to be stood out for a period. For this purpose clay pots are best as they allow passage of some moisture from the peat to the potting compost.

it is required to force, increase the temperature slowly also over a week or so. Even for forcing, temperatures over about 18°C (64°F) should be avoided. In fact, most of the favourite hardy spring flowering bulbs will give their best show in an unheated greenhouse or conservatory.

GENERAL POTTING

There is no need to pot storage organs for the greenhouse deeply. Often the 'nose' of the bulb, or the top of any other organ, can be left just protruding from the compost (Fig. 27). This gives maximum room for the roots. For greenhouse or conservatory work, proper flower-pots or half-pots with drainage holes are better than fancy undrained bowls. Clay pots are best for hardy organs to be saved.

Do not use fibre or a compost containing no nutrient if you wish to save your storage organs. Use a proper conventional potting compost. Do not overcrowd when potting. The number of organs to set to each container usually depends on their size (Plate 22). Overcrowding, and the use of containers too small, may cause roots to push the organs out of the compost. All composts should be nicely moist before potting, and the moisture evenly maintained whilst the organs are growing. A plunge bed must also be kept moist, but prevented from waterlogging.

GENERAL CULTURE

Storage organs vary considerably in their preferences according to type. However, a general rule is to feed well whilst the foliage is forming and until it shows signs of dying down. However, a few types are not deciduous and need special treatment outlined where necessary in this book.

The tender organs described in the following pages should be started into growth in warmth – *not put into a cold plunge*. They can be started into growth by immersion in moist peat in a propagator, and most of the true bulbs can be directly potted into individual pots of potting compost and placed in the propagator or in the greenhouse itself, depending on warmth requirement (Plate 23). 'Prepared' bulbs (specially treated for extra early

flowering) usually need special forcing temperature and treatment according to the supplier's instructions – they are more suited to the home than to the ordinary greenhouse. Organs started in moist peat must be potted into potting compost *as soon as shoots or roots are seen to be forming.*

Plate 20 (*Above*) A bowl of bulbs planted in potting compost and ready for plunging. Illustrated are hyacinth bulbs, three of which have been selected to be of the same variety and of similar size. Even flowering at about the same time, of the whole group, is then more certain. Large flowered bulbs, like hyacinth, should be well spaced and not crowded together.

Plate 21 (Below) A simple plunge bed can be improvized from a bath or similar container filled with moist peat and covered to prevent rain from waterlogging.

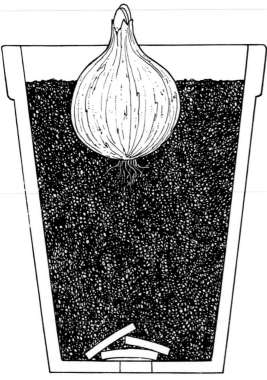

Plate 27 (*Above*) Potting greenhouse bulbs. Since weather protection is given there is no need to plant deeply. Leave the 'nose' well above the compost to give more root space.

Plate 22 (*Below*) Small, and smaller flowering bulbs like the crocus illustrated can be potted generously for best colour effect. Again try to select all the bulbs to be of similar size and condition and avoid mixing varieties unless you know they have the same flowering times.

SAVING STORAGE ORGANS

Hardy bulbs and the like should be allowed to retain their foliage for as long as possible. After flowering they can still be fed and are best put outdoors with their pots plunged in soil. If clay pots are used, the roots will remain nicely moist. In autumn the pots can be dug up and the bulbs cleaned and repotted.

The tender organs are often stored in their pots set on their side in a frost-free place over winter. In autumn, when the foliage shows signs of deterioration, watering and feeding is reduced until the pots go dry. The faded top growth should then be removed. Do not allow the compost to become wet during storage, or the organs may well go rotten. With some types, the organs can be removed from the pots in autumn and stored in dry clean sand over winter. Special methods will be given where appropriate in the following pages.

Storage Organs: Selected List

ACHIMENES

These are grown from curious, elongated catkin-like storage organs called tubercles. Although the named cultivars are great favourites, there are many charming species and varieties obtainable from specialist growers. Some tend to be rambling in habit and are fine for hanging containers. Others are more erect, but may need a few twiggy sticks for support.

Start by immersion in moist peat in late winter, 16–18°C (61–64°F). Pot three to five per 13-cm (5-in) container, or more according to size, as soon as growth is detected. The average basket will take about ten to fifteen. Grow on avoiding chill as much as possible. The plants like moderate humidity and shade in summer. Store over winter with the pots on their side. At replanting time the tubercles will usually have multiplied.

Some popular cultivars are 'Michelssen Hybrids' having very large flowers, and good for pots; 'Purple King' which is dwarf and easy for beginners; the taller 'Early Arnold' which is quite sturdy and self supporting and has very large violet flowers; the pendent

Plate 23 Storage organ started into growth and ready for potting. Illustrated is a gloxinia (p. 95) and at the stage shown it is obvious which way up the tuber should be potted.

'Cattleya' with blue and white flowers; the neat and beautiful 'English Waltz' with pink and yellow flowers; and the dainty 'India' with a profusion of lilac-purple bloom.

BEGONIA

The giant flowered exhibition tuberous begonias are one of the most eye-catching plants at the major flower shows. These named cultivars are also rather expensive, and beginners may prefer to make a start with cheaper offers often to be found in the rear pages of seed catalogues. Start into growth as described for achimines. The top of the tubers is usually the concave or flat side and this should be subsequently potted just level with the compost surface. For large blooms allow only one shoot to develop per tuber. If more form, they can be carefully detached and rooted as cuttings if desired. The stem as it grows will need careful support as it tends to be brittle and easily snapped. Buds usually develop in threes, the male flower forms the central bud and is the large showy bloom. It is accompanied by a pair of females, one either side, with winged seed capsules attached. Both can be snipped off as soon as possible to divert the plant's resources to developing the male

bloom. This liberty is usually only practical in the case of giant flowered begonias. Those described below need no stopping, disbudding or interference.

Other types making extremely beautiful pot plants are the multiflora kinds with lots of smaller flowers; fringed begonias with ruffled petals and very attractive; marmorata types with quite large blooms exotically marbled and splashed usually in rich shades of red; crispa begonias with single flowers daintily picotee edged and frilled in contrasting colours; and fringed begonias, which are double with frilled petals. See also pendulous types, p. 140. Begonias do not like chill, and they should be given moderate humidity and shade during summer. Store dry in their pots over winter or in dry sand.

CANNA

All cannas can be grown in the greenhouse but the shorter forms like 'Lucifer' are more convenient in the average home greenhouse. Start the fleshy rhizomes as already described during late winter, and pot-on to individual pots just large enough to take them. Try to give as much moderate warmth as possible; about 16°C (61°F) minimum is ideal. Where temperatures are low, development is slow, and during a poor summer flowers may come too late to mature properly. If the summer weather is good, the pots can be stood outdoors. Final pots of about 20 cm (8 in) size or larger may be needed for vigorous specimens.

The foliage of all cannas is impressive and some cultivars have beautiful bronze or maroon shades. The flowers are like giant gladioli and very striking. A fair number of fine named cultivars are available from bulb specialists. For best results give excellent light conditions. In autumn let the pots go gradually dry and cut off all top growth. Store the pots on their sides where it is perfectly frost free. Mature rhizomes may become quite large and can be cut up when restarted for propagation, one 'eye' to each piece.

CRINUM

Crinums are probably seen at their best where they can be planted either in a greenhouse border, or in very large pots or tubs, and left to form sizeable clumps. Despite their demand for space, only conditions just free from frost are required – they are often hardy outdoors in mild areas. They consequently make excellent conservatory plants. Probably the best for under glass is *C. moorei*, which has stems bearing numerous large pink and white trumpet flowers from summer to autumn. The height of this species is about 45 cm (1½ ft). Rather less tall and a little more compact is *C. × powellii* which was obtained by crossing the first mentioned with *C. bulbispermum*. This has pure white to shell pink flowers during the same period. The foliage in both cases is strap shaped, arching and evergreen.

The bulbs are very large with long necks. In the greenhouse they can be potted like hippeastrum with the necks protruding – but *not* outdoors where exposed to chill. They must then be well buried. Give a position of good light, water freely in summer, but keep only slightly moist in winter. The bulbs are best left undisturbed as long as possible, but can be propagated by dividing the clumps in spring which is also the time for potting and planting.

CYCLAMEN

The easiest way for beginners to grow cyclamen is to start from young plants bought from a nursery in early spring or to start corms, bought from a bulb specialist, from mid- to late summer. The corms should be started as described for begonia but in this case the convex side should be placed *downwards* when potting, and about one third of the corm should be above the compost surface. No artificial warmth is usually necessary, and one corm should be set to each 13-cm (5-in) pot. Place the pots in a shady cold frame and keep them moist. Take the pots into the greenhouse in autumn and endeavour to maintain about 10°C (50°F) minimum. If the floral display is required for mid-winter and spring, any premature flower buds should be carefully pulled away complete with stem from the base, to prevent rotting.

To save the corms after flowering, gradually reduce watering and keep the pots in a shady cold frame during summer. During this time keep watering to a minimum, but sufficient to maintain foliage. Aim at resting the plants without letting them go dormant and allowing drying out. In autumn return to the greenhouse and treat as already described. Although some people have had cyclamen they have grown on for years, this is not the general rule. After about two years, when the corms become 'corky', flowering often deteriorates. The young seedlings bought in spring usually give the fastest and easiest show of bloom for the beginner. For the cold and unheated greenhouse, the hardy cyclamen make charming plants for half pots.

EUCHARIS

E. grandiflora is one of the more 'exotic' bulbs in that it needs more care to avoid chill. The bulb is large and very much like hippeastrum. It also needs the same potting procedure. The flowers are quite different being rather like the daffodil in structure but very large and powerfully fragrant, usually filling the greenhouse with scent. With reasonable greenhouse warmth, these delightful blooms come at intervals throughout the year. The ideal minimum temperature is about 16°C (61°F). It is unlikely that most home greenhouses will be held at this temperature during winter, so it's worth transferring the bulbs to the window sill of a warm room of the home where you may get further flowers during the winter months.

In summer water freely and when active growth is being made. In winter also water sufficiently to maintain the foliage, but more cautiously. Never allow complete drying out. Established bulbs are best left undisturbed as much as possible, top dressing rather than potting-on. Excessive chill may cause the bulbs to rot.

EUCOMIS

The best known species is *E. bicolor*, the pineapple flower. The popular name is inspired by the strange pineapple-like tuft of spiky foliage sited at the top of the flower spike. The spikes are hyacinth-like, the individual florets being greenish with lilac edging. The bulbs are almost hardy and can be potted early in the year, one to each 13-cm (5-in) pot. The flower spikes appear about mid-summer and reach about 30 cm (12 in) in height. Unfortunately, the flowers sometimes emit a very unpleasant smell, but are unusual and spectacular in appearance. For winter the bulbs can be left dry in their pots.

GLORIOSA

The species usually readily obtainable is *Gloriosa rothschildiana*, but others appear in catalogues from time to time. This very lovely plant is much more easy to grow than some of the older gardening books lead one to believe. It is grown from large elongated tubers. The most convenient way to cultivate gloriosa is as a climber – the leaves develop twining tendrils at the ends. However, it can, with care, also be grown from hanging baskets and allowed to trail down if there's space – it could need about 1.5 m (5 ft). The flowers are extremely eye-catching, freely borne, and coloured in a striking combination of bright crimson and yellow. In shape, they are like reflexed lilies.

My own method of growing the tubers, is to start them by immersion in moist peat in a warm propagator. February to April is a convenient time. As soon as a shoot or roots are seen to be forming, from the thick end of the tuber, pot immediately. Pot so that the sprouting end is *centrally* placed in the pot. About an 18-cm (7-in) pot is usually suitable. It does not matter if some of the tuber protrudes over the pot edge, as long as the growing end is covered with compost. As the plant grows the old tuber slowly shrivels and new ones are formed below the compost. At the end of the year, let the pots go dry. Store the pots dry in a place well free from frost over winter. Next planting time, *carefully* turn out the pots; you will usually find at least *two* new tubers to start again. Thus you soon build up a stock. The new tubers may be joined and should be carefully separated with a razor blade. The tubers are very brittle and easily damaged. They are then liable to rot. To support the stem during growth a bamboo cane will be needed. Tie the stem to this or other suitable support, rather than rely on the leaf tendrils.

GLOXINIA (SINNINGIA)

This is one of the most showy and exotic looking pot plants with huge trumpet blooms borne freely in erect clusters and handsome velvety foliage. The colours are usually rich and vivid and sometimes the blooms have a contrasting striking white border. There are a number of fine named cultivars. The tubers should be started from late winter onwards by plunging well into moist peat. It is often difficult to tell which is the top of the fibre covered tubers, but this will easily reveal itself when the shoots and roots begin to appear, at which time potting should be immediate. For starting, a temperature of about 16°C (61°F) is adequate. Give each tuber a 13-cm (5-in) pot. Flowering is from late summer to autumn. The plants should have a moderate humidity, warmth – but not excessive heat in summer – and shade. Do not allow water droplets to remain in the foliage, since this may cause brown marking.

After flowering, reduce watering allowing the pots to gradually dry out. Clean the tubers from adhering compost and store in dry sand over winter. Old 'corky' tubers are really best discarded. A useful way to propagate named varieties is from leaf cuttings, using young leaves and the 'cut vein' method.

HEDYCHIUM

Hedychiums are popularly called 'gingers' and certainly belong to the ginger family (Zingiberaceae) but, although grown from rhizomes, are not sources of commercial ginger. Three species usually to be found listed in the catalogues of specialist bulb merchants, are the scarlet flowered *H. coccineum*, the white flowered scented *H. coronarium*, and the very fragrant red and yellow flowered *H. gardnerianum*. The last mentioned is a particular favourite.

The gingers have a generally 'tropical' looking appearance forming clumps and with bamboo-like stems. The flowers are borne as spikes, and in time the plants can reach an appreciable height and become as tall as a man. Pot the rhizomes in March choosing a pot size just large enough. Subsequently, pot-on each spring as necessary. Large pots or small tubs will be required in due course. Although making large clumps, only frost-free conditions are needed in winter. Give a position of good light, and keep almost dry during winter. Plants need to become established before they flower well. When in their final pots, they should be left *undisturbed* and just top dressed with fertilizer or fresh compost each year.

HAEMANTHUS

Although there are several showy species, *H. multiflorus* is one of the most readily available and easiest for the home greenhouse. It is a large bulb with a remarkable crimson flower resembling a gigantic dandelion clock in structure. It needs similar cultural treatment as *Hippeastrum* below, and belongs to the same family. The flowers usually appear from late summer, and foliage coming afterwards. However, contrary to my recommendation for *Hippeastrum*, keep the bulbs *dry* over winter or they may tend to rot if conditions are chilly. In a warm greenhouse the bulbs are more vigorous and the flower stem may rise to about 60 cm (2 ft) at least. It is specially important to feed well during the foliage development period, and flowering seems more generous if the pot is kept to the minimum size.

HIPPEASTRUM

This bulb, often incorrectly called amaryllis, and so well known for its enormous trumpet flowers, is often sold in the 'prepared' form for early flowering. For the home greenhouse these are best avoided. There are a number of very choice named cultivars available from bulb specialists. These are expensive, but an excellent investment, and are best potted in early spring for summer to autumn blooms. Give each bulb an 18-cm (7-in) pot and leave the 'nose' of the bulb well above the compost. Do not let the compost dry out, but water cautiously at first. With new bulbs, the flower may appear well before the foliage, and at this stage there may be no roots to anchor the plant. Be careful that it does not topple out of the pot. When the leaves are growing, water freely and feed as necessary. In autumn reduce watering and keep the pots *very slightly* moist

over winter, just enough to allow the plants to retain their foliage. It is not generally realized that hippeastrums are *evergreen* bulbs. If you have the space and a winter temperature of about 7°C (45°F) *minimum*, far better results are obtained by *not drying off* the bulbs as so often practised. There is no need to repot for at least three years, but the pots should be top dressed. If you only have a cold or chilly winter greenhouse, let the pots go dry in late autumn and store in a frost-free place.

HYMENOCALLIS (Ismene)

The bulbs of this species can be grown very much in the same way as described for *Hippeastrum*, but should be given, if possible, a slightly higher temperature. Varieties of two species are generally available, but may be found in catalogues under the name 'Ismene'. A one time favourite is *H. narcissiflora* 'Advance' (*H. calathina*). This is known as the Peruvian daffodil, and has large white daffodil-like flowers delightfully fragrant. Similar, but with longer stamens, is *H. × festalis*. This is not quite so exacting as the previous species and will survive outdoors in sheltered places. A very beautiful variety, 'Zwaneburg' is sometimes available, and so is a rather rare form 'Sulphur Queen'. The latter is pale yellow with green stripes. Avoid buying small bulbs – they are quite large when of flowering size. A first quality bulb will flower year after year. Avoid potting-on more than necessary and keep practically dry during winter or the bulbs may rot. Pot up initially as early in the year as possible to allow subsequent maintenance of about 13°C (55°F) minimum. Flowering is usually from about March to April but may be later.

IXIA, SPARAXIS and TRITONIA

Unlike many flowers suitable for cutting, these three can make charming pot plants. They are all grown from corms in the same manner, and all bear simple, but beautiful, flowers in rich lovely colours, on wiry stiff stems. The corms can be potted much in the same way as described for freesia. The best potting time is October and they should then be plunged like the spring flowering bulbs generally. From

January onwards, the pots can be brought into a cool greenhouse. If you want extra early blooms they can be *gently* forced, but high temperatures must be avoided. The normal flowering time is spring to summer. Particularly good for pots and the greenhouse is *Tritonia crocata* 'Orange Delight' and is worth looking out for. The sparaxis usually best suited are *S. tricolor* and *S. grandiflora*. A popular old favourite is 'Fire King'. Ixias come in just about all colours of the rainbow. Indeed, an excellent offer by leading bulb merchants is called 'Rainbow Mixture'.

NERINE

There is often confusion about the types of nerine suitable for pots in the greenhouse, as the potting time and culture differs according to type and species. A specialist catalogue should be consulted for details (see Appendix). By far the most impressive are the named cultivars which are again expensive but well worth having. The large umbels of flowers come in wonderful colours and often have a glistening sheen. These bulbs should be potted, as described under *Hippeastrum*, in late summer (preferably August). Put the pots outdoors in a sunny frame and only apply water when the bulbs commence to grow. Return the pots to the greenhouse in autumn for flowering into early winter.

Remove the faded flowers and continue watering until the foliage deteriorates. Then let the pots go dry and store in a frost-free place over winter. When the weather becomes warmer and sunny, expose the bulbs to full sun until next starting time, but avoid repotting more frequently than about once every three years, top dressing the pots when necessary.

SMITHIANTHA

Smithiantha does not seem to be commonly grown in the home greenhouse. The modern named cultivars are delightful plants combining beautiful spikes of foxglove-like flowers with subtle colour tones of velvety foliage, sometimes with iridescent lustre. Descriptions will be found in specialists' catalogues, but a very popular and easy one for beginners is

'Orange King'. Start the rhizomes as described under *Achimenes*. Pot one per 13-cm (5-in) pot or three to each 18-cm (7-in) pot. Try to maintain reasonable warmth and humidity. Plants started early can be stopped to produce bushy growth, but this may delay flowering. Normally, flowering will occur from late summer to autumn. After flowering gradually dry off and store the pots on their sides frost-free over winter. Tip out when it is time to restart – the rhizomes should have multiplied.

SPREKELIA

S. formosissima, Jacobean or Aztec lily, is eye-catching because of its thin-petalled, bright crimson flowers which usually appear before the foliage in summer. It should be potted as described for *Hippeastrum*, but should be stored dry over winter. In the usually rather cool home greenhouse, this bulb often unfortunately has a tendency to rot.

VALLOTA

V. speciosa, Scarborough lily, bears a group of handsome, trumpet-shaped, scarlet flowers on stout stems during autumn, and it ought to be better known as a home greenhouse plant. Pot as for *Hippeastrum, in summer* in this case; otherwise treat similarly. Also keep growing slowly over winter. Vallotas usually produce offsets freely, and these can be detached and potted individually at repotting time. Offsets may take three years to reach flowering size.

VELTHEIMIA

V. capensis is particularly useful in cool conditions and for its unusual flowers appearing from winter to early spring. These look like those of the red hot poker of the garden, but the colour is far less exciting and usually a dull pink – an opportunity for plant breeders here! Pot in autumn in 13-cm (5-in) pots. No artificial heat will be required in areas where the greenhouse is just frost-free over winter, and the pots can, in any case, go directly on the staging. Keep the pots *very slightly* moist during winter.

11 PESTS AND DISEASES

CULTURAL PROBLEMS

When growing or acquiring a plant of the less well known or popular type, it is always useful to find out as much as you can about its natural environment. This will obviously help you to produce conditions to at least give it some encouragement for growth, and it will help to avoid obvious mistakes in simple matters like suitable temperatures and water requirement. However, strict rules cannot be applied – many plants do seem to flourish in environments completely unlike their natural one, so experiment is always well worthwhile.

What can be remembered as a general rule is to avoid DRASTIC CHANGES of all kinds. Large and sudden fluctuations in the condition of the environment will always bring about a disaster of some kind, e.g. leaf shedding, bud or flower drop. In edible crops, fruits may fall at an immature stage. It is for this reason that every effort must be made to maintain even conditions of moisture around plant roots and reasonably slow changes in temperature within the range suited to the plants.

By making slow and gradual changes plants can often be acclimatized to get accustomed to environments quite different from their natural one. For example, very many tropical and sub-tropical plants will be perfectly happy in remarkably cool conditions if the temperature is *slowly* lowered over *several weeks or more*. A wide range of popular house plants such as marantas, numerous foliage begonias, aphelandras are typical examples, but many are safer housed in the home for winter.

Watering faults

These have been discussed on p. 49. Leaf yellowing and sometimes shedding is a frequent symptom of overwatering. The compost may also become sour and sometimes smelly. It is sometimes possible to save overwatered plants by repotting into fresh, slightly moist compost. The old sour compost should be washed away from the roots as much as possible, and any rotted roots cut cleanly out. Underwatered plants usually show obvious wilting and the compost will also be obviously dry and the pots light in weight. When rewatering dry plants make sure the water does penetrate to the roots. The amount of water to apply and the time of year to carry out watering often depends on the nature of the plant, and some may have to have definite rest periods when water is greatly reduced or withheld entirely. Failure to acknowledge a plant's rest period may cause abnormal development and the failure of flowering and fruiting.

Overfeeding

This has been discussed along with overwatering and symptoms are similar. 'The more the better' does *not* apply when feeding plants. In some cases overfeeding can also upset the growth pattern of a plant. For example, many climbers can become very rampant forming masses of stems and leaves but hardly any flowers or fruit. Annual flowers may tend to bloom poorly too and form an over-abundance of leaves.

Feeding plants with 'straight' chemicals or concentrates – which contain only a few of the necessary nutrients – is nowadays rarely necessary. The proprietaries are scientifically formulated to contain the optimum balanced mixture and often the most important trace elements.

Light

Light conditions have an important influence on plants. Inadequate light leads to weak, lanky growth and poor leaf colour which may be pale or too yellowish. However, too much light for those plants *known to be shade lovers* can have a similar effect. The variegation and colour intensity or contrast of plant foliage can also be greatly affected by light conditions – developing well or badly according to the light required by the plant type in question (see Chapter 14).

Temperature

Temperature greatly affects growth rate. Too much heat causes fast weak growth of poor colour. Seedlings are often prone to be 'forced' excessively by beginners. In all cases the range of temperature recommended for the plants must be kept, and it is often better to err to the lower region of the range if in doubt. High temperatures given to the *more hardy* types of plants can upset flowering or fruiting, or even inhibit it altogether. If the overall temperature is too low for sub-tropicals and tropicals they usually first grow slowly, finally yellowing and shrivelling. A browning of the leaf edges is a common first symptom. Frost entry into the greenhouse frequently causes similar symptoms in most tender plants, followed by a 'glassy', 'scalded' appearance of the foliage, and ultimate blackening. Leaf-edge browning may also occur if there are toxic fumes in the greenhouse – from sterilizing chemicals, or gas or paraffin heaters, for example.

pH

A few pot plants can be considerably influenced by the pH of the compost – the degree of acidity or alkalinity or lime content. Outdoor gardeners are well familiar with this matter, and in this book it is brought to attention where necessary. There are special composts available.

PESTICIDES AND THEIR APPLICATION

Research in the subject of pesticides is expanding so rapidly that nowadays it is difficult to make any specific recommendations that will not be liable to becoming out of date. The reader is therefore advised to keep in touch with the leading manufacturers of such products – current literature, useful pests and disease charts, and information, is regularly published by most reputable firms, and can be obtained from garden centres. In all cases the makers' advice regarding application and safety precautions must be strictly obeyed.

In the confined space of the greenhouse it is specially important to avoid inhalation and contact with the eyes and skin as much as possible. On the other hand, application must always be thorough and special attention given to covering the undersurface of foliage, where pests and diseases usually first congregate. Many pesticides can be applied as fumigants, either from 'firework'-like preparation, lit by a fuse, or by aerosols in pressurized cans. This is obviously a very penetrating and effective method. The *special instructions* will be found *printed on the packs*. Pesticides with a systemic action are also very useful and long lasting, but should be used with care on food crops. One of the latest formulations of outstanding value for the greenhouse is a mixture of heptenophos and permethrin, sold under the trade name of Tumblebug. This can be used to eliminate and control *all the common sap-sucking pests*, including some of the previously troublesome ones like red spider and scale insects. It is also relatively safe for amateurs, if used as the label instructs.

Certain types of plant may, in some cases, be damaged by a particular pesticide – read the labels to check. Plants in bloom and bearing long lasting flowers or blooms for exhibition should not be treated with fumigants (which may cause discoloration) or have their bloom wetted by sprays (which may cause browning). It may be safer to use dust pesticides if necessary, but dusts are not usually so effective. I do not personally approve of 'automatic' pest control where pesticides are *constantly* vaporized and are all the time present in the greenhouse atmosphere.

STERILIZING THE GREENHOUSE

The importance of strict hygiene has already been discussed. When possible, and where a greenhouse can be cleared of plants for a few weeks during the winter, sterilizing each year is an ideal way to maintain excellent hygiene. Pests and diseases rarely become seriously troublesome or build up to become a problem, and the very tenacious red spider can be practically eliminated. This is because sterilization kills off *all* hibernating pests, eggs, and spores that normally hide away in the greenhouse structure to reproduce rapidly as soon as temperatures rise.

Use of the ground soil of the greenhouse has also been mentioned. Should the soil be used it will almost certainly become necessary to carry out some form of sterilization sooner or later, but owing to quick recontamination from the surroundings regular sterilization will probably become an annual chore. The methods described in most books on general gardening can be employed, but it should be noted that formalin often recommended is no longer freely available to the home gardener. Preparations based on cresols are usually used, and for greenhouse soil it is important to leave about eight weeks for fumes to clear and before planting.

Cresol agents, such as ICI Clean-up which is excellent for greenhouse application, can be employed for washing down the greenhouse structure and for sprinkling on the floor to give surface sterilization. In such cases, the greenhouse can usually be safely used after a very much shorter lapse of time, because the vapours and fumes clear quickly if free ventilation is given. Full instructions for dilution and application will be found on the makers' containers, and again the safety recommendations must be carefully followed.

The diluted cresols are also useful for sterilizing pots, seed trays, and equipment. Plastic or metal objects can be merely rinsed and washed free of the sterilizing agent under running water. Clay pots, wooden trays, or other porous or absorbent objects, must be left to 'air' before use, until the odour of cresol has become very faint or has gone.

When in doubt about the safe clearance of sterilizing agents, you can make a check by growing cress – the 'cress test'. Merely sow in the treated soil or in the greenhouse that has been washed down, or in containers that have been given treatment and need testing. Nor-mally cress is fast germinating and grows quickly. If there is any marked delay, slow development, or any abnormality in growth, allow a longer time for fumes to clear and then test again.

Quick sterilization of an *empty* greenhouse can be done by burning sulphur: 500 g to every 28.3 cu m (1 lb to every 1000 cu ft). Seal the greenhouse as best you can leaving a door for your escape. Mix the sulphur with a few wood shavings on a deep tin lid or old tray and set fire to it, making sure the sulphur is burning with a very pale blue flame – **do not inhale the gas** (sulphur dioxide) evolved, or linger once the flame is seen – the gas is **extremely poisonous** and pungent. Leave the greenhouse closed over night. The next day, open the door but do not enter for some hours. Finally open all vents. A sulphury smell may persist for some time, but it is safe to use the greenhouse for plants, since the gas quickly clears. This method is obviously unsuitable for greenhouses attached to dwellings, and should only be carried out by those who are used to handling dangerous chemicals. Clearly children should be kept away from the sphere of operations.

Remember that the methods of sterilization described here *kill all life, including plants*. Greenhouses **must** be **empty** before treatment.

ALGAE AND SLIME, MOSS AND LIVERWORTS

These are in fact minute plants and, although not directly harmful, they can give a very unsightly impression. They grow anywhere where there is light and moisture and can be especially troublesome to automatic watering systems, staging and the surface of composts. Sometimes algae encourage pests such as springtails, they may emit an unpleasant odour, and may interfere with the germination of seeds and development of seedlings when they cover the compost in which the seeds are contained. Algae will of course grow in water in the presence of light. For this reason irrigation tubes, valves, tanks, and the like, involved with automatic watering, should always be *opaque* to light. Clear plastic should not be employed for such equipment.

(**Left**) Tuberous begonias with fringed petals (fimbriata) in the author's greenhouse. Inexpensive and easy to grow. Pot one tuber to each 13-cm (5-in) pot.

(**Below**) *Begonia marmorata* in the author's greenhouse. Also inexpensive but very showy. One tuber to each 13-cm (5-in) pot.

Punica granatum nana, dwarf pomegranate, is easy from seed and forms a neat pot plant. Flowers are followed by tiny ornamental pomegranate fruits.

Fine smithianthas can be grown from seed, as illustrated, and flower the first year if sown early. The rhizomes formed can be saved.

Hippeastrum (Amaryllis) special hybrids. The illustrated plants were grown from seed, but the bulbs take several years to reach flowering size – worth waiting for!

Gloxinia (*Sinningia speciosa* hybrids). Gloxinias are among the most showy pot plants. Illustrated is 'Waterloo', one of many varieties easily grown from tubers. The plant shown is in a 13-cm (5-in) pot.

Whitefly. This is a tiny insect, but easily recognized by its triangular wing shape. Weeds outside and around the greenhouse may also harbour the pest.

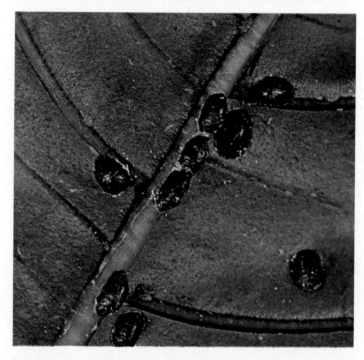

Scale Insects. These tiny 'limpet'-like insects attach themselves firmly to plants. They favour smooth leaved plants, cacti and other succulents.

Fortunately both slimes and algae can now be easily controlled by spraying or treatment with the product Algofen, also safe to use on edible crops. The container label gives full instructions. It is best used as a preventative – do not wait until the algae has gained a hold. Algofen further seems to have a mild disinfectant action and has a deterrent effect on mosses and liverworts, although it is quite safe to use on nearly all plants. Sprayed plants are less prone to diseases caused by fungi and bacteria.

APHIDS

These are well known and include a number of different coloured species as well as the common 'greenfly' and 'blackfly'. There are now innumerable proprietary products that will give very effective control.

In the greenhouse, aphids can be troublesome all the year round where frost-free conditions are maintained – the use of the systemic type pesticide is therefore specially recommended.

BOTRYTIS CINEREA
(GREY MOULD)

This is a grey to brownish furry mould that grows on dead plant tissue, but can soon also attack living tissue, especially if there is slight damage. When disturbed, a cloud of dust-like spores will arise to spread infection everywhere (Plate 24). On some plants it can produce a variety of undesirable effects such as spotting of fruit or bud drop (see also Tomatoes, p. 158).

The methods of clean and hygienic greenhouse routine do much to reduce trouble from this fungus, and dead or decaying plant remains left lying around or on the plants will encourage it. Crude manures are a frequent source of severe infection.

A good air movement whether by the use of ventilators or electric fans is a powerful discouragement to botrytis. A very effective chemical control is fumigation with TCNB (Tecnazene). Benlate (containing benomyl) is a product that can be sprayed. These chemicals should preferably be used as a routine preventive measure, especially for plants known to be dangerously prone to botrytis

Plate 24 Grey mould (*Botrytis cinerea*) attacking a 'geranium'. It has completely destroyed the section of the plant left of the picture causing stems and leaves to collapse.

attack, like lettuce in winter. Generally, in winter, keeping down humidity will help to deter the fungus.

DAMPING-OFF

Several different types of fungi can attack seedlings at the base causing them to topple over. These fungi can spread with amazing rapidity soon wiping out an entire batch of seedlings. Again lack of general greenhouse hygiene is often the cause, and if the advice given in this book is followed damping-off should not occur. (See Cheshunt compound, pp. 73 & 187.)

EARWIGS

This pest can be the cause of much 'unexplained' damage in the form of holes and ragged edges found on leaves and petals. The insects hide away in cracks and crevices during the day and fly out at night – like vampires – to create havoc among our prize blooms and plants. They will also eat seedlings. There are numerous proprietary baits and dusts that will control the pest, dusts being the most suited for application to blooms. Most ant baits will also kill earwigs. Where prize blooms are grown it is wise to use these products as preventives.

RED SPIDER MITE

This is probably the most serious and troublesome of all greenhouse pests (Fig. 28). It attacks insidiously, usually causing slight yellowing and mottling of foliage, but by this time the infestation may already be severe and serious plant damage unavoidable. Look at foliage affected as described, with a hand lens. Red spider mite will then become visible and there will also be minute spherical whitish eggs present. If no action is taken, the mites swarm and multiply to thousands forming sticky webbing and becoming easily visible through sheer numbers. All is then lost! Infestations are usually most serious where there is lack of humidity and the temperature is kept too high in summer. The most effective modern chemical control and preventive is Tumblebug, a combination of heptenophos and permethrin. However, where this pest is an annual nuisance sterilization of the greenhouse with a cresol product usually has a dramatic effect, and I have known the pest to be completely eliminated. Many of the older pesticides, such as liquid derris, used for spraying plants, seem to have lost their effectiveness. Possibly this is due to mutations producing resistant strains of the mite.

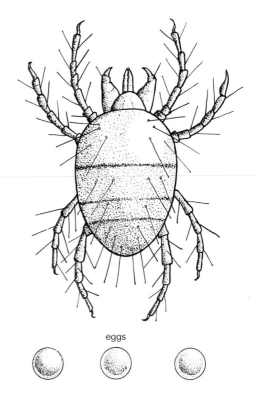

eggs

Fig. 28   Red spider mite.
The tiny mite can readily be seen with the aid of a hand lens, especially a watchmaker's eye glass.

SCALE INSECTS (COCCIDAE)

These, like aphids and whitefly, often cause a stickiness of the foliage below where they congregate. They appear as tiny cream, yellowish, or brownish scales of waxy texture firmly clinging to the foliage. They often attack plants with thickish foliage and cacti and other succulents. The heptenophos and permethrin pesticides are now a very effective preventive and control, whereas at one time this was a difficult pest to eradicate.

SCIARID FLY MAGGOTS

This is not a well-documented pest, yet it can be very troublesome, especially now that peat based composts are widely employed. It takes the form of very tiny worm-like maggots which eat plant roots and the base of seedlings causing wilting or toppling over. The maggots are the larvae of several species of minute fly, often seen flying around where there are peat composts especially, or where conditions are very humid such as where there is automatic watering. Slime and algae covered areas encourage them too.

A constant watch should be kept where this pest is likely to occur, and the flies controlled. Most general purpose pesticides will kill the flies, but the maggots are not so easy to deal with and once these are seen the damage may already be severe. Reduce moisture and watering as much as possible and then water with a solution of diazinon (Fisons Combat soil insecticide or Gesal Root Guard).

SLUGS, SNAILS, AND WOODLICE

These common garden pests will invade the greenhouse where general hygiene and clean working are not the routine. It is sometimes not realized that woodlice can cause severe plant damage by eating roots and seedlings. BHC (HCH) dusts usually give effective control, but there are other proprietaries that can be used. Similarly, slugs and snails can now be efficiently killed with modern baits which, in the greenhouse, remain very effective over a long period.

THRIPS

Thrips are tiny insects which cause whitish patches to appear on foliage. These are often surrounded by black specks. Put the plant over a sheet of white paper and give the foliage a shake – the thrips will fall out and become easily visible wriggling on the white surface. it is an easy pest to control; most general pesticides are effective, particularly the systemics.

VIRUS DISEASES

These are caused by organisms resembling huge chemical molecules that can reproduce themselves. They can be spread by cutting or pruning tools, by sap-sucking insects, or sometimes by merely handling infected plants. Symptoms may be stunting, distortion, leaf yellowing and mottling, or striping of flowers and general malformations. Sometimes a plant may show all these ill effects.

There is no cure yet known, and affected plants should be *burnt* to prevent spread of infection. Strict general hygiene as emphasized in this book greatly helps to reduce virus disease problems (see also Propagation, p. 63). Some plants can harbour the diseases without ill effect to themselves, but be a source of infection to other types. In a few cases some viruses seem to be harmless, and sometimes even beneficial in producing attractive plant colours or variegations.

WHITEFLY

This is a very tiny triangular-winged whitish fly that often occurs in swarms if left uncontrolled. It can colonize nettles and weeds around the greenhouse and these sources of infestation must be destroyed. The larvae suck plant sap causing a yellow and sickly appearance. A sticky sugary secretion may be produced – like aphids – and this often grows a black fungus further adding to the plant's discomfort and your displeasure. Malathion aerosols give good control, but a specially efficient new pesticide is resmethrin (PBI Sprayday) which is safe for use on the cucumber family, unlike many other pesticides.

WEEDS

These are rarely a serious problem in the greenhouse, but the odd weed or two, from airborne seed or that has remained in the compost, may appear in pots and seed trays. Prompt manual removal is the best way to deal with them. Properly made John Innes compost should be weed free, but sometimes peat can convey some persistent weeds, such as species of *Oxalis*. Again prompt hand removal is the safest remedy.

The greenhouse floor can often grow many of the usual weeds found outdoors, the seeds being mostly carried in on shoes or having remained dormant since the structure was erected. The safest weedkiller of the 'total' type is sodium chlorate. This should not be applied close to where plants are growing in the ground as it may find its way to the roots. It is best applied as a 5% solution at the rate of about 4.5 1 to 8.3 sq m (1 gal to 10 sq yd).

Weedkillers of unknown composition should *not* be used under glass, particularly if liable to contain 'hormone type' agents. These can seriously upset plant growth even in traces, which may become airborne in dust kicked up from the floor. Hormone weedkillers should also *not* be used outdoors in the greenhouse vicinity and where spray may drift in. Certain greenhouse plants, like tomatoes, are remarkably sensitive. Distorted or stunted growth and taint are common symptoms of damage. Fruit may have a curious 'disinfectant' taste.

PART III
GREENHOUSE PLANTS

12   POPULAR FLOWERING PLANTS

GENERAL NOTES

The range of greenhouse flowering plants is formidably vast. In the following very small selection I have included only those that I think practical for the average home greenhouse – plants that do not demand great expertise, that are not difficult to obtain, and do not need high temperatures. I have also tried to choose plants that will be more or less happy in company with each other. This is important if the greenhouse is to be successful. Nearly all should do reasonably well in a greenhouse with a minimum winter temperature of about 7°C (45°F). Some may need a few extra degrees to remain in perfect condition. Others only need to be kept frost free.

Greenhouse Flowering Plants: Selected List

AGAPANTHUS

There are a number of agapanthus that can be greenhouse grown, but the well-known Headbourne hybrids, hardy in many places outdoors, make very easy pot plants. With protection they usually look far more decorative too, flowering earlier and lasting longer. Pot one plant to each 25-cm (10-in) pot, and water well in summer and sparingly in winter. The large umbels of blue or white flowers appear from summer to autumn. During this time the pots can be stood out on a terrace or patio if desired.

AZALEA (Rhododendron)

There are two types of azalea grown in pots in the greenhouse – one is hardy and the other is *not*. It is important not to confuse them! The florists' azalea, that makes a popular Christmas gift, is usually *Rhododendron simsii*, the Indian azalea. These plants have been specially forced by commercial nurseries and are more suited to warm greenhouses. However, they can be stood out during the summer and kept well watered. If returned to a warm house in late autumn flowering may occur during winter, but not usually so early as when purchased.

By far the easiest to manage are the hardy evergreen outdoor types sold by most good garden centres, but for pots they must be *dwarf in habit*. Garden centres and nurseries in southern and western parts of the British Isles will have slightly more tender types which are particularly useful for the greenhouse. There are a host of names to select from, giving a very wide range of colours and flowering times. The plants are invariably container grown and merely need transfer to a pot just large enough to take the root ball. Use an ericacious or acid compost, and water with clean rainwater. When the pots are stood out in summer, on no account let them go dry. The effect of drought may not become apparant until some time after it has occurred – yellowing and falling foliage.

BEGONIA

Many species, hybrids, varieties and cultivars, are notable for attractive flowers as well as for foliage, but often the ones suggested in many general greenhouse books are hardly suited to the chilly conditions of the average home greenhouse. In fact, very few begonias like it cold, but some are better suited to coming through the winter than others. Even so, they may end it looking rather scruffy. The following are some that usually survive about 5–7°C

(41–45°F) minimum and soon make fast new growth with the return of warm weather. When temperature is low, water very cautiously, if at all, and avoid a high winter humidity. In summer a high humidity is usually appreciated and moderate shade. Remove any foilage that has gone brown around the edges or yellowed in early spring when new growth commences.

Easy and very handsome for foliage and its large cluster of pinkish winged flowers is *B. corallina* and the similar *B.* × *corallina* 'Lucerna'. The stem is 'cane'-like and maroon coloured and the heart-shaped foliage exotically spotted in silver on an olive green background. The very showy flowers are generously produced from spring to autumn. It is not unusual for this plant to lose all its leaves in winter chill, but it will soon recover as it warms up. In continuous warmth it will reach a very appreciable height and flower almost the year round. Normally use final 18-cm pots.

Similar too is *B. coccinea* and its hybrid 'President Carnot' with spotted leaves. In the former the flowers are vivid red, but in the latter much paler. *B. boweri* is quite striking with hairy, chocolate-edged foliage and pretty pale pink flowers in spring. Also attractive is *B. manicata* with red-edged foliage having tufts of hairs underneath and a profusion of pink flowers during the winter, if not too chilled. Another pink-flowered species is *B. haageana* with foliage dark green above and red below. Rather different is *B. fuchsioides* which is a winter flowering, neat shrub. The flower form is reminiscent of fuchsia and the colour bright red to pinkish, but the blossom is borne in small clusters. The fibrous rooted bedding begonias, grown from seed, also often flower through the winter in a bright greenhouse well free from frost. In slight warmth they may flower quite prolifically. The 'Lorraine' begonias were at one time renowned for masses of winter bloom, but they do need warmth to do well, and are not the most practical for the average home greenhouse.

BELOPERONE (Drejerella)

B. guttata is the well-known shrimp plant, so named because of the appearance of the bracts surrounding the flowers, and giving colour from spring to winter. It can usually be acquired as a small house plant and should be given an intial 13-cm (5-in) pot. Take off the first flowers and bracts to divert the plant's resources to developing a good shrubby shape. There seems to be a difference of opinion in the culture of this plant. Instead of shade often recommended, I stand plants in full sunlight during summer – not neglecting to water of course – which induces a rich colour generally. The plants go back into the greenhouse in early autumn. Overwinter at not less than about 7°C (45°F) if possible. If plants deterioriate cut back in early spring. With warmer conditions quite rapid growth to produce sizeable plants usually occurs.

CALLISTEMON

Several species, popularly called bottle brushes because of their extraordinary flowers – just like real bottle brushes in fact – are grown, and are almost hardy. Certainly the easiest is *C. linearis* which can also be grown from seed, then flowering in a few years. The plants form small shrubs, but the stems and foliage are graceful and they respond well to pruning to prevent invasive growth. The flowers, borne in summer, are a bright vermilion colour. This species can be grown as a standard with time and patience, and will flower well in a final 25-cm (10-in) pot. Another fine species often suggested is *C. citrinus*, but this is more tender and takes up more room. Plants can of course be stood out for summer – but rains may spoil the flowers making them look very bedraggled!

CAMELLIA

These popular evergreens make splendid pot plants often flowering extremely well in surprisingly small containers. Moreover they are ideal for cold conditions and are one of the few pot plants that do well in the conditions of a vinery. Numerous named cultivars are listed in nursery catalogues, mostly derived from *C. japonica*. In the greenhouse camellias bloom earlier, and lovely flowers remain in perfect condition, and last longer.

Pot into an *acid* compost and never allow

drying out. Water with clean rainwater and, in the greenhouse shade with Coolglass; do not allow high temperatures at any time. Erratic cultural conditions of any kind cause bud shedding, and leaf yellowing and falling often encountered by beginners. The trouble may occur a long time after the ill treatment has been given. By choosing a selection of varieties, flowers can be enjoyed from winter to spring. Any pruning needed to keep plants compact should be done after flowering and before active growth begins. Pots can be stood outdoors in summer in a shady sheltered place, but not allowed to dry out (plunge if possible, preferably in clay pots).

CITRUS (ORANGE, LEMON, LIME, GRAPEFRUIT)

It is often a waste of time to grow these from seed if you want good, reliable, flowering and fruiting plants for decorative effect. Buy definite species or named plants from a nursery. Seed saved from marketed fruit is unlikely to yield plants true to type owing to special methods used commercially to produce plants for cropping. The 'fruit shop' lemon, may however give a satisfying plant from 'pips'.

For the average small home greenhouse, *C. mitis*, popularly sold as a house plant, is very useful and often does extremely well. The waxy white scented flowers and small oranges may look attractive almost the year round with a winter minimum of 7°C (45°F). Pot into an *acid* compost, shade only to protect from excessive sunlight. and try to maintain even conditions of moisture. Rapid changes of any kind may cause leaf, bud, flower, and fruit shedding. Yellowing of foliage is common if conditions become too alkaline. Water with clean rainwater and, if leaf yellowing becomes severe, treat with aluminium sulphate, a pinch dissolved in a teacup of water now and then. *C. mitis* can be drastically pruned if it tends to become too large.

CLIVIA

C. miniata is an easily grown, very showy spring flowering plant with great umbels of large orange trumpet flowers, and bold strap-like foliage. It is almost hardy, but *must* be

kept frost free. Give 25-cm (10-in) pots and leave to grow undisturbed for as long as possible, top dressing the pots when necessary. In time the roots will become seriously pot bound. When this happens divide the plants by cutting through the roots with a very sharp blade rather than attempting to pull apart.

CYTISUS

Two 'brooms' are commonly grown in the greenhouse and are frequently offered as 'house plants'. Both can, if given large pots or planted in a greenhouse border, reach an appreciable size and the height of a man. However, restricting pot size and careful cutting back, makes them quite manageable. *C. canariensis* commonly called genista, is evergreen with short spikes of scented yellow flowers from spring to summer. *C. × racemosus* has greyish-green foliage and quite showy bright yellow fragrant flowers from winter to late spring. To keep both plants reasonably compact it's best to cut back the stems after flowering and to stand the pots outdoors for the summer. Plants in large pots or greenhouse borders should be slightly shaded over summer. In all cases a winter minimum of about 7°C (45°F) should be maintained. Plants left in the greenhouse during summer should be carefully watched for red spider attack, to which they are prone. Never allow the roots to dry out.

C. × racemosus must be propagated from cuttings rooted from summer to autumn; it will not come true from seed.

DAPHNE

D. odora is a charming compact shrub for the frost-free greenhouse with purplish heads of lemon-scented flowers from winter to spring. The evergreen foliage is also attractive. It is happy in a 25-cm (10-in) pot for several years. The variety 'Aureomarginata' has very pretty cream-edged leaves and is especially decorative at all times.

ERICA (HEATHER)

E. gracilis, which is pink or white, and *E.* 'Hyemalis', which has pink tubular flowers and elongated foliage, are often forced commercially for an extra early market. Pot into an *acid* compost and stand them outdoors for summer, watering and feeding well. Return to the greenhouse in autumn and overwinter at about 7°C (45°F) as near as possible, watering with clean rainwater at all times. There are many named hybrids with variations in form and flower colour, most flowering from about Christmas time onwards.

ERYTHRINA

E. crista-galli, coral tree, is an easy herbaceous shrub for 25-cm (10-in) pots, and flowers with eye-catching effect from early to late summer. The flowers are large and pea-like, shiny red with waxy texture. The plants die back in autumn when all top growth should be cleanly removed. Restart the roots in spring, giving slightly elevated temperature if possible. The pots can be stood out in summer, or after flowering, but keep well watered. In winter keep almost dry. A minimum of about 4°C (39°F) is then all that is required.

FRANCOA

F. appendiculata may well be unknown to many readers, yet it was at one time extremely popular. The long arching racemes of flowers were often cut and used in making up wedding decorations. This suggested the common name of bridal wreath. The plant is a perennial easily grown from seed. The foliage forms a neat rosette. The flowers can give a 'different' look to the greenhouse. They take the form of long stems of numerous florets with long petals, the stems often exceeding about 90 cm (3 ft). In the form *F. a. ramosa* the colour is white and the racemes tend to branch. In *F. a. sonchifolia* the colour is shell pink. Seed of both is usually available, and sometimes plants.

Sow in spring at a temperature of about 16°C (61°F). Prick out into small pots and pot-on as required. A final 13-cm (5-in) pot is adequate for flowering. When growing from seed, it is convenient to accommodate the plants in a slightly shaded cold frame during summer to save greenhouse space. During winter a minimum temperature of about 7°C (45°F) is required. During winter ventilate freely whenever outside temperature permits

and keep humidity down as much as possible, otherwise foliage may turn brown and deteriorate.

When the plants begin to grow rapidly from late winter onwards, give more water and feed as necessary. The flowers usually appear from early summer onwards and may need support with thin split canes. To get the finest flowers the plants are best grown as biennials, but it might be worth holding over a few plants for further flower production.

FUCHSIA

Undoubtedly one of the most popular pot plants and remarkably adaptable to give fancy shapes, standards, climbing and trailing effects, and with numerous flower forms and colours. It is impossible in the space allotted to give full description here, and a catalogue from a specialist should be consulted (see Appendix).

For the home greenhouse it is usually best to start with rooted cuttings from late winter to early spring. These usually give a good show of flowers the first year. Most fuchsias lend themselves well to training into a variety of shapes such as standards, bushes and pyramids. This can be done by judicious pinching out or stopping of shoots during a plant's development. Most plants will benefit from stopping from time to time, since this encourages more stems that will produce more flowers. However, always leave a plant untouched for about eight weeks prior to the time you want it to flower. For the first year, rooted cuttings may flower well in 13-cm (5-in) pots, but slightly larger ones may be needed for some vigorous varieties. A final 18–20-cm (7–8-in) pot will usually be adequate. Old plants can usually be repotted, or top dressed. For hanging baskets about three rooted cuttings are usually needed.

Most of the choice greenhouse fuchsias are not hardy. Over winter they must be kept frost free, and rested by watering sparingly, except where some form of training demands constant slow growth. It is not unusual for foliage to be shed, but the stems should *not*, ideally, die back. If conditions are chilly, this may happen but growth will usually commence from the base in spring.

From spring onwards the plants like good light but should be protected from excessive sun by shading with Coolglass, which is the ideal shading material. Ornamental foliage varieties have a special need for good light to develop the best colours and contrasts. Shoots removed from plants in spring, when training, make useful cuttings for propagation.

HYDRANGEA

Hydrangeas are useful pot plants for the greenhouse, because they lend themselves to a certain amount of cultural trickery to control flowering time and quality, but do not demand high temperatures. Most seen in pots are varieties of *H. microphylla*, but *H. paniculata*, which has large conical panicles of creamy flowers, is also delightful.

Plants are often bought in flower from florists or garden centres – you can then be sure of the bloom size, quality, and colour. After flowering, cut off the faded flowers and also any weak growth, and stand the plants outdoors in a shady position. Plunge the pots in moist peat or sand to keep the roots cool and moist. If the pots are plastic, cover the rim well. During summer new shoots will grow and the old stems that have produced flowers should be cut out just above the highest of these. The new shoots will bear the blossom for the following year. Water with *clean* rainwater, not hard water known to contain lime, and feed well.

In autumn take the pots into the greenhouse when the foliage is shed. Water only sufficiently to keep the compost moist and *do not* allow temperatures higher than about 10°C (50°F), which could inhibit flowering. In February, pot-on if needed. The temperature can then be allowed to go a little higher if early blooms are required.

To grow quick flowering plants from cuttings, take the cuttings, about 10 cm (4 in) long from flowering shoots. Root them at about 18°C (64°F) and pot-on to small pots of lime-free compost. When the pots are full of roots, stop them to leave only two pairs of leaves. Then pot-on to 13-cm (5-in) pots and plunge outdoors as already described. In July stop all shoots produced by the first stopping to two pairs of leaves. This treatment should

give plants bearing about five flower heads during summer. To get spring flowering you can *gently* force going no higher than about 16°C (60°F) from late December.

Yet another trick is to develop one enormous flower head. This is done by rooting cuttings in early autumn, but not stopping. Allow only one stem to develop.

H. paniculata requires different treatment. Blooms should be removed after flowering, but pruning should not be done until autumn. Then cut back each stem to about three buds from the base. All weak and straggly wood must also be cleanly removed.

The 'blueing' of hydrangeas is often a matter of controversy. Some varieties are *naturally pink, red* or *white*, and no attempt should be made to blue them. Blue varieties will lose their richness and become faded or 'washed-out' if poor or alkaline potting compost is used. An acid or ericaceous compost must always be used for hydrangeas. Special blueing compounds are sold at garden shops, but you can achieve the same result by watering the plants with a solution of aluminium sulphate (½ oz/gal (3 g/litre) rainwater) from time to time during growth.

MYRTUS

Two species make delightful pot plants for the greenhouse being attractive for their foliage, scent and flowers. They are also easy and need only frost-free conditions. Perhaps the best known is *M. communis*, the common myrtle, which is hardy outdoors in favoured positions. It also does well in pots and the fragrance of the foliage is quite pronounced when captured under glass. The summer-produced white flowers with their mass of 'fluffy' stamens are dainty and attractive. Particularly good for pots in the greenhouse are the compact forms such as 'Tarentina' which is worth looking out for. There is also a pleasing form with variegated foliage.

M. bullata has dark green corrugated foliage against which the masses of flowers show up in starry contrast. The foliage is not quite so scented as with the common myrtle, but the flowers come from late spring to summer. Both species can be grown from seed and will need a final pot size of about 20 cm (8 in) or

Summer to autumn colour. A group of decoratives in the author's greenhouse banked for effect and comprising some of the plants described in this book. Note that exotic foliage plants, such as *Begonia rex* (top right), *B. masoniana* the iron cross begonia (centre), and *Sanseveria*, mother-in-law's tongue (centre), should *not* be left in a chilly greenhouse during mid-winter.

Fuchsias. Illustrated are some varieties with elongated flowers that hang well – ideal for training into standards and for hanging containers or pedestal pots.

Gerbera 'Happipot'. This very new introduction, with dwarf habit, is easy from seed, flowering about 18 weeks from sowing. Makes a fine pot plant.

Streptocarpus 'New Hybrids'. Good quality seed can give fine plants, as illustrated, but growing from seed does need a little extra care.

Freesias from seed. Sow about seven seeds to each 13-cm (5-in) pot. The small corms produced can be saved for further plantings.

Carnation 'dwarf mixed'. Illustrated is an example of the fine blooms that can be obtained from high quality seed.

Ricinus communis 'Impala' is a new highly decorative form of the Castor oil Plant. It's quick and very easy from seed.

Caladiums. These very exotic and gloriously coloured foliage plants are easy to grow for summer/autumn decoration. Store the tubers in warmth, over wintering them in the home.

larger. They prefer a bright airy position, and are ideal for cool conservatories.

NERIUM (OLEANDER)

N. oleander is a very easy to grow evergreen shrub needing only frost-free conditions, yet becoming smothered in glorious single or double flowers from summer to late autumn. The colours are shades of red, pink, carmine and white. Personally I prefer the single-flowered forms. The doubles sometimes tend to have flowers too heavy for the supporting stems, especially when borne in large clusters, causing an untidy floppy appearance. The singles are much more graceful.

Plants can be grown in 25-cm (10-in) pots for a long time, top dressing when necessary. Correct pruning is essential. From the base of the flower trusses, it will be seen that new shoots, usually about three, easily form. These should be *removed* as soon as possible; you can use them as cuttings if you wish. In autumn after flowering cut back shoots of the previous year's development to within a finger's length of their base. If pruning is neglected plants will become straggly and too large for a small greenhouse. Plants can be stood out for the summer if desired, but at all times, except mid-winter, the roots must be kept nicely moist.

Sometimes long pods of fluffy seeds will form. These germinate quite well if sown in spring, giving flowering plants in about three years. However, propagating is very easy from cuttings, which usually root by merely placing in a jar of water. (*Warning:* the sap is poisonous).

PELARGONIUMS

For the ivy-leaved basket types, see p. 141. The two main types for pots are the popular, so-called 'geranium' and the show or regal pelargonium. The latter has very flamboyant, showy blooms but these are not usually produced so freely as in the zonals or the ivy-leaved forms.

Zonal pelargoniums
Growing the F_1 hybrids from seed is described on p. 80. A wide range of named cultivars will be found in specialist nursery catalogues and are best bought as rooted cuttings in spring. Although often grown outdoors the flowers can often be better appreciated under glass. During a bad, wet summer the heads can be ruined and may often turn brown in the centre. A bright airy greenhouse is essential for best results and the plant must not be over watered.

It is easy to overwinter plants in a frost-free greenhouse, but they should always be cut back severely – many people are afraid to do this and the result is that frequently extremely straggly, leggy and untidy plants are seen. During the cutting back the material removed can be useful for propagation when used as a source of cuttings. Cuttings root easily at about 16°C (61°F) in the usual cutting compost. Old plants saved over winter should be repotted in early spring. A general pot size is 13 cm (5 in) but vigorous specimens may need larger ones. Some of the named culivars will in fact form quite large shrubby specimens if grown on in a temperate greenhouse.

Regal pelargoniums
Culture is much the same. Cuttings in this case are usually best taken during summer. Young plants from rooted cuttings should also be stopped to encourage a bushy habit and potted in final 13-cm (5-in) pots. Old plants may need considerably larger pots, and again quite drastic cutting back when just restarting into growth in spring or, if overwintered in a frost-free greenhouse, in late autumn. All pelargoniums are prone to grey mould attack if dead vegetation is left on them.

STRELITZIA

S. reginae, bird of paradise flower, is one of the most striking of all flowers. Despite its exotic appearance, and the fact that it is described incorrectly as a 'stove plant' in so many books, the frost-free home greenhouse is a suitable environment. Young plants are now sold which start flowering within a year or two. Seed can be germinated at warm summer temperatures, but the seedlings are slow growing at first and several years must pass before flowering can be expected. Flowering usually takes place when the plants are in 25–30-cm

(10–12-in) pots and the roots are slightly pot bound. My own mature plants, originally grown from seed, flower during the summer and again at around Christmas time, but are often erratic. For winter flowering I take the plants into the higher temperature of the home, but a great deal of warmth is never given. The evergreen banana-like foliage and the spectacular blue and orange flowers, like a bird's head are always welcome. The plants can be left in their large pots for a number of years and eventually form several fan-shaped clumps. These can be divided for propagation, in early spring, by cutting through the roots with a sharp blade. Give plenty of water in summer, little in winter when conditions are cool.

STREPTOCARPUS

Excellent plants can be grown from seed, but this is not the easiest way to obtain stock for beginners. It's easier to buy in young plants produced by division, seed, or perhaps leaf cuttings, from a nursery. The named hybrids cannot be grown from seed, and a good selection will be found described in specialist nursery catalogues. There are both small, multiflowered form and large flowered types. I personally prefer the latter. A pretty old favourite is 'Constant Nymph' and recently the John Innes hybrids have attracted much attention. However, there are now many splendid seed strains offered, and plants from these can be most impressive. The trumpet flowers are often very large, sometimes with frilling, and come in a wide range of colours and contrasting markings. There are even now strains with shorter neater foliage – the disadvantage with streptocarpus is long brittle and easily damaged leaves. Flowering often lasts from summer to well after Christmas.

Although the plants like moderate humidity and congenial warmth, once established they will winter reasonably well with about 5°C (41°F) minimum, although often looking a little tatty at the end. Growth soon resumes with the advent of warmer, conditions, and the plants can be very easily increased by simple root division. Indeed, frequent division is an advantage, since old plants may become too leafy and this may interfere with the formation of the flower stems.

TIBOUCHINA

T. semidecandra is an actually incorrect name that has persisted for *T. urvilleana* and is still used in most catalogues. It is best obtained in the form of rooted cuttings. Pot these and take out the tips, stopping the laterals that form when about a finger length in size. Pot-on to 18-cm (7-in) pots for flowering, giving a strong cane for support. Enormous, glorious, violet, pansy-like blooms are produced from summer to autumn. This used to be a favourite Victorian conservatory plant, but seems to have gone out of fashion in recent years. Water well during active growth, sparingly in winter when a minimum of about 7°C (45°F) is desirable. The leaves often take on reddish tints in autumn. In late winter prune back severely. Propagate from cuttings taken from non-flowering lateral shoots in spring. These should be rooted at 18°C (64°F). Seed is also available but, in my experience, unreliable.

13 CHRYSANTHEMUMS, CARNATIONS AND CUT FLOWERS

Chrysanthemums

The culture of the chrysanthemum demands a little more care and attention than most plants, but the satisfaction it can give makes the extra trouble well worth while. It is a first class cut flower, lasting for an exceptionally long time when the stems are placed in water. There is also a remarkably wide range of glorious colours and flower sizes and forms, which make them absolute treasures for the flower arranger. Some, however, like the Charm and Cascade types, make wonderful pot plants.

The most important are the *late flowering* chrysanthemums. These are grown out in the open during summer and taken into the greenhouse for flowering from about autumn to winter. Classification of types is roughly as follows:

EXHIBITION INCURVED: Petals close and turning *inwards* to form a spherical bloom.

REFLEXED DECORATIVE: Petals more loose and turning outwards.

INTERMEDIATE DECORATIVE: Central petals turn inwards and the outer petals outwards.

ANEMONE FLOWERED: Flowers of anemone-like form.

OTHER FORMS (with self-descriptive names): SINGLE, POMPON, THREAD PETAL, SPIDER, and SPRAY.

The name Exhibition is given to those types with gigantic flowers – so often admired at shows. However, these, and also Decoratives, Singles, and Anemone Flowered, have medium flowered as well as large flowered forms.

CULTIVATION

It is vital to start by getting a descriptive catalogue from a specialist nurseryman. You will then be able to choose current varieties to please you. New varieties are introduced so frequently that any list of recommendations given here would soon become outdated.

Any home greenhouse will provide excellent accommodation for chrysanthemums, provided there is plenty of light from autumn onwards and a winter minimum of about 7°C (45°F) can be attained. A few degrees lower for short periods will not matter. The plants, grown outdoors during summer, can usually be moved in after a tomato crop has been cleared. A position where tomatoes have cropped well will also be a good one for the chrysanthemums.

Buy in rooted cuttings from the specialist from late winter to early spring, and pot into individual small pots. Grow on in the greenhouse, with the temperature not falling below about 4°C (39°F), until about mid-spring when a potting-on to 13-cm (5-in) pots should be given. Slightly larger pots may be needed for some vigorous varieties, and plants should not be allowed to become pot bound.

At this stage, after the plants have become established in their new pots, they can be transferred to a cold frame, since no further artificial warmth is necessary. The plants must also be hardened-off but be sure to close the frame overnight if there is a risk of frost. In early summer pot-on the plants to their final pots; about 23 cm (9 in) is usually a suitable size.

The next stage is an important one. A suitable site for standing out must be found. Somewhere bright but *sheltered from strong winds* is essential. Stand the plants in rows, preferably on a strip of polythene to prevent worms and other pests from entering the drainage holes, and thrust a strong 1.5-m (5-ft) cane in each pot. Put a stout stake at each end of the row and run a wire from end to end, securing the tops of the canes to the wire. This is to make quite sure the plants *do not blow over*. The pots must not be allowed to dry out, and some automatic form of trickle irrigation is very helpful if you have to be absent for long periods of time. Feeding is not usually necessary until mid-summer, and then a special chrysanthemum feed (from the specialist nursery) should be given according to instructions. A very frequent pest is the leafminer, whih makes brownish wandering lines on the foliage. It is wise to spray with Hexyl (see Appendix) as a *preventive* – systemics may damage chrysanthemums – do not wait until the pest is seen.

As the plants develop they will need training and stopping, see below, and can usually be taken back into the greenhouse about early autumn. See that the greenhouse and the site is thoroughly cleaned before they are put in. From then on shade slightly with Coolglass should there still be hot autumn sunshine, and keep a close watch for fungus *Botrytis cinerea*.

TRAINING AND STOPPING

If a chrysanthemum is allowed to grow without interference, it will form a single bud at the tip of its stem – called the *break bud*. This comes to nothing, but below, several shoots, called the *natural break*, grow from the stem. The shoots form buds, called *first crown buds*, which develop flowers if left alone. More breaks will form below producing *second crown buds* and so on (Fig. 29). To get the best quality blooms it is necessary to intervene, and we control development by 'stopping', 'securing buds', and 'disbudding'.

The catalogue of a leading specialist (see Appendix) will give up-to-date advice on stopping and training, particularly useful for newly introduced varieties. Stopping is the simple procedure of merely snipping off the break bud. The best time to do this depends on the variety. A catalogue will give a guide, but only experience and trial and error can attain perfect results, since the climate of your area may also have an effect on growth.

'Securing a bud' is, as the term suggests, allowing it to develop, not removing it. 'Disbudding' is the removal of small buds or shoots that may form around or below the secured bud. This should be done as early as possible so that the plant's resources are directed to the development of the secured bud.

Exhibition chrysanthemums

These are usually flowered from the *first crown buds*, but some from the *second*. Only one to three blooms should be allowed to develop on each plant. Two to three stems should be

Fig. 29 Stopping chrysanthemums.
(*A*) Break bud, which comes to nothing and should be removed. (*B*) First crown buds – remove other shoots if these buds are wanted and are to be 'secured' for blooms. (*S*) Unwanted shoots removed. (*C*) Second crown buds – remove all other shoots as in (*B*) if these are to be 'secured'.

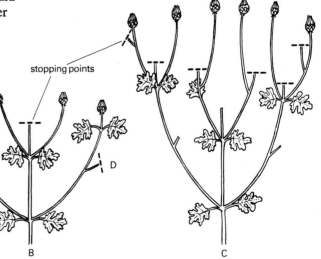

permitted to grow during late mid-summer and lower side shoots subsequently removed. For really giant blooms, plants can be stopped in early summer and only one bud on a single stem secured – all other shoots should be removed.

Exhibition incurved

Three to six blooms should be allowed for each plant. Secure buds late summer to early autumn, promptly removing any earlier ones. When stood out in summer, this group does better if given *slight* shade and when not overfed.

Decoratives

As many as about eighteen blooms can be allowed. Plants should be stopped when about 18 cm (7 in) high and when in their first small pots. The shoots that form should be reduced to about three or four and permitted to grow-on. These shoots should be stopped in turn from late spring to early summer.

Other types

Singles need little stopping and should not be stopped after spring, and buds should not be secured before early autumn. Anemone flowered can be treated as described for decoratives. Most other varieties are usually left to grow as they will, and without interference of any kind.

AFTER FLOWERING

Cut back to about arm's length, and at the beginning of the year to about finger length. With a temperature minimum of about 7°C (45°F), plenty of new shoots to use as cuttings should be formed. Exhibition types can be rooted early, and little extra warmth is required. Root decoratives late winter to early spring and singles in the latter period.

CHRYSANTHEMUMS FROM SEED

Particularly easy to grow from seed are the modern F_1 and F_2 hybrids. Very easy indeed are 'Autumn Glory' and 'Petit Point' which make splendid pot plants, nicely bushy and only about 45 cm (1½ ft) in height at the most,

needing the minimum of attention. The Korean hybrids, at one time very popular, are similar in habit but taller. Considerably taller, and useful for cutting, are F_1 hybrids 'Superjet' and 'Fanfare'. The former can be disbudded for extra large flowers if desired. All of these should flower from late summer to autumn during the year of sowing, if a start is made in early spring. Merely pot-on the seedlings to about 18-cm (7-in) pots.

Charm and Cascade types

These are grown from seed best sown in February, germinating at about 16°C (61°F), but the main flowering of the cascades is in the second year. The cascades also need special training. The early culture is the same for both. Prick out the seedlings to seed trays like bedding plants, later to individual small pots and from then on pot-on as required. The seedlings must be stopped, when about three leaves have formed, by careful removal of the tips. This is essential to encourage subsequently *bushy* development. During summer a cold frame will give convenient accommodation so as not to waste greenhouse space, as it can also for the F_1 hybrids already mentioned. Potting-on should be done similarly too. Both the charms and the cascades should flower from late summer to autumn. This is the time to select the plants with the best colours and flower form for saving – there may be quite a few not up to standard. The Charms form huge cushions of bloom up to about 75 cm (2½ ft) wide and almost as high, and may make an impressive display. The cascades will be taller and less exciting – their performance comes the following year.

Training cascades

The cascades that have been selected and saved will form basal shoots during late autumn, and these should be removed and used as cuttings for propagation. Take them when about 7.5 cm (3 in) in length. Pot up, when well rooted, into small pots and grow on over winter in a greenhouse preferably with a minimum of about 7°C (45°F). In spring, move on to larger pots using J.I. No. 3 potting compost. Harden off the plants gradually when they are about 30 cm (1 ft) tall and stand them outdoors with the pots plunged. As the plants get higher move to 25-cm (10-in) pots and provide a cane for support, thrusting this into the ground by each pot at an angle of 45°, and so that you can tie the plant to the cane at about 15 cm (5 in) from the plant's base.

As the plant develops, shoots will form in the lower leaf axils: remove their tips when three leaves have formed. This encourages more shoots to form on the new side shoots and these, in turn, should be stopped similarly. Continue the stopping until about late September. The plant will become very bushy and tapering towards the top, and as this development proceeds the plant should be carefully tied to the supporting cane. To get the ultimate flowering as evenly distributed as possible, try to arrange the final stopping so that the base of the plant is pinched out during about mid-September, the centre at about the end of the month, and the top parts about a week later.

In October the tricky operation of removal to a frost-free greenhouse is due, and you will need the assistance of a helper. The plant must be cut from the supporting cane and, with your helper supporting it with the utmost care, you must carry the pot into the greenhouse and place it on staging already prepared to give sufficient height for the cascading effect. To reduce risk of breakage of the stem, bent stiff wires and canes can usually be improvized to help at this stage, and the plants tied to these. The procedure sounds complicated, but with practice you will soon achieve success – and the results are pretty spectacular. It's well worth doing where you want to put on an impressive conservatory display; and there will be plenty of people or friends coming to view your efforts!

Carnations

Provided there is good light, a few pots of PF (perpetual flowering) carnations can usually be found a space in a mixed home greenhouse collection. However, their charm and beautiful colours, and the exquisite fragrance of some varieties, together with their great value as an almost year round cut flower, often tempts people to set aside a small special greenhouse for them. A glass-to-ground house is ideal, and a winter minimum of about 4–7°C (40–45°F) is adequate for good bloom production, but there should be provision for plenty of ventilation when necessary.

Buy plants from a specialist nursery. There are innumerable named varieties, but bear in mind that not all have a strong scent. In recent years height to which plants grow has been drastically reduced in many cases. These low growers are especially useful for the home greenhouse.

Rooted cuttings are best obtained from winter to spring, the latter being most convenient for home gardeners. Pot immediately into small individual pots, and from then pot-on as required to final 18-cm (7-in) pots. The young plants may have been stopped by the nurseryman. If not, stop when about five pairs of leaves have formed. The side shoots that form should be further stopped. Stop the longest or fastest growing shoot first; do not stop them all at the same time. The side shoot stoppings should be done when the plants are in their final pots, and yet further stopping can be carried out as required. The best stopping procedure may depend on variety and is soon learned with experience.

Disbudding is absolutely essential to obtain top size first quality blooms (Fig. 30). All the little buds that form around the large crown bud should be removed as early as possible. This is best done by carefully bending them backwards, when they usually snap off cleanly. Canes can be used for supporting the stems, but it is neater and more secure to use special wire supports sold by the specialist nurseries. Special carnation feeds are also obtainable, but the high potassium feed used for tomatoes also gives good results. In summer light shading with white Coolglass may be necessary, but in winter let in all the light that is possible.

Plants are best not saved for more than two or three years, and old plants are best not used as a source of cuttings for propagation. Use shoots with about six pairs of leaves taken from young plants – these root easily by the usual methods if taken early in the year.

Of the host of named perpetual flowering carnation varieties now available, the 'Sim' varieties deserve special attention. The name is

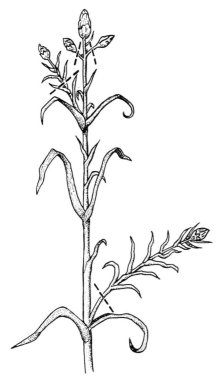

Fig. 30 Disbudding carnations.
The small buds that form around the large leading bud are best removed by gently bending downwards when they snap off cleanly. Other buds often form from below and are borne on weak spindly stems. Remove these also, since they waste the plant's energy and only produce poor blooms if left.

derived from William Sim, a Scotsman who originated the first remakable free-flowering seedling, also with fine quality blooms. There are now hundreds of sports embracing just about every colour imaginable. Another advantage, I have personally noticed, is that the Sim varieties seem less prone to calyx splitting (see below). A possible disadvantage is that they do tend to grow rather taller than some of the other varieties now available. However, for beginners the Sim varieties will be found extremely encouraging, and they are highly esteemed by many professional cut flower growers.

AMERICAN SPRAY CARNATIONS

These are fairly new to the carnation scene. The name is self-explanatory. To get the spray effect, the plants are stopped once by taking out the first bud produced by a rooted cutting. In other respects, culture is identical to that required for the normal PF types. The sprays, however, are perpetual too, and will continue to flower through the year. The flowers are slightly smaller and there are far fewer varieties. In very recent years, there has been a decline in popularity.

CARNATIONS FROM SEED

Thanks to the expertise of modern plant breeders, this is now an exciting field to explore. It is doubtful whether you can expect to get blooms of such fine quality as with the named perpetuals, but the growing is extremely easy, you can get some lovely colours, and often the fragrance has not been lost. Some seed-grown varieties make excellent pot plants, and others can be used for cut blooms. They are grown similar to – but are a great improvement on – the old fashioned annual Chabaud carnations. Seed of the latter is still available; 'Giant Chabaud' can be specially recommended.

A dramatic introduction in recent years is the 'Knight' carnation. This is F_1 hybrid seed, available in separate and mixed colours. The plants grow to about 30 cm (1 ft) in height, and make fine neat pot plants as well as having stems long enough for cutting. The blooms, usually fragrant, are of remarkably good quality and some of the colours are particularly striking – 'Crimson Knight' has become a particular favourite. To go with this, 'White Knight' is another beauty. There are also some delightful picotee flowered forms. From a late winter to early spring sowing, the Knight group will flower from summer to autumn. A little earlier flowering is the new F_1 hybrid 'Mini-Skirt' which, despite the name, grows a little taller. So far it's only available to give a mixture of colours, but they are astonishingly diverse. Worth trying in pots for cutting is another newcomer, the F_1 hybrid 'Scarlet Luminette'. This too is early flowering, with very good colour and strong long stems. All these annual varieties are easily grown, needing little in the way of support. Some can be disbudded, if you want to go to the trouble, to produce extra large blooms, but for many this is not essential, as it is for the PF types.

123

CALYX SPLITTING

This is one of the most common problems encountered by carnation growers. Its exact cause still seems to be a matter of controversy. The name describes what goes wrong – the green calyx, from which the flower petals emerge, splits down one side. This causes the petals to bulge out at that spot, completely ruining the shape and symmetry of the bloom. This can happen to all the carnation types. There is good evidence that the main cause of the trouble is erratic and rapid changing of environmental conditions, particularly temperature and watering. It may be noticed most during changeable summer weather, for example. Too much nitrogen in a fertilizer, and erratic or excessive feeding, should also be avoided.

To overcome the trouble to some extent, calyx menders can be used. These are merely short lengths of thin pliable wire covered with very thin green plastic strip to look as inconspicuous against the calyx as much as possible. The menders should preferably be applied *as soon as any suspicion of splitting is noticed*, but sometimes a repair can be made afterwards. You will not win prizes with such blooms, but at least they will be serviceable for cutting and flower arrangement. At one time tiny elastic bands were used, but modern 'menders' are much easier to apply and are less conspicuous. They are obtainable from most carnation nurseries.

Miscellaneous Flowers For Cutting

With a few exceptions these often make untidy pot plants. Flower arrangers and similar enthusiasts would be well advised to set aside a small greenhouse expecially for their culture. Little more than weather protection is usually needed, and a plastic greenhouse may provide this adequately. If such a house can be moved from site to site, the ground soil can often be used for growing a generous number of stems for cutting. Some of the cut flower subjects also grow better in the soil than when confined to pots. In all cases good light is essential.

ANNUALS (HARDY)

Many popular hardy annuals of the type with strong stems for cuttings, can be sown in autumn and grown on over winter for very early flowering. Antirrhinums can be grown as single spikes by removing all side shoots as development takes place. Choose tall large spiked types for this, not the dwarf compact varieties. Stocks are also valuable cut flowers and should be grown from the Hansen all-double strains of seed. Save only the *light green* seedlings which are those giving double-flowered spikes. Very impressive are the 'Giant Column' stocks which can be grown as single spikes like antirrhinum. Delightful for winter colour are the 'Beauty of Nice' stocks. Clarkia, larkspur, calendulas and asters are among others that make excellent cut blooms.

FREESIA

This is a highly prized flower for cutting. Corms potted during summer should flower in winter if about 10°C (45°F) can then be maintained. From bulb specialists choice named varieties can be obtained. Some of these are notable for scent, but not all freesias have fragrance. Named varieties are, however, usually vigorous and extra large flowered.

From a sowing made early in the year flowers can be produced for summer to autumn cutting. Sow about seven seeds to each 13-cm (5-in) pot, and give a few thin canes for support. A tie with cotton may be needed to keep the foliage from straggling.

GERBERA

Gerberas are extemely important to the flower arranger. The flowers are very large and showy, yet always graceful and never too flamboyant. They usually have a simple daisy shape with fine petals (although there are more double forms) and the range of colours is unusual and subtle.

The finest plants are obtainable as named hybrids from a few specialists. The plants should be potted in pots large enough to just take the root ball comfortably as soon as they are received. Do not plant too deeply: the crowns should be very slightly above the surface of the compost. A common trouble with gerberas is rotting of the root crown. However, from then on culture is relatively simple and consists of potting-on as necessary, thorough watering in summer with slight shade, good light and very modest watering in winter. Such plants will often take two to three years to produce blooms generously, and often there's plenty during winter if about 7°C (45°F) or a few degrees higher can be maintained – the plants like much the same conditions as carnations. To take the flowers *do not* cut the stems. Pull them sharply so that they detach cleanly from the root crown. Pieces of stem left attached usually rot, and this may spread down into the root crown resulting in complete death of the plant.

A number of different kinds of gerbera will be found offered as seed by the leading merchants. These seed strains are sometimes 'fancy-flowered', but whether double or semi-double types are desirable is a matter of personal opinion. When you grow from seed, the flowers are also usually smaller. However, very recently a remarkable new strain called 'Happipot' has been introduced. This can be highly recommended as a pot plant, because its habit is compact and neat. The flowers are also borne on much shorter stems – although the length is variable – but they are quite long enough for pulling if you wish. Another feature is that flowering occurs only a few months after sowing. An early spring sowing gives plants flowering from summer onwards. The flowers are smaller than in the named hybrids, and the petals are thicker, but the colours are delightful and include cream, yellow, orange, salmon, pink and red shades. A final 15-cm (6-in) pot is adequate for flowering.

GLADIOLI

With little more than weather protection huge handsome spikes, of great value to the flower arranger can be easily grown. Plastic protection can be given to soil plantings, taking care that ventilation is perfect. If pots are used they should be large. Planting can be done early in the year, and this should not be done deeply – about 5 cm (2 in) is adequate. Make sure a firm stick is given to support the blooms, even under cover these can topple over.

Dwarf gladioli such as 'Nymph' (*G. nanus*) and 'The Bride' (*G. colvillii*) are easy if planted three to each 13-cm (5-in) pot in late autumn. Keep frost free until spring, then allow extra warmth and water freely. Both are pure white, but 'Nymph' is streaked carmine.

HELLEBORUS

Many species are valuable for cut flowers, particularly during the winter months. They are hardy, but outdoors the flowers are very liable to weather damage during the harsh months from January to March. With a little protection you can also get flowers earlier and over a longer period. The genus includes evergreen and deciduous species. The former are especially desirable for greenhouse growing if a constant reasonably ornamental appearance is to be maintained. However, for purely cut flower production, it's more convenient to accommodate plants in plastic houses or frames, no artificial heating being necessary.

Very popular is the Christmas rose, *H. niger*. The cultivar 'Potter's Wheel' is a fine aquisition for permanent unheated greenhouse decoration. It has spear-shaped rather shiny foliage often with fine contrasting veins. The flowers are pure white with a central cluster of anthers and much larger than the original species. They come from December to March and last well when cut and put in water.

The Lenten rose *H. orientalis*, is also evergreen. The flowers are usually later and smaller, but there is a much wider colour range and, as well as white to cream, shades of red and purple occur. Sometimes there is attractive speckling of the petals. Both these plants are fairly compact in pots reaching about 60 cm (2 ft) in height. Potting and planting should be done in autumn. From then on the less disturbance the better, and it's wise to give containers with ample room for subsequent development. Hellebores can make a useful decorative plant where there is a shade problem apart from its cut flower value.

LILIUM

Lilies make exotic cut flowers, but many are strong stemmed and low growing enough to be suited to pots in the greenhouse or conservatory. There are now many extremely beautiful hybrids, and descriptions will be found in the catalogues of specialists. An ideal compost for lilies is a mixture of 4 parts fibrous loam, 3½ parts sterilized leafmould (by pouring boiling water on and allowing to drain), 2 parts of grit, and ½ part of crushed charcoal. A little bonemeal can be added, but lilies do not generally like richly fertilized soils or composts.

Autumn to spring is the best planting time. For pots just cover with compost. Some lilies are base stem rooting. If roots are seen to be forming, fit a 'collar' to the pot – made from a strip of thin metal or plastic, and heap more compost above the base roots (Fig. 31). After potting it is essential to give cool conditions and the pots are best plunged as described on p. 90. Most of the long stemmed lilies can be grown for cutting. The stem-rooting *Lilium longiflorum* (Easter lily) is particularly prized and is grown as a commercial cut flower; it is often forced by nurserymen. The finest variety for pots is 'Holland's Glory' and without forcing it flowers from June to July.

L. regale is one of the best known lilies and one of the easiest to grow. The bulbs are often sold in two size grades – it's wise to pay a little extra for the larger.

L. auratum is well known too and one of the most exotic lilies – it also makes a fine specimen pot plant. There are some especially fine named types available and most bloom from about August to September. They have reflexed petals with exciting markings and a tremendously powerful scent.

Not so well known is *L. brownii*. This, however, can also be useful for floral art work. The flowers are white and trumpet shaped, the exterior being richly shaded with chocolate-brown. This is a stem-rooting species.

Very dainty, and a good pot plant if the bulbs are grouped, as well as useful for cutting, is *L. japonicum*. This grows only to about 60–90 cm (2–3 ft), and the fragrance is notable but not so overpowering as some species.

A more delicate perfume, too, can be found in *L. speciosum*. There are a number of extremely beautiful named varieties the colours ranging from pure white to rich crimson.

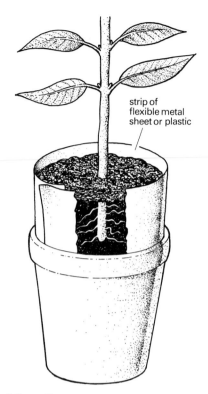

strip of flexible metal sheet or plastic

Fig. 31 Lily collar.
To give stem rooting lilies the desirable extra compost, a pot 'extension' can be fitted as shown.

The flowers have reflexed petals, usually exotically marked, and come from August to September. Look out for 'Lucie Wilson' (pink and white speckled red, and very long flowering period), 'Grand Commander' (crimson and white with dark red spotting, and quite outstanding), 'Album' (pure white with a lovely scent). Speciosum lilies are stem rooting.

The tiger lily, *L. tigrinum*, is a very old favourite, but there are some new delightful forms of unusual colour, still retaining the tiger spots on the reflexed petals. 'Flaviflorum' the yellow tiger lily, has a pure yellow colour with sharply contrasting purplish spots. It's very good for cutting. 'Splendens' is a rich orange with black spots. There are also double forms. Most flower about August.

Highly esteemed for cutting for special occasions, is *L. umbellatum*. These also make superb pot plants owing to their low growing habit. They have erect extremely exotic flowers in an enormous range of colours and there are many named forms. They are often forced, or the bulbs 'prepared' for early bloom.

A charming lily you can usually flower from seed the first year of sowing – if this is done early – is *L. formosanum pricei*. During the first year put about 5 seedlings to each 25-cm (10-in) pot, and in subsequent years about three of the bulbs which will form to the same pot size. This species has white trumpet flowers. Most other species take some years to flower from seed.

These species and forms, and many others, have been hybridized to give a host of marvellous fancy named types. You could spend many years exploring these alone.

ROSA

With a greenhouse you can enjoy the beauty of unblemished roses as early as spring. To do this, buy first quality hybrid tea roses in October. Wash any soil from the roots with clean running water and pot into an approved potting compost. Use 20-cm (8-in) pots and trim the roots if necessary so that the plants can be made to fit this size. At the same time cut away cleanly any roots that may be damaged or unhealthy. Potting done, stand the pots outdoors on a layer of shingle to prevent ingress of soil pests, until December when they should be taken into the greenhouse.

Now prune the plants removing all weak stems. You can do this quite drastically to leave only a few strong stems, this gives far better results.

From then on avoid temperatures over about 10°C (50°F) and ensure good light and ventilation. With such teatment you should get flowers by April.

Finer blooms, if you have patience, can be obtained by standing out the pots for a year and disbudding continuously to prevent flowering. This directs the energy of the plant to development. During the standing out the pots are best plunged.

Plants given the extra standing out should be returned to the greenhouse in November and gently forced during January not exceeding about 10°C (50°F). Prune the plants, but much less drastically this time.

SPRING AND SUMMER BULBS

Among the miscellaneous spring and summer bulbs can be singled out some noted for cut flowers. All the popular narcissi and tulips need no introduction. Do remember to grow them cool and to ventilate freely when possible. Of the summer flowering bulbs, two have become popular cut flowers. *Ornithogalum thyrsoides*, chincherinchee, with creamy-white spikes is a very untidy plant, but a wonderful cut subject. The same can be said for the famous, highly scented tuberose, *Polianthes tuberosa*. The variety 'The Pearl' is the one usually grown with spikes of white double flowers. Put about three bulbs to each 18-cm (7-in) pot. The bulbs can be forced gently in warmth at almost any time of the year, but rarely flower again.

More useful sources of cut flowers from storage organs are *Acidanthera*, *Crocosmia*, *Galtonia* (summer hyacinth), bulbous iris, *Anemone* and *Ranunculus*. All can be spring potted.

SWEET PEA

As delightful as sweet peas are, they can sometimes prove a tricky crop under glass. Sowing is best done during October and the plants overwintered in a frost-free greenhouse, but some growers prefer to sow from January to February. The plants are, either way, grown on under glass and hardened off for early planting outdoors and consequently early flowers.

Actually flowering under glass needs more care. Sowing is best done in September – but it's essential to *select suitable varieties*. The early flowering types should flower reasonably well under the limited daylight conditions from winter to spring. The popular Spencer types with large flowers will perform well in the greenhouse but are difficult to get to flower *before* about April; the buds often tend to be shed. The smaller flowered Cuthbertson types are much easier to manage and their stems are of reasonable length to make them useful for cutting. For success generally, good light is vital. Headroom of at least about 1.5 m (5 ft) is also necessary. All seedlings must be stopped in the manner usual to outdoor growing.

14   FOLIAGE PLANTS

GENERAL NOTES

From my investigations, a minimum winter temperature higher than about 5–7°C (41–45°F) is not common for the average home greenhouse these days. Often the temperature may fall to just frost free.

This means that very many of the popular plants recommended in general greenhouse books are unlikely to be practical; they are often more suited as house plants. Grow them in the greenhouse from spring to autumn, by all means – they will usually thrive and do better than in the home. However, in the chill of a winter greenhouse, many will severely deteriorate. Some may die, and some may survive and grow away again when conditions become warmer. Unless you have a greenhouse minimum of about 10–13°C (50–55°F), most of the more exotic foliage plants are best overwintered in the home, and should be taken there in the autumn. Typical examples of such plants are foliage begonias, marantas and related plants, ficus with a few exceptions, aphelandras, sansevierias, palms with few exceptions, dracaenas, dieffenbachias, and codiaeums.

In planning this chapter, I have therefore had a rethink. The following suggestions are plants that should be reasonably practical and keep their good looks *the year round* in the relative winter chill of the average home greenhouse. They should be happy in the company of each other too, in winter as well as in summer. A few are very easy from seed, and so are simple to replace if they do deteriorate. Most of the following are also useful for the small home greenhouse, although a few may outgrow themselves eventually. Large foliage plants are described in the conservatory section. Displaying flowers on a greenhouse bench should be given as much thought as a flower arrangement in the home. Suitable foliage plants to enhance the blooms are essential for that 'professional' look. The following offer a variety of leaf shapes, forms, and tints, to act as a foil for flowers, but some are quite beautiful in themselves.

Greenhouse Foliage Plants: Selected List

ARAUCARIA HETEROPHYLLA (syn. A. EXCELSA)

This is popularly called Norfolk island pine and is somewhat Christmas tree-like in appearance. Although it will reach the height of a man, it can be kept relatively small in a 20–25-cm (8–10-in) pot for a long time. If desired plants can be stood out in summer to make more greenhouse room, but watering then should not be neglected. During winter keep just slightly moist. The plants like slight shade in summer and ventilation whenever possible in the greenhouse. If plants become large or leggy, cut back early in the year and use the new young shoots that form as cuttings for propagation.

ACACIA

Most acacias are attractive for their graceful fine ferny foliage, and many are esteemed for their charming blossom which is often fragrant. The best known, and very easily grown from seed, is *A. dealbata*, the 'mimosa' of the florist. This quickly makes a beautiful foliage plant for the frost-free grenhouse, and it's hardy outdoors in mild areas, growing to the size of a small tree. However, in pots, I find it slow and reluctant to flower readily. To show blossom it needs a small tub and a large conservatory. As a foliage plant, this acacia, like most others, has got the disadvantage that the leaflets tightly close from early evening until early morning, and during this time looks far less pleasing! For normal greenhouse or conservatory use this probably will not matter, but may be undesirable if plants are wanted for the home.

Another graceful species for foliage, easily raised from seed, is *A. baileyana*. This too will reach a considerable size in time. There is an especially interesting variety, *A. baileyana purpurea*, with maroon tinted foliage and shoots. Hardy in mild places, and with very lovely foliage, is the shrubby *A. podalyriifolia*. The overall colour effect of this species is silvery-white, the young shoots and 'leaves' being covered with a white down-like farina. The plant often flowers well during winter, too, these being elongated and golden yellow. Ideal for the smaller greenhouse and a very reliable flowerer in small pots, is *A. verticillata*. This does, however, have sharp 'prickles' rather than 'leaves', but the blossom, also elongated, is borne in profuse clusters and is a delightful lemon-yellow colour. The popular name is prickly Moses. Seed of all these species germinates well at about 20°C (69°F). Soak the seed overnight before sowing.

ASPARAGUS

There are three important species, often incorrectly called 'ferns', with graceful, fine needle-like foliage. This is highly prized for enhancing flowers, and is often picked to go with blooms like sweet pea or carnation. All three described here are easy to grow from seed and to further propagate by simple root division. The finest for growing as a neat *erect* pot plant is the not so well known *Asparagus densiflorus* 'Myersii'. This has no tendency to spread and trail or 'climb', but is very much slower growing and takes at least two years to make a sizeable plant in a 13-cm (5-in) pot.

Most popular and generally useful is *A. densiflorus* (syn. *A. sprengeri*). This is often fairly erect in the early stages, but as the stems lengthen they become more trailing, it is very

attractive in hanging baskets and is often employed to accompany flowers. For this purpose about two years should be allowed for growing from seed.

A. setaceus (syn. *A. plumosa*) is a curious species with extremely fine needle foliage. Young plants usually have the habit of the cedar of Lebanon in miniature, with flattish spreading fronds, and make very neat compact specimens. After a time, often variable, a dramatic change in habit usually takes place. Very long stems are rapidly sent out and sometimes these may twine round any support that happens to be near. Otherwise they will trail down, again making the plant pleasing foliage for hanging containers.

These three species are happy in little more than frost-free conditions, and seed germination is easy in spring if sown at about 16°C (60°F).

ASPIDISTRA

A. elatior was once very well known as the cast iron plant because of its remarkable resistance to neglect and ill treatment. In recent years it has gone out of fashion, and indeed has even become difficult to find in some areas. However, the Victorians were very wise plantsmen, and anything they grew extensively is well worth reconsideration. The reason for the loss of interest in the aspidistra is undoubtedly because it is so frequently badly grown; its reputation seems to make people want to treat it indifferently! In fact, well-grown specimens are extremely handsome and positively delightful if the smooth lance-like leaves are given treatment with a leaf-shine product. However, for something a little different, do look out for the *variegated* form, not so often seen. This has the foliage striped with a contrasting pale cream.

Aspidistras are splendid for slight shade, and will usually survive little more than frost-free conditions – ideally a winter minimum of about 7°C (45°F) should be maintained. Water freely in summer but keep only very slightly moist in winter.

BEGONIA

There are numerous forms of beautiful foliage begonias, well documented in most greenhouse books. Unfortunately, unless you can maintain a winter minimum of about 10°C (50°F) the foliage is liable to turn brown or be entirely shed. *B. rex* with large heart-shaped leaves, exotically marked and coloured, is very popular. It can be grown from seed, which is very fine and dust-like, and available from most seedsmen. Well known too is *B. masoniana*, the iron cross begonia, so named because of the remarkable contrasting dark mark just like the Iron Cross, on the pale green leaves. Not so well known, but often doing especially well in the greenhouse, is *B. cathayana*, similar to *B. rex*, but red veined and with red hairy stems.

All these are liable to become scruffy in chill over over winter, but usually grow new leaves with the arrival of warmer conditions. Give moderate shade and a good summer humidity. All the common house plant begonias make excellent greenhouse plants.

CALADIUM

This is one of the most striking of the exotic foliage plants; it is definitely not a plant for chill. Fortunately, it can be grown like an annual, from tubers started into growth in spring and using a warm propagator. The large arrow shaped leaves will be enjoyed from summer to autumn when the foliage then fades. Let the pots go almost dry – not completely so – and store somewhere in the home over winter, where the temperature does *not fall below about 13°C (55°F)*. Various cultivars are available with richly marked and veined, showy leaves in shades of red, green, and cream.

CHLOROPHYTUM

C. capense is well known as the spider plant. It is best grown as the variety 'Variegatum' with green and cream long grassy arching foliage. From the clump grow numerous, very long stems bearing tiny plantlets at the ends and creating a pleasing 'spidery' effect. It is an ideal plant for wall pots, hanging containers, or pedestals. Ideally give a winter minimum of about 7°C (45°F). It will survive very much lower if kept on the dry side, but is then prone to foliage deterioration. The little plantlets can

be layered for propagation, or the parent plant can be simply divided.

CINERARIA

C. maritima. This is best known as a beautiful graceful silvery grey foliage plant for summer bedding. Young specimens also make delightful winter foliage plants if grown in pots, a fact rarely brought to attention. However, it is not usually wise to keep the plants for more than a year or so, since they begin to grow away too fast and become leggy and untidy. The masses of yellow flowers are also untidy and floppy.

An interesting companion for this cineraria is *Dodonaea viscosa* 'Purpurea', easy from seed available from rare seed specialists (see Appendix). This plant has purple-red foliage, brighter than ever in winter, and makes a striking contrast with the silver of the cineraria. It makes a neat and compact pot plant, and has the common name of hopseed bush.

CISSUS

C. antarctica is an attractive climber with pale green spear-shaped leaves with toothed edges. Its ultimate height seems to depend on pot size, and in a final 18-cm (7-in) pot it will grow to a man's height. In a large tub or planted in a border it can much more than double this, and may then need training up into and along the greenhouse roof. It is easy to grow, but is prone to aphid attack and should be carefully watched for this pest. A winter minimum of about 5°C (41°F) is adequate.

Another species, *C. discolor*, which is best grown as a trailer, is one of the most beautiful of all foliage plants with gloriously coloured silvery patterned leaves of spear shape. Unfortunately, it is *essential* to overwinter this in the home, or where the temperature does not fall below about 13°C (55°F). It also likes a high humidity, and so is not a particularly easy plant to keep in good condition.

COFFEA

C. arabica is an interesting plant to grow because it is a source of the commercial coffee bean. The beans are now available from most seedsmen and germinate easily at about 24°C (75°F). This can be reached without a propagator in the greenhouse during spring and summer. The plant forms a neat bushy shrub, the seed sold usually being the dwarf form *C.a.nana*. The leaves are spear shaped with slightly undulating edges, a rich green colour and quite glossy. It is often reported that you will get flowers and berries – this may be somewhat optimistic! Moreover, in the average cool home greenhouse, it is extremely unlikely! To achieve flowering and fruiting, a very congenial constant warmth and humidity is required.

DESMODIUM

D. gyrans is another foliage plant grown for its curiosity value rather than for beauty. Its leaves exhibit movement but, unlike *Mimosa pudica* (p. 137), it does not have to be touched; the leaves will move of their own accord. It is a tropical subject, but can be grown as an annual in much the same way as *M. pudica*. Soak the seed overnight and sow in rather more warmth: about 24°C (75°F) is ideal. Pot-on to 13-cm (5-in) pots. Fresh seed should germinate well, but it is not unusual to encounter problems because seed of doubtful freshness is supplied. Greenish coloured seed, rather than black, seems to germinate more freely.

The leaves are trifoliate and are made up of one large leaf with two small ones at the base. It is the small pair that *move*. Small seedlings do not form the small active leaves; give the plant a chance to develop. When they have formed and are properly mature they will be seen to move. The movement is somewhat semi-circular and often jerky. This has lead to the common names of telegraph plant and semaphore plant. The phenomenon is seen at its best when the temperature is fairly high, such as during a warm day. It is sometimes reported that bright sun is necessary, but this is *not true*. When the plant is at its agile best, the leaflets will be seen to move together, clasp each other, and then spring apart. In ideal conditions this tropical annual produces pea-like violet flowers. This is very unlikely in the home greenhouse except possibly during a long warm summer to autumn.

EUCALYPTUS

The hundreds of species could well be explored as a source of attractive foliage plants for pots. Even those species that grow into enormous trees usually have pleasing juvenile leaves, and can be very useful when young. Since most eucalyptus are fairly easy from seed, replacement when a plant has become too large is usually little problem. However, there are many dwarf and shrubby species, and some will flower well in pots too.

Very easy and well known is *E. globulus*, the blue gum. It is relatively hardy, but is often used for sub-tropical bedding features. *E. gunnii* is also popular because of its eye-catching greyish juvenile foliage, but it is a fast grower and soon has to be found a place outdoors. *E. citriodora* is often specially recommended for the greenhouse, or as a house plant when young, but it really needs a winter minimum of about 10°C (50°F) to retain its good looks. The foliage has a powerful lemon scent when gently pressed between the fingers. *E. cordata*, heart-leaved silver gum, is little known, yet it forms a delightful, greyish-leaved foliage plant also suitable for bedding out for effect. The common name is an apt description. Excellent for retaining in relatively small pots for a long time are *E. archeri*, the alpine gum, which is by nature a dwarf tree, and particularly *E. eximia nana*, the dwarf golden gum. The latter I can especially recommend; when grown in pots it usually forms lovely yellow flowers about three years after sowing, as an extra bonus to the pleasing foliage.

EUONYMUS

Dwarf evergreen varieties of euonymus make excellent pot plants and, although almost hardy, the foliage is beautifully marked and coloured to a degree found in exotics. It is very surprising they are not grown in pots more often, since they are also a good choice for places where light is poor. *E. japonica* 'Variegata' and 'Aurea', and *E. fortunei* 'Vegeta' and 'Silver Queen' are four examples of very charming varieties often sold as container plants by garden centres. 'Silver Queen' will grow tall if allowed, but is very slow. The others rarely exceed about 30 cm (1 ft) and have spreading habit. Leaf colour is often enhanced in the chill of winter.

FATSHEDERA

This is unusual in being a bigeneric cross between *Fatsia* and *Hedera* and, being hardy it has become a favourite house plant for cold places. The choicest form is × *F. lizei* 'Variegata' which has shiny, ivy-like leaves attractively variegated in cream. By pruning back each year it can be grown to give a bushy shape. If left alone it can be trained up canes as a climber. The variegated form is best given not less than frost-free winter conditions.

FATSIA JAPONICA

This is often called the false castor oil plant because the leaf shape is very similar. It is quite hardy, but the most desirable cream variegated form is not quite so easy or vigorous and is best kept frost free. Although eventually growing to a considerable size, plants can be kept in relatively small pots for a long time. New plants can be easily raised from seed, but the variegated form must be propagated from stem cuttings taken in the early summer. The foliage is excellent for creating a 'tropical' effect and is especially attractive if treated with a leaf-shine product.

FICUS

Most of the exotic *Ficus*, including, the notorious rubber plant, *F. elastica*, will not survive the average home greenhouse with temperature lower than about 10°C (50°F). In chill there will be severe leaf shedding. Exceptions, even hardy in some places are *F. deltoidea*, called mistletoe fig because of its reddish to yellow berries borne the year round, and *F. pumila*, creeping fig, which has a trailing habit but can also be grown up short supports. In both these species the foliage is relatively small and dainty.

GREVILLEA

G. robusta is a favourite greenhouse and conservatory foliage plant easily raised from seed provided it is grown in an *acid* compost.

To remain in good condition is should have a winter temperature of about 7°C (45°F). When lower there is risk of leaf shedding. The foliage is graceful, finely divided and 'ferny' in appearance, and the plants make a particularly decorative foil for most floral displays. By the second year from seed, plants are often sufficiently tall to be used for outdoor effect during summer. It is wise to raise new plants from seed every two years or so to replace those that have outgrown their usefulness.

HEDERA

There are many species and varieties of *Hedera*, and several cultivars of *H. helix*, the common ivy, with variously shaped foliage and very pretty variegation and markings. All are ideal for the frost-free greenhouse, and can often be grown as climbers or trailers according to vigour. A specially striking species is *H. canariensis*, a species growing to considerable size and height if allowed. Its large leaves are variegated in dark and light green and cream. This species appears to be hardy if gradually acclimatized to cold, and its leaves often acquire pleasing reddish or purple tints in winter. In warmth it can grow quite rampantly, but drastic changes in temperature should not be given suddenly, or leaf shedding is probable. A well-grown specimen, in a 25-cm (10-in) pot, can be trained up canes to reach the greenhouse roof making an impressive sight. It is easily propagated from cuttings, but these may need reasonable warmth to get them quickly established when rooted.

HYPOESTES

H. phyllostachya (sanguinolenta) is a most attractive foliage plant often seen sold as a house plant. Its habit, at first, is neat and compact. The small spear-shaped leaves of the best forms are a beautiful olive green freely covered with contrasting deep rose-pink spots and speckles. There are, however, less colourful variations.

A disadvantage is that the plant soon tends to become straggly and often almost semi-trailing, and the distance of the stems between the leaves becomes excessive. To overcome this, plants on sale have often been treated with a dwarfing chemical, but they will revert

(**Left**) *Clianthus formosus* flowering well in a drain pipe in the author's greenhouse – a spectacular flower not so difficult as often thought.

(**Below**) *Lilium speciosum* 'Rubrum'. The shorter forms of this lily make excellent pot plants with a delicate fragrance. They flower later than most lilies (August/September) and are excellent for the conservatory.

Thunbergia alata. This is a new variety called 'Susie', with extra large flowers and a wider range of colours including cream and sometimes white. I personally discard seedlings that do not have the striking black eye, a few of which usually occur in a batch. This species can be used as a climber or trailer.

Luffa gourds, *L. cylindrica*, the source of the bathroom loofah, growing in the author's greenhouse. Easy from seed.

Petunias displayed in a hanging basket in the author's greenhouse – they need bright airy conditions to flower well.

F₁ hybrid pelargoniums. A group in the author's greenhouse flowering in early summer from early sown seed. Rear back and rear extreme left can be seen the very new 'Startel' variety with smaller blooms but with unusual 'spiky' petal shape. All in 13-cm (5-in) pots.

to straggling in time. The best way to always have neat plants is to grow from seed – this is very easy and the usual methods can be employed. It is also possible to propagate from cuttings, but these may begin straggling more quickly than seedlings. However, any particularly good colours in a batch can reliably be reproduced from cuttings. Generally, give slight shade in summer, sow and take cuttings in spring.

JACARANDA

J. mimosaefolia is a graceful plant similar in habit to *Grevillea robusta* and can be grown from seed similarly. It is, however, easy to grow in any normal potting compost. The leaves are very 'ferny' in appearance and pale green in colour, and this beautiful plant ought to be more extensively cultivated in the home greenhouse. In its native habitat of Brazil, or when planted in warm countries, it also bears glorious blue flowers, but these are not produced on small plants in the cool greenhouse.

MIMOSA

M. pudica may not be one of the most showy foliage plants, but it certainly ranks among the most fascinating. It is the famous sensitive plant, and everyone should grow it at sometime or other. Children find it most intriguing.

In the home greenhouse it is best grown from seed as an annual. It is very easy to germinate by the usual methods and can be potted-on to final 10-cm (4-in) pots in which size it will remain neat and compact. The foliage is rather like that of the 'mimosa' of the florist being composed of numerous leaflets. At the base of each leaflet there is a tiny pale swollen spot, called a 'pulvinus'. If this is gently touched with a thin sharp object the leaflet will instantly fold back. More general disturbance results in all the leaflets folding, and if the whole plant is agitated it will collapse completely in a most dramatic manner. This apparently does no harm, and recovery can be expected in an hour or so.

A few small fluffy purplish to pinkish flowers may be produced, shaped like those of the well known mimosa, but these are insignificant.

Keep reasonable warmth, give good light and do not over-water. The species is a short-lived tropical perennial, but you will have no difficulty in growing it as an annual. Better germination may be obtained by soaking seed overnight before sowing.

MONSTERA

M. deliciosa is the well known house plant popularly called Swiss cheese plant, the leaves, when young, being 'slashed' or lobed and, when mature, perforated with holes. It can grow to a very impressive size, about 3 m (10 ft) in good conditions, yet seems to be happy in remarkably small pots. It will usually send down aerial roots which may enter the compost and, again in good conditions, may produce arum-like flowers followed by fruits like elongated pineapples. These fruits, as grown in cultivation, are usually too fibrous to be pleasantly edible.

Although tropical in appearance and origin, the plant can be amazingly hardy. Ideally the minimum should be about 13°C (55°F), but there are many cases where plants survive unheated homes, offices, and public buildings, for long periods.

To grow plants from seed is easy, *provided the seed is fresh*. Seed very quickly loses its viability. Fortunately, some seed firms are now taking *special* care to supply fresh seed. This must be ordered well before June which is the delivery time. During this time quite high temperatures can be reached in the greenhouse and germination of the seed should take place readily.

PELARGONIUM
(SCENTED LEAF TYPES)

Full details of these will be found in the catalogue of any specialist pelargonium nursery. There are very numerous named varieties and species with a variety of leaf forms. All are notable for the remarkable leaf scent and the common names are usually inspired by what this may suggest. Thus we have 'rose', 'lemon', 'orange', 'nutmeg', 'peppermint' and similar. A few types have pretty flowers, but this is not the rule. Most can be overwintered in a fost-free greenhouse if kept on the dry side, and in much the same way as other 'geraniums' and pelargoniums. They generally like bright airy conditions in summer and in the warmth at that time the scent can become quite delightful.

RICINUS

R. communis is the true castor oil plant. It has large palmate foliage of very tropical appearance, yet is extremely easy and quick to grow from the beans. From an early spring sowing, with a germination temperature of about 21°C (70°F), fine plants can be obtained by summer. A particularly splendid quite new variety which should be given preference is 'Impala'. This is quite destinctive in having the foliage beautifully flushed maroon-red, and borne on reddish stems. The flowers too, are more attractive than other forms and the spiky seed capsules are quite eye-catching, being brilliantly tinted a glowing vermilion colour. It makes a fine neat annual pot plant. *Ricinus* is also often used for sub-tropical outdoor bedding and, during a good summer, the plants can reach a man's height and look most impressive.

The bean-like seeds are prettily marked and should *not* be allowed to fall into the hands of small children who may find them attractive: the beans contain an *extremely poisonous* substance called 'ricin'.

SAXIFRAGA

S. stolonifera (*S. sarmentosa*) is the well-known mother of thousands, so called because it sends out long runners bearing baby plantlets which can be easily detached and rooted. It is useful for the edge of staging, shelves, or wall pots, and also has pretty white flowers in summer. The variety 'Tricolor' is of special interest because of its very attractive pink-edged, roundish, veined green leaves, but is not so fast growing. Only frost-free conditions are needed in winter.

SCHEFFLERA

Two species make first class pot plants for the home greenhouse, but they are rarely described and then usually incorrectly. *S. actinophylla*, the umbrella tree, which reach a man's height in a large pot, but is very slow

growing. Its stems have a ring of large spear-shaped glossy leaves radiating like the spokes of an umbrella. *S. arboricola* is similar except that it is lower growing and more compact.

Both deserve to be much better known and are extremely easy to grow from seed. The foliage looks brilliant if given a leaf-shine treatment, since it is naturally extremely glossy. It is usually reported that these species need winter warmth. I have found both to survive well, with little deterioration, when temperatures have fallen to little above freezing. However, in chill, keep the roots almost dry.

SOLEIROLIA

S. soleirolii is a dainty little creeping plant with the common name of mind your own business. It is an ideal carpeting subject and can be grown on the compost surface in pots containing other taller plants such as standards or small shrubs or trees, as well as in hanging containers. However, it is a moisture lover and should not be allowed to dry out at any time. It is very easily propagated by division, but is best grown at not less than about 5–7°C (41–45°F).

STENOCARPUS

S. sinuatus has the impressive common name of Queensland firewheel tree because of its brilliantly showy red flowers. It is often reputed to bear flowers when small and shrubby but, in my experience, it has not done so when grown as a foliage plant in pots in the cool home greenhouse. It is easy from seed and has large lobed glossy green foliage, also worth treating with leaf-shine. Frost-free conditions are adequate, and it is hardy in mild places in the British Isles.

TOLMIEA

T. menziesii is called pig-a-back plant because tiny plantlets form around the leaf edges and these root easily. It is a low growing creeping plant with dainty, prettily marked foliage. The spikes of pinky white flowers in summer are also attractive, and the plant is generally useful for trailing effects.

15 TRAILERS, CLIMBERS AND WALL SHRUBS

GENERAL NOTES

This group of plants tends to get neglected by home greenhouse gardeners, probably because a little more care is needed in their growing, training and application. However, they are indispensable if you want to get that 'professional touch' and to give interest and variety – particularly when a greenhouse is used for display or as a conservatory.

Trailers are perhaps most often planted in hanging containers, but they are also useful for growing from along the edge of staging or on shelves and in wall pots. In such cases make sure the pots are well weighted or secured, so that one-sided growth of the plants does not cause 'top heaviness' and toppling over. To give height to a container of trailing plants, it can be stood on an inverted flowerpot or other support. For conservatories ornamental pedestal stands, usually adjustable in height, make attractive and ideal supports. Fancy effects can be obtained by wiring two or more plastic pots one above the other. Planting up in each pot then eventually produces a hanging column of flowers or foliage and the pots become hidden from view.

For the home greenhouse, climbers should be chosen with care. Evergreen types can seriously cut light entry and, if you use your greenhouse for a wide range of general growing, good light is always important. Some climbers also tend to be rampant if allowed to grow unchecked. In a small greenhouse, they are best grown in pots or given a restricted root run. Also make sure you do not overfeed.

The annual climbers are more easily managed and are easy from seed. They pose few problems and can be discarded at the end of the year.

Wall shrubs are more suited to the larger conservatory or lean-to used as a garden room. In this chapter I suggest a few of the more practical types that can be kept in check and that do not demand high temperatures. Where both climbers or wall shrubs are grown against a wall, the wall is best rendered and given a coat of white emulsion before commencement. This is to block any cracks and holes where pests or diseases may hide away. If support is needed, use wire or plastic-coated wire or mesh, *not* plastic by itself. Plastic often becomes brittle and loses its strength after a short time in the greenhouse, and a well-trained plant may suddenly be left without any support.

Trailers

ACHIMENES

These have been described on p. 92. Certain varieties are especially suited to hanging containers. Some recommended ones are 'Pendent Blue', 'Pendent Purple', 'Blue John', 'Cameo Triumph' (pink), 'Alamandine' (purple), 'Chalkhill Blue' (white eye) and 'Peacock' (pink with eye).

AESCHYNANTHUS

This trailing genus of the Gesneriaceae seems less well known than the more frequently described *Columnea*. It bears certain resemblance, but is generally easier for the home greenhouse and will survive a winter minimum of about 7°C (45°F) if kept on the dry side then. Plants are sometimes sold as house plants, the most frequently seen being *Aeschynanthus speciosus* (*Trichosporum splendens*). This can trail to a length of about 60 cm (2 ft), has waxy-textured spear-shaped pale green leaves, and bright orange-red, yellow-throated tubular flowers in clusters, borne from summer to autumn. There are hybrids which are even more easy to manage. *A. pulcher* can be grown as a climber or as a trailer. The flowers are of similar shape but more crimson in colour, and are produced at intervals from summer through winter.

The plants must be potted into an open fibrous compost A mixture of peat potting compost, of not too fine texture, and sphagnum moss is suitable. Wire or slatted baskets make the best containers. During summer give slight shade, water well, and spray with a mist of water from time to time to maintain good humidity. In winter, keep conditions much more dry but do not let the compost dry out completely.

BEGONIA

The 'pendula' tuberous begonias make splendid showy plants for hanging pots or baskets. The 'Lloydii' types have tassel-like flowers in a wide range of colours. Very showy indeed are the choice 'Sensation' strains of pendulous begonias. These are usually available in separate colours. The tubers can be started and grown on, and about three to four are usually needed for the average basket.

CAMPANULA

The favourite species for trailing is the very old fashioned *C. isophylla*. This has a blue and a white form, and both smother themselves with blossom from summer to autumn. It can be used to trail over pots and on the staging edge or on shelves, and can be easily propagated from cuttings – it cannot normally be grown from seed. However, 1983 saw the introduction of the remarkable new 'Kristal Hybrids' which flower in summer from a February sowing, and are exceptionally free flowering. Sometimes shoots will spontaneously show cream-and-green leaf variegation. These can be isolated and rooted to form variegated plants. However, in my experience, these are not so free flowering and the blossom is often smaller.

Similar, and very attractive, is *C. fragilis* which is fairly easy to raise from seed.

CARDIOSPERMUM

C. halicacabum is little known, but deserves to be grown more often. It is a climber, but is ideal for hanging baskets and as a very quick growing charming foliage plant. The dainty vine-like leaves make a graceful background for other flowering plants. The flowers are tiny and of no interest, but the large inflated seed pods that follow are delightful and an added attraction. The common name of the plant is balloon vine, and it is extremely easy to raise from seed as an annual.

CLIANTHUS

C. formosus (*C. dampierii*) is the famous Sturt's desert pea said to be notoriously difficult to cultivate, and many readers may be surprised to see it recommended in a home greenhouse book! In fact, from personal experience over a number of years, I suggest that it's well worth a try. The flower is so extraordinary and beautiful, that it's a pity to miss. The plant rambles or trails and will flower the same year as sowing. The flowers are of most unusual appearance and are usually borne in circular groups around a central supporting stem. The individual flowers are of curious 'hooded' structure and consist of an upper 'standard' and lower 'keel'. These are coloured brilliant crimson-scarlet. In dramatic contrast, there is a jet-black central glossy 'boss' from which two red petals hang down. The groups of flowers are surprisingly generously borne from late summer to autumn.

Seed is freely available. Try my method as follows. Soak the seed overnight and sow it individually – it's small but can be handled easily with tweezers. Put each seed in any of the approved potting composts contained in a *fibre sweet pea tube*. Put the tubes in a propagator at about 21°C (70°F). Sowing is best done in early spring. Germination can be expected to be poor and variable, but a packet of seed will usually yield several seedlings. The point of the tube pots is to avoid disturbance of the long tap root formed. It is therefore important to transfer each tube to the final container soon after germination has taken place. I have found the best containers are made from pieces of plastic 10-cm (4 in) pipe, cutting each to a 40-cm (16 in) length. Put some drainage pebbles in first and fill with potting compost. Set the pea tube, complete with *undisturbed* seedling, in the pipe's compost leaving the top of the tube a few centimetres above the compost. This reduces risk of the seedling's base rotting, a common cause of failure. From then on no special care seems necessary except that watering should be cautious and the water applied around the pea tube. I find many of the seedlings grow poorly and may wither for no apparent reason and come to nothing. However, there's usually a few that go on to flower with amazing vigour. The plant is actually a perennial, and there are reports of it being saved over winter in little more than frost-free conditions. A bright airy position is preferred and I have stood plants outdoors in sheltered places during summer. Some people graft the seedlings on to *Colutea arborescens* seedlings, but I have not found this necessary.

The main secret of successful cultivation seems to be avoiding disturbance of the seedling roots and to provide adequate depth of compost for the root's later penetration.

FUCHSIA

There are very many named varieties of fuchsia particularly suited to hanging baskets and pedestal pots. In the case of baskets, about three rooted cuttings are usually needed for each. When the stem reaches the basket edge, stop the plant to encourage more shoots to form at that point. These in turn can be further stopped to get enough growth to form a cascading effect. (See also p. 111.)

LACHENALIA

L. bulbifera (*L. pendula*) is a small bulb especially suited to growing in baskets. Line a basket with moss and plant the bulbs on top of the moss about 5–8 cm (2–3 in) apart and with their tips pointing down. Fill with potting compost and plant a few more bulbs normally around the edge. The bulbs will grow through the moss and the hanging basket will become a

'ball' of bloom from December onwards if planting is done from early to mid-autumn. The flowers are brightly coloured in a combination of red, yellow, and purple. After planting, put the baskets in a cool greenhouse with a minimum temperature of 7°C (45°F). High temperatures above 13°C (55°F) must not be permitted or flowering will be checked. After planting water sparingly until the foliage is growing vigorously.

L. aloides 'Nelsonii' can be grown similarly, but is best grown normally in pots and *not* hung. After flowering allow the containers to dry when the foliage has died down and give a position of full sunlight. The containers can be tipped out and the offsets separated when it is repotting time.

LOBELIA

The trailing lobelias have always been neglected, and when used are often regarded as mere companions for other more showy subjects. A very recently introduced variety, 'Cascade' is an extremely showy mixture of colours including red and carmine and all the usual blue and lilac shades found in lobelia. Many of the flowers have contrasting white eye, and a basket planted up with this variety alone will create a very beautiful effect. For 'self' colours 'Red Cascade' and 'Blue Basket' are also two outstanding varieties. Lobelias grow readily from seed. When pricking out, take up little clumps of the seedlings and space out, a technique called 'patching-out'. It is impossible and pointless to try picking out the minute seedlings individually.

PELARGONIUM

The ivy-leaved pelargoniums are among the most pleasing of all basket plants. The leaves are in themselves attractive enough, but the flowers in numerous lovely colours, in single, semi-double, or fully double forms, continue to appear, without any notable off periods, from summer to late autumn. Planting up, from rooted cuttings, can be much in the same way as described for fuchsia in this section. A number of fine named varietes will be found described in the specialist catalogues. Very new and striking are 'harlequin geraniums' having white petals with bold colour contrast edging in a number of different shades of red, pink, mauve and orange as named varieties. These latest 'ivy-types' were developed from 'Mexicana' forms with red and white blooms. New, too, is 'Red Fountain', which can be grown from *seed*! Overwinter and propagate as described on p. 117.

PETUNIA

Petunias are easy to raise from seed and most can be grown in hanging baskets provided the site is *bright* and airy to encourage free flowering. Some varieties, if you study the seed catalogues, are described as more compact than others and these are best reserved for bedding, rather than for hanging. An outstanding and quite spectacular petunia for baskets, and the protection of the greenhouse, is the variety 'Titan'. This has enormous single flowers in a wide range of all the usual petunia colours, and these are extremely freely produced over a long period, At first the plants tend to be compact, but the stems soon begin to lengthen and cascade over the container edge. Do not cover petunia seed when sowing. The new picotee-edged petunias such as 'Red Picotee', and other F_1 hybrids of this group, are also exceptionally striking.

PLECTRANTHUS

P. oertendahlii is another trailer often sold as a house plant, sometimes under the extremely misleading popular name of Brazilian coleus – it looks nothing like a coleus, but is of the same family! It is quite an attractive evergreen foliage plant with oval to roundish leaves delicately veined in cream and sometimes with slight pinkish flush. The flowers are very dainty and born as longish erect spikes of white to purplish tubular florets from summer to early winter. The plant rambles or trails and stems will often root into compost where they touch. Such pieces can be cut off for propagation if desired. This species is an easy one, putting up with some neglect, and even surviving little more than frost-free conditions – others of the genus are far more exacting and need congenial warmth.

SWEET PEA

Compact and dwarf sweet peas make easy colourful basket plants for a bright airy greenhouse or conservatory, during the summer to autumn months. They are less satisfactory for heavily shaded places, but slight shading with white Coolglass, for example, as required for most of the summer greenhouse plants, is all right.

These sweet peas are newcomers to the scene. They are *not* climbers and have *no* tendrils to cause an untidy tangle, and they grow to little more than about 75 cm (2½ ft) at the most. In hanging containers they will tumble over the sides beautifully. The first of the type was 'Snoopea' with an excellent colour range and with some flowers scented. Very recently a further improvement has been made with 'Supersnoop'. This has even finer quality flowers and the stems are long enough for cutting if you wish – no particular advantage for basket growing. Other short sweet peas can be grown in hanging containers, but their tendrils will encourage a climbing rather than a trailing habit. Culture is very easy and often a fine display is possible by sowing the seed along with other bedding plants, but pricking out directly into the baskets. Several seedlings should be put into each basket which will later cascade with kaleidoscopic colour.

THUNBERGIA

T. alata is the well-known black-eyed Susan. It is really a climber and can be grown up a fan of short canes thrust into the pot to give very quick colour. However, left to themselves the stems tend to trail and in a hanging container soon tumble over. The striking feature is the jet black eye that many of the flowers have, which contrasts so dramatically with the brilliant orange, cream or white background. Not all the plants from a batch of seedlings will have the 'eye' so, since even the small seedlings produce flowers, I throw out all those without it – before planting up the pots and baskets. The plant grows very easily and freely from seed so you can afford to carry out this 'rogueing'. (A 'rogue' plant is one showing undesirable, unwanted or abnormal characteristics.) A recently introduced and greatly improved variety is 'Susie' with larger flowers and especially suited for hanging containers.

VERBENA

The verbenas used for bedding are known botanically as *V. hortensis* 'Compacta'. In fact they involve extensive hybridization and over the past few years some amazing improvements have been made. Early forms, despite the botanical name, often became straggly or leggy as they grew. This may be all right for hanging containers, window boxes, and the like, but the production of flowers often tended to ease off from late summer onwards. The delightful newer varieties are much more compact, but they will still make splendid trailing subjects. They flower freely and continuously, the colours have a wide range and are often brilliant, and some still retain the sweet scent. Particularly good new varieties excellent for growing in hanging baskets include 'Springtime' which is early flowering with many bright colours, 'Showtime' with very vivid colours with white-eyed florets, and 'Blaze' which is a dazzling scarlet. These verbenas are extremely easy to grow from seed in the manner usual for bedding plants. They should flower from early summer well into autumn, but should be given a bright airy position.

Climbers and Wall Shrubs

ABUTILON

A. megapotamicum can be grown as a climber or trained as a wall shrub. It is almost hardy and survives outdoors in mild areas if given a sheltered wall. By growing in pots, it can be kept down to about 1.5 m (5 ft) or less. Given a free root run, it will grow up into the roof of a tall conservatory if allowed. The flowers appear from late spring to autumn. They are pretty and unusual, like small lanterns, and red and yellow in colour. There is also a form with creamy-yellow variegated foliage to add to the attraction. If plants tend to get out of hand in the small greenhouse, cut back by about a half in early spring, and at the same time cut out all the weak growth.

BOUGAINVILLEA

A number of species and named varieties constitute the most showy of all climbers or wall shrubs, but it is not always apreciated that most can be trained to form bushy specimens for pots if preferred. The brilliant colour comes from the bracts that surround the inconspicuous flowers. The best effect is obtained by growing the plants as wall shrubs if there is space available, or plants can be trained up wires and into the greenhouse roof, or up roof supports in a conservatory. However, at minimum temperatures below about 10°C (50°F) there is serious risk of deterioration and die back. In winter it is safer to keep plants dryish, but in summer water freely and maintain a good humidity. A lovely variety is *B.* × *buttiana* 'Orange King', and fairly easy too is *B. glabra* with mauve bracts. Both start to give colour when quite young. The best time for pruning is late winter if you wish to drastically keep plants in check. Some light pruning can also be done after flowering.

CAMPSIS

C. grandiflora (*C. chinensis*) makes a very beautiful climber for a frost-free conservatory or lean-to where it can be grown up a rear wall. However, it can also be trained up any suitable support if desired. A disadvantage is that it's deciduous. The trumpet-shaped flowers are a showy orange red, about a finger's length, and borne from late summer to autumn. This species has finer flowers and is less vigorous than the more hardy, and more commonly seen *C. radicans* grown outdoors, but the latter can be planted under glass where the area may be particularly cold. Where it's very chilly, campsis can be poor flowerers, so there could be distinct advantage for greenhouse protection. Fairly drastic pruning is usually necessary. Cut back new plants to about 13 cm (5 in) to promote as many basal shoots as possible. The main pruning is best done during about February – how hard you prune must depend on the space available. Campsis are not suitable for greenhouses that are very shady; flowering will be meagre. Both species produce aerial roots but, in the case of *C. grandiflora*, they should not be relied on to give support. Plants need to be several years old before they flower well, and they flower best when the summer has been bright, long, and warm. The flowers form on the current year's growth, and this is useful to remember when pruning.

CESTRUM

Cestrums are easily grown wall shrubs and are hardy outdoors only in the milder areas of the south and west. They make excellent subjects for the frost-free greenhouse or conservatory and, where space is limited, can be grown in large pots or small tubs. Perhaps the most popular is *C. aurantiacum*. This is only partially evergreen, but it has very bright orange tubular flowers from summer to autumn. *C. purpureum* is attractive too. It has clusters of pendent reddish purple flowers from late spring to late summer, and is evergreen. The flowers of most cestrums are borne on the current year's growth so, even if the frost does get into the greenhouse sufficiently to kill off top growth, flowers can be expected on the new shoots that subsequently arise. Under glass, the plants should be given slight shade in summer. In a frost-free greenhouse, preferably against the wall of a lean-to conservatory, cestrums can give a very beautiful display, yet they are not all that well known!

CLIANTHUS

C. puniceus is a very attractive wall shrub hardy outdoors only in mild areas. It is ideal for a bright frost-free greenhouse or conservatory – particularly where there's not much height. It tends to grow fan-shaped, rather than ascend. The foliage is very graceful and remindful of 'mimosa'. The flowers are usually described as 'claw-shaped' but have suggested the common name of parrot's bill. They are usually a vivid rich scarlet and are produced in clusters from late spring to early summer. There is also a white form, less frequently seen. A very charming effect can be obtained by growing a plant of each colour near to each other so that the stems can intermingle.

To keep the shrub nicely trained, wires will usually be needed for support, or some other means of securing. Keep good ventilation during summer, but do not let the atmosphere become too dry, and do not neglect watering. A great menace to this species is red spider mite. It's wise to make continuous routine inspection with a hand lens so that instant action can be taken – plants can be completely ruined by this pest very quickly.

COBAEA

C. scandens is easily grown as an annual from seed. It is known as the cup and saucer plant because of the shape of its quaint flowers. These are usually purplish. There is said to be a white form, but I have never seen it. With me, seed claimed to be from white flowered plants has produced only purple! Under glass it can be perennial, but it is very vigorous and can be too rampant as a permanent resident. It will climb up sticks or trellis supporting itself with tendrils. The flowers appear over a long period from early summer to late autumn.

ECCREMOCARPUS

If sown early, *E. scaber* will often give flowers the first year. These are freely produced from summer to autumn, are tubular and borne in clusters, and are usually a showy orange colour. There are also yellow and red forms. It is a perennial climber hardy in many places out of doors, but unreliable for surviving a really severe winter. It is self supporting by tendrils and can quickly reach the greenhouse roof. However, in my experience it is not a long-lived plant and is best grown in pots which can be replaced every three years or so with new plants. Prune back plants in spring and cut out all weak straggly growth.

HOYA

H. carnosa is a very attractive evergreen useful for its foliage, the starry cluster of pinkish flowers, sometimes slightly fragrant, being a bonus from late spring to autumn. There are also very desirable forms with cream variegated and spotted foliage, but these are not usually so vigorous or so chill resistant as the normal. Even so, in my experience little more than frost-free conditions is necessary in winter, provided the plants are kept on the dry side. When grown from rooted cuttings, generous flowering usually takes about two to three years. Well-established plants can be grown up into the greenhouse roof where the dangling blossom will look especially charming. Give a position of good light to encourage flowering. In summer maintain a moderate humidity and spray the slightly glossy succulent foliage with tepid water from time to time. The stems bearing the thick foliage can become heavy and will need supporting.

IPOMOEA

The well known and loved morning glory is usually listed in the seed catalogues as *I. tricolor* (syn. *I. rubro-caerulea* and *Pharbitis tricolor*) and, although there are now several fancy varieties, this is still one of the finest; its lovely blue colour is delightful. For best results sow in spring, germinating at about 18°C (64°F), and pricking out into individual small pots. Grow on, avoiding chill as much as possible, finally putting about three plants to each 25-cm (10-in) pot, or one to each 13-cm (5-in) pot. A long cane or strings will be needed for the plant to twine around. Always prick out the seedlings promptly, or the long root formed may become damaged and the seedlings may be set back or die off. Plants grown in small pots should be stopped in the seedling stage to induce branching and reduce ultimate height. Groups of plants in large pots are best trained up a wall trellis or wires and fanned out. A position of good light ensures freedom in flowering, and each morning the plants should become smothered with bloom which fades in the afternoon. Discard plants at the end of the year.

'Heavenly Blue' is still the finest blue variety. 'Flying Saucers' is blue and white striped. 'Early Call' is rose pink, and 'Scarlet O'Hara' is red. *I. nil* 'Daybreak Red' has recently become available. This is not a vigorous climber and can be used to trail from a large basket. The flowers are huge and outstanding – rich, deep red.

Calonyction aculeatum, the moonflower, is closely related to morning glory. It is interesting in that it starts flowering at dusk. The flowers are similar but larger and pure white – they are intensely fragrant. The moonflower is

well worth growing in conservatories or greenhouses visited in the evening or that communicate with the dwelling house; the scent is really delightful and will waft in. Culture is much the same as for *Ipomoea*, but the climber is perennial in a warm greenhouse.

JASMINUM

J. polyanthum is another species renowned for its exquisite scent. Ideally it needs a winter minimum of about 4–7°C (39–45°F), preferably the higher, otherwise it is liable to shed foliage and deteriorate. In good conditions it can become very rampant and smother everything else, but the masses of lovely white tubular flowers in late winter usually makes people excuse its invasive habits. However, be sure to stop shoots to check growth when necessary, and it is best to give 25-cm (10-in) pots to restrict roots. A well-lit site should be found and wires or trellis used for support. Do not overfeed, but water well during summer.

LAPAGERIA

L. rosea is a charming evergreen climber, particularly suited to rather shady sites where it is only just frost free over winter – not often popular with many plants! Moreover, it is not at all rampant. The very beautiful red flowers are elongated, bell shaped and of waxy texture. There are white and pink forms, but these are not easy to come by. The flowers usually give pleasure through the entire autumn months. In sheltered places in the south and west the species is hardy, and garden centres in those areas are usually the most likely places in which to find plants for sale. In the greenhouse grow in a 25-cm (10-in) pot. The stems are twining but should not be allowed to become too entwined and tangled.

LUFFA

L. cylindrica (*L. aegyptica*) is someting different to grow as a 'fun' plant – it is the source of the bathroom loofah! Seed is freely available and can be germinated and grown on exactly like cucumber. However, it is simpler to merely grow the plant up a cane or wire, since the crop is hardly likely to be of great

Plate 25 Passifloras, such as *P. caerulea* illustrated, grow well on the wall of a sunny lean-to but need to be drastically pruned if they are not to take over the entire greenhouse! In the picture a wire mesh is being used as a means of support.

importance, merely of interest. If left alone to grow as it will, insects will usually carry out pollination for you; to get setting of the gourds pollination is needed as for melon. You can pollinate yourself as described under melon if you wish. The best results are obtained in a bright position. The gourds look almost exactly like cucumbers but usually have stripes along their length and are more decorative. Leave them on the plants *as long as possible*, even after the plant has withered if necessary. This is to ensure a period of developing and ripening that's as long as possible. You are more likely to get a strong fibrous interior, which forms the loofah. To obtain this, peel off the skin and wash away the pulp of the interior under running water, teasing the fibre to free it. The likelihood of producing a loofah of the quality of a shop-bought specimen is low – we do not usually have a long enough summer – but the plants bearing the gourds are quite ornamental.

MINA

M. lobata is now the correct name for the very pretty half-hardy annual climber which will also be found listed in catalogues as *Ipomea lobata*, and *Quamoclit lobata*, and sometimes as

Ipomea versicolor. The flowers are nothing like those of the *Ipomea*, morning glory; they are tubular, about the length of a thumb, and inflated. The colour is interesting: it starts dazzling crimson, but gradually changes through orange to yellow and finally to cream. The clusters of flowers are borne on quite long stems and they can even be used as cut blooms. It can be easily grown much in the same way as *Ipomea*. It can reach a height of 3 m (10 ft) and will flower from summer well into the winter of a frost-free greenhouse. It is in fact perennial in a warm climate. It should be better known.

PASSIFLORA

The best known passion flower is *P. caerulea*. This is often grown in greenhouses and conservatories, but is usually hardy outdoors and can become extremely invasive and rampant. However, the extraordinary blue and white rayed flowers are very attractive and have been attributed a religious significance. Given a bright site under glass, the species often sets fruit. This is ovoid and turns a rich golden brown, but is usually too seedy to eat! The species is very easy to raise from seed, but may take several years to reach a good flowering size (Plate 25).

PLUMBAGO

P. capensis is best treated as a wall shrub proper, although it can be grown shrubby if well trained and pruned. It is not generally known that excellent plants can be raised simply from seed. These plants usually flower very well the second year. From seed the flowers, remarkably phlox-like and very beautiful, are usually blue. White forms are also available from time to time. A delightful effect can be obtained by growing blue and white together so that the flowers intermingle. Grow on to 25-cm (10-in) pots and preferably train up a wall trellis. After flowering, which is from mid-spring to autumn, prune back by reducing all growth by about two-thirds. Ideally, avoid winter temperatures lower than about 7°C (45°F). In chill, leaves may be shed, although growth usually begins well enough with the return of warmer conditions in spring.

16 FRUIT AND VEGETABLES

GENERAL NOTES

Most edible crops need conditions of good light, expecially those grown for winter use. Good, controllable ventilation is also important. Thanks to the development of new varieties and F_1 hybrids, many crops are now easier to grow in each other's company, and are less fussy about environmental conditions. A typical example is the case of cucumber and tomato – there is now no problem to find varieties that crop splendidly together and given the same growth conditions. To make the most use of space, most small edible plants, such as lettuce, radish, and the like can be grown as 'catch crops', i.e. between or with larger or taller subjects. However, do not forget how useful frames can be in saving greenhouse space when height is not essential.

The lean-to type of greenhouse is often a useful shape for fruit growing. It is adaptable for grapes, cucumbers, melons, figs, peaches or nectarines – and similar plants – grown against the rear wall.

In the home greenhouse splendid crops can be obtained by growing in growbags or large pots or similar containers, or in trenches lined with polythene and slitted for drainage, sunk in the greenhouse floor, and filled with a potting compost. For economy, try a DIY mix as described on p. 55. A 15–20-cm (6–8-in) depth for the trench is usually adequate depending on the root space demanded by the subject.

When using pesticides on edible crops in the greenhouse, be especially careful to follow instructions regarding safety and period of harvesting after treatment. On no account use pesticides of doubtful composition or identity and that have no label assurance of *edible*-crop suitability.

Greenhouse Fruit and Vegetables: A Selection

AUBERGINE

This too can be grown like sweet pepper, but is generally much taller and will need a longer cane. In this case only about two to three fruits should be allowed to form on each plant. Stopping plants at an early stage will encourage lower more bushy development. If there is reasonable height, the plants can be allowed to go up to about 1 m (3¼ ft) without stopping. In some varieties the fruit is large and quite heavy, and will need the use of strong canes for support.

CABBAGE and CAULIFLOWER

A bright airy greenhouse can be of service to these crops in the early stages, and sometimes to cropping. A number of cabbage varieties can be sown from January to March for later planting out and harvesting from May onwards. The varieties 'Hispi' and 'May Star', both F_1 hybrids, are especially suited. Grow seedlings on in seed trays and pot-on into small pots. Where the winters are very harsh and liable to damage spring cabbage, make sowings in autumn and plant out from early March. Cool conditions in the greenhouse are essential for the growing on.

Cauliflowers particularly useful for starting under glass are those varieties suited for sowing during September and harvesting from May to June. Study catalogue descriptions carefully to make sure you choose the right varieties. Very useful is winter cauliflower (curding broccoli). It can be sown from April to May to crop in January. There are varieties that are hardy and those that are not so hardy – choose according to the greenhouse winter minimum. The former are ideal for the unheated house. Grow the plants much as you do bedding plants. A cold frame can be used for summer accommodation. Subsequently, the plants can be set in a greenhouse bed in rows. Space the plants about 45 cm (1½ ft) apart. They can also be grown in 25-cm (10-in) pots.

CAPE GOOSEBERRY

In recent years this easily grown fruit has excited considerable interest. The true Cape gooseberry is *Physalis peruviana* (*P. edulis*), but it is possible that there may be some confusion with *P. ixocarpa*, the tomatilo or jamberry, and with *P. pruinosa*. All have rather similar fruits. For growing in the greenhouse the presumed variety called 'Golden Berry' gives good results. The seed germinates easily and can be raised and grown on much like tomato, moving on to the same size pots and using the same compost. A warm bright position gives the best crop. Variable heights seem to be reported, from 60 cm (2 ft) to three times this figure, which further suggests more than one species is involved. In any case a cane should be given for support and it's as well to assume the maximum height will be reached. To get bushy development, and more stems on which fruit will form, the plants can be stopped with advantage – but too much stopping must be avoided. The fruits mature and are usually ready for harvesting from about late summer, depending on conditions. In appearance it is very like the well known Chinese lantern fruit of *P. alkekengi* of gardens. The berry inside the husk, however, should be a rich golden colour and about the size of a large cherry when ready to gather. It is quite delicious and refreshing to eat raw, but it can be employed in all manner of culinary adventures, including jams and desserts. Left in the husk, it keeps for a considerable period. The flowers are small, but quite pretty, being pale yellow with bold dark purplish spots at the base of each petal, and the fruit is said to have a very high vitamin content.

CHINESE GOOSEBERRY

This is the fruit of *Actinidia chinensis*, and it is now much more frequently seen in high class greengrocers. It is hardy outdoors where the climate is not excessively harsh, but it also makes a fine ornamental wall shrub for an unheated greenhouse or conservatory, except that it's deciduous. The foliage is heart-shaped and the flowers are cream at first maturing to a mustard-yellow. The fruits are brownish, slightly 'furry' and about the size of a very large egg, but more cylindrical. The skin is quite thin, so there's plenty of fleshy interior, and this is juicy, refreshing, and delicious; quite a luxury fruit in fact. The flavour is difficult to define and has been likened to gooseberry and grape.

To ensure setting of the fruit, a male plant is essential. Nurseries sell pairs of one male and one female, and these should be clearly labelled. There is no need to plant both in a greenhouse – provided the male plant is put somewhere *near* outside. Pollinating insects will find their way in and out of the greenhouse vents. However, to be sure, there is no harm in hand pollinating the flowers with a piece of fluffed-up cotton wool.

The best site is the rear wall of a south-facing lean-to, but slight shading may be needed in summer. Large pots can be used for the greenhouse female plant if desired. Stop the young plants to encourage spreading development, and subsequently train against the wall with wires. Once plants are established growth can be vigorous. Prune during February to maintain shape and size.

CLIMBING FRENCH BEAN

Several varieties can be sown in late winter and germinated and grown on as described for cucumber. Earlier sowing in the home greenhouse is best avoided unless a congenial temperature can be maintained. Ideally a minimum of about 13°C (55°F) should be the aim, but lower for short periods does not usually do much harm. A position of good light is vital. Grow the plants from floor level as for tomato, spacing about 38 cm (15 in) apart. Train the plants up strings and stop the laterals and secondary laterals at the third joint. The crop is usually ready by late spring and should be gathered as soon as ready for maximum quality and flavour.

'Selka' is a 1983 introduction especially recommended for the greenhouse, and with very long, stringless pods in profusion.

CUCUMBER

The popular idea that you cannot grow cucumbers and tomatoes in the same greenhouse is now a myth. Visitors to my greenhouses in summer will see both growing close together and bearing splendid crops. This is partly because new cucumber varieties are much easier to grow, but also new pesticides have been introduced, which are safe to use on both crops. Consequently there need be no pest problems. Most of the older pesticides were severely damaging to all the cucumber family including melon – but modern products, containing resmethrin or a combination of heptenophos and permethrin, for example, have no ill effects, and are particularly useful for controlling pests like whitefly, which was a menace to both tomatoes and cucumbers (p. 107).

For the home greenhouse I strongly recommend choice of one of the modern varieties listed in Table 4 (p. 159). At one time accidental pollination of the cucumber was a problem. Ordinary varieties bear both male and female flowers and if pollination occurs the fruit becomes club shaped, seedy, and often bitter. All flowers *not* bearing a tiny fruit consequently have to be promptly removed. Modern all-female varieties bear few if any male flowers and can usually be left to grow without interference apart from training. The new varieties also less fussy in their environment, and do not demand the higher humidity and shading required by the old ones.

The flattish seed is large enough to sow in individual small pots, and should preferably be set on edge in the compost. Germination is usually rapid at about 18°C (64°F) (Plate 26). Further growing on can be in much the same way as tomato, and in large pots, growbags or similar; ring culture is also possible. However training is quite different and is important for maximum cropping and quality.

Plate 26 The author with modern F_1 hybrid cucumber plants grown from seed and at a stage ready for planting. The plants as illustrated are in 10-cm (4-in) pots, and are ready for transfer to their final growbags or large pots placed at staging level.

Plate 27 A fine cucumber of good shape and quality in the author's greenhouse. You are much more likely to obtain quality cucumbers such as this if you grow the modern, all-female varieties which are also vigorous and easy. For best flavour always pick as soon as the fruit is of adequate size.

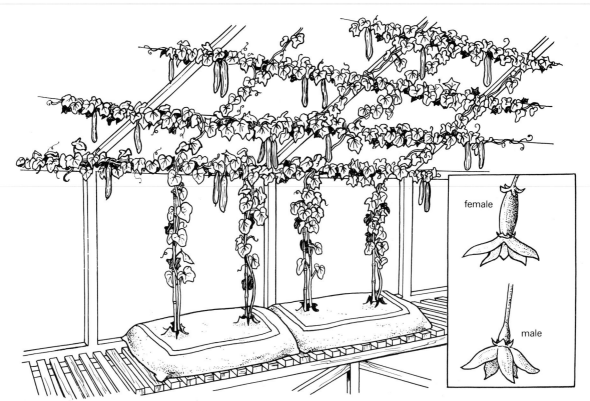

Fig. 32 Growing cucumbers
The plants are best grown and trained as shown. Growbags or pots (about same size as for tomatoes) can be used. Inset shows the obvious difference between the female and male flowers. All the latter should be promptly removed to prevent pollination. For sake of clarity, the leaves are shown smaller than they are in life.

Growing is best done from staging level (Fig. 32). The roof slope just above should have strings or wires stretched from end to end and spaced 15–20 cm (6–8 in) apart. Grow the plants as single stems up the greenhouse side and up into the roof under the wires, stopping each stem when the last wire is reached. Laterals (side shoots) will form and should be tied to the nearest wire and led along. Female flowers should form on these laterals after about four leaves have developed. When a cucumber appears, stop the shoot bearing it about two leaves further on. Secondary laterals should form and can be similarly trained. As mentioned male flowers, if any, must be promptly snipped off, and it is a good idea to also snip off tendrils. A mature fruit is shown in Plate 27.

The compost must be kept evenly moist and overwatering avoided – cucumbers are *not* bog plants! Wet conditions will cause the fruits to rot and fall before reaching maturity. The section of the greenhouse where the plants are placed is best shaded with white Coolglass in summer.

FIG

The fig (*Ficus carica*) gives a much more reliable crop when planted under glass. Outdoors, the fruits may not ripen in cold areas. By far the best way to grow the plant for maximum production, is to fan-train against the wall of a south-facing lean-to or conservatory; the plant is also quite decorative.

However, given a free root run, it becomes rampant. If set in a border, the planting hole should be about 75 × 75 cm (2½ × 2½ ft), and lined with slate, old tiles, plastic, or similar, but don't forget drainage, to prevent the roots from wandering. Alternatively, planting can be done in a large clay pot which can be plunged. If desired, figs can also be grown in free-standing large pots or small tubs, and these, if it's thought convenient or an advantage, can be stood outdoors during summer. In such cases, the plants can be allowed to grow as 'bushes', but will of course be less productive.

The variety best suited to under glass culture is 'Brown Turkey'. This fruits abundantly on both the previous year's and the current year's shoots, and has excellent flavour. Potting or planting is best done in spring, although container-grown plants are now often sold by garden centres and can be planted almost any time. When they are destined for wall and fan training, wires will have to be run along the wall for securing the stems as they develop. For the first few years after planting, little feeding is required, provided the soil was well prepared or a good potting compost used. After this, and as the plants become established and begin to bear fruit, regular feeding during the period of active growth is important.

Pruning consists of removal of all tangled weak, or unwanted excessive growth in early spring, to keep plants within bounds. In early summer young shoots bearing fruits should be stopped at a point about four leaves along their length. Better quality fruits are obtained by restricting them to about three or four per shoot. The fruit is held erect as it develops – it is ripe and ready for picking when it becomes pendent – usually from late summer onwards.

GRAPE

Many beginners feel that they must have a grape vine in their greenhouse (Fig. 33). In fact, few of the other popular greenhouse pot plants and crops will get on well with a vine. To get the best yield, grapes are best given a vinery to themselves. Variety is important and a specialist nursery catalogue should be consulted when buying. The ideal site is a south-facing lean-to. Plant the 'rods', as the plants are called, alongside the greenhouse *outside* in a well prepared border. Lead the rods through gaps made in the base of the greenhouse and train them up inside and on to wires run under the roof. It is best to get potted plants early in the year and site them about 1.5 m (5 ft) apart or just under. After planting cut back the rods to about 45 cm (18 in). In the first year allow the leading shoot to grow on as far as possible. If just one vine is

Fig. 33 Training vines. This shows the method of planting the root outside the greenhouse, which often gives the best results. Holes can of course be made in a boarded base if necessary.

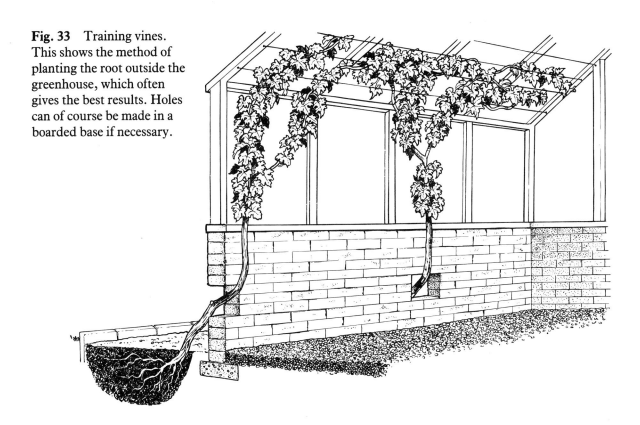

being grown in a small house, you can let two leading shoots grow. These should be trained horizontally in opposite directions, and from these, top laterals can be allowed to develop and trained up vertically.

All side shoots from vertical growth must be stopped when about 60 cm (2 ft) long and, in winter, cut back completely. In winter, too, cut back the main leading vertical shoots.

In the second year the side shoots must be fastened to wires. Further winter pruning involves reducing all laterals to one or two buds. The second year may yield a few bunches of grapes, but the third should give a good crop.

Each lateral should be allowed to give only one bunch of grapes. To get well developed bunches, thin as soon as possible to prevent the berries becoming overcrowded, and to form a pleasing shape for each bunch. Use finely tipped vine scissors and do not touch the berries with the fingers.

During flowering, a temperature minimum of about 13°C (55°F) is advantageous, but after cropping there is no need for warmth and no artificial heating is necessary in winter. Good ventilation is always important, otherwise there is a risk of mildew trouble.

It is convenient in the small home greenhouse to grow grapes *in pots*. The best to grow in 30 cm (12 in) pots are 'Black Hamburgh' and 'Royal Muscadine' since they are known to be suitable. Some modern varieties may also be satisfactory if you wish to experiment. Train the plants up canes to give about six bunches per plant. Pot up at about Christmas time, and plunge the pots *outdoors* until late winter. Then bring into the greenhouse and give a temperature of 10–13°C (50–55°F). For best results put two 1.5-m (5-ft) canes in each pot and fasten a short length across the top to form a 'loop'. Train the vine up one side across the top and down the other. The laterals formed should be thinned so that those remaining are about 30 cm (1 ft) apart. Stop these laterals about two leaves beyond where the bunch develops.

When the plants are dormant the following winter, remove half the cane formed the previous season, and reduce the laterals to two buds. Plants can only be grown for about three years, and then a fresh start has to be made.

If a warm propagator is available, pieces of lateral removed during pruning can be used as cuttings for propagation. Cut up so that each piece has a well formed bud with a length of stem about 2.5 cm (1 in) long above and below. Press the cuttings into the compost so that the bud just protrudes.

LETTUCE

Certain varieties (Table 4) of this extremely popular salad crop, are useful for growing in the greenhouse from winter to spring. Best results are obtained when the plants are grown in pots, troughs or polythene-lined beds, filled with a suitable compost, but ideally it is a frame crop. Many people do use the ground soil, but there is then a greater risk of grey mould attack (p. 105), to which lettuce is especially prone. Good ventilation is essential at all times. Seed is best sown and the seedlings pricked out, to grow on in seed trays, in the same manner as for bedding plants (p. 8). Take note that *not all* lettuce varieties are suitable for growing under glass.

MELON

The finest melons for the greenhouse are the Cassabar type. These are very large and named after the Turkish town where they are a famous market crop. The very much smaller Cantaloupes, or musk melons, named after Cantaloupo, near Rome, can be grown too, but these do perfectly well in frames and need little height.

Grow melons much the same way as cucumbers but there are some very important differences in culture. Space the wires about 25–30 cm (10–12 in) apart and, in this case, *deliberately pollinate* the female flowers. Pick off a male flower – with no tiny melon behind it – pull off the petals, and transfer pollen to the female flowers all at the same time. The female flowers should have a tiny melon behind and, if pollination has been successful, these should quickly begin to swell.

There is no need to shade melons, unless conditions become very hot and sunny. Do not allow more than about three to four melons to develop on each plant and, when the fruit has reached full size, keep humidity down, in-

Cucumbers are an ever-popular greenhouse vegetable for the amateur.

Melon 'Emerald Gem'. The supporting nets may not be easy to find, and may have to be improvized from net curtaining, string shopping bags etc.

The greenhouse is a convenient place to produce 'seed sprouts', such as alfalfa illustrated, thought to be an important aid to healthy eating – tasty too!

Lettuce 'Kloek'. A popular variety for sowing in October to crop March/April in cold or slight warmth.

Aubergine 'Dusky'. Another expensive-to-buy vegetable but easy to grow in the greenhouse.

Capsicum 'Gypsy'. The sweet pepper, or pimiento, is also an expensive-to-buy vegetable, but again is easy to grow yourself in the greenhouse.

Growbags can be used as a simple trouble free way to grow many crops and flowers. Illustrated is tomato 'Alicante'.

Tomato 'Alicante'. This variety has tended to become far more popular than the once favoured 'Moneymaker'. It is vigorous, a good cropper yielding excellent quality fruit of fine flavour, and is less prone to the usual tomato troubles.

Marrow 'Little Gem' 13 weeks after sowing. One of many outdoor or frame vegetables that can be hurried by initial pot culture in the greenhouse.

A fine crop of grapes in a greenhouse at Clack's Farm. Variety is 'Buckland Sweetwater'.

crease ventilation, and give less water. Large fruits will need support with nets secured to the wires. These are not often stocked by garden shops but can be improvized from any suitable textile material. The fruit is ready for harvesting when the end furthest from the stalk is resilient when pressed with the finger; a pleasant fruity scent may be apparent too.

MUSHROOM

This is the fungus *Psalliota campestris*. It can be a very useful crop for the understaging area of a base wall-type greenhouse. A section can be partitioned off so that a temperature of about 10°C (50°F) minimum can be maintained economically. The section can be warmed with electric warming cables if necessary. Mushrooms are expensive to buy and always in demand, so the crop could be very worthwhile. The understage area should be fitted with a trough about 25 cm (10 in) deep. Old timber can be used for this. It must be filled with a horse manure compost, or a proprietary ready-made mushroom compost. Horse manure is often sold in bags. This may be all right to use if it has not a strong smell. Fresh manure must be turned over several times at intervals of a few days until the odour is only faint. Manure that has had fertilizer or chemical additions is *not* suitable. When the manure is ready, transfer to the trough and press down. Insert a soil thermometer and keep a check on temperature. At first there may be fermentation elevating the temperature, and then there should be a cooling off. The ideal 'planting' time is when the temperature is at about 24°C (75°F), after it has come *down*. Darlington's Grain Spawn should then be spread as evenly as possible over the compost surface and mixed in to a depth of about 5 cm (2 in). There are other spawns that can be incorporated with the compost before filling the bed, but sometimes results are less even. A packet of Grain Spawn is usually sufficient for a bed of about 3 m² (roughly a bed under the staging about 10 ft long and 2 ft wide). After a few days it may be possible to see fine white mycelium (fine thread-like roots) impregnating the compost. A covering of preferably sterilized soil should then be applied. This helps to support the mushrooms as

they grow through. They should start appearing from about eight weeks after distributing the spawn, and cropping should be over about three months. It is important to make sure the compost is nicely moist, not wet, before spawning. It is *not* necessary to black-out the area, but covering may be helpful in winter to conserve warmth. Any covering must *not* impede ventilation.

For those who do not desire such elaborate preparation, ready-spawned 'buckets' can be obtained. They are sold by most seed firms and full instructions are provided. These buckets are, however, hardly practical or economical if you want a crop of reasonable magnitude. The mushroom can be an almost year-round crop.

PEACH, NECTARINE and APRICOT

These are also best given the rear wall of a sunny lean-to and fan trained. Culture is much the same as for outdoors, but to keep height down, try to encourage growth from low on the plants. In the greenhouse artificial pollination is necessary. Use a piece of fluffed up cotton wool, lightly brushing over the flowers at about midday when possible.

Maintain a moderate humidity but do not spray the flowers or the ripening fruit with water. In a small home greenhouse, plants can sometimes be grown up one side and along wires under the roof, espalier-like. Good varieties are 'Hales's Early' and 'Duke of York' (peach), 'Lord Napier' and 'Early Rivers' (nectarine), and 'Moorpark' (apricot). Apricots must be given very good ventilation as the flowers form, or they may fall, particularly if the temperature rises too high. Lately especially dwarfed peach forms have become available from some nurseries. These are excellent for growing in pots.

SEED SPROUTS

Sprouting seeds providing a source of health-giving vegetables is another matter that has aroused much attention over the past few years. Sprouted seed are in fact rich in proteins, vitamins, minerals, and other important biochemicals necessary for health, but low in carbohydrates and fats. Apart from this they are delicious, and this is a good enough reason for growing them. With a greenhouse you can do the job on a reasonably useful scale. Gone will be the days when the home window sills were cluttered with messy trays and pots! The ideal apparatus for sprouting seeds in the greenhouse is a simple cold frame fitted with warming cable. A minimum temperature of about 20°C (68°F) is desirable. This can easily be achieved by covering the frame with bubble polythene. For some seeds, a black polythene 'black-out' may be needed too. The seeds can be sprouted in jars or spread out on clean seed trays lined with clean capillary matting (which can be washed when necessary in a domestic washing machine). The best method of sprouting is usually given on the packets of seed as bought from the seedsman.

Best known is of course, mustard and cress (*Brassica alba* and *Lepidium sativum*). When you grow your own you can eat these together, which gives the best flavour. Sow the cress three to four days earlier than the mustard to make sure they keep the same stage of development. Most so-called cress sold in shops is, in fact, rapeseed. This seems to retain its quality and freshness better during the warm summer months, so it may be worth changing from mustard and cress during that period.

Very popular now is the Chinese bean sprout, derived from the Mung bean, *Phaseolus mungo*. The sprouts can be eaten raw or cooked, and the yield of sprouts is just over four times the weight of beans used. Germinate in the dark. Alfalfa (*Medicago sativa*) is very tasty with pea-like flavour and the sprouts are ready in about five days. The yield is about 12 times the weight of seed. The ideal harvesting time is when the sprouts are about 2.5 cm (1 in) long.

Adzuki beans (*Phaseolus angularis*) are used in Japan like the Chinese sprouts. They can be eaten raw or cooked and have a 'nutty' flavour.

Fenugreek (*Trigonella foenum-graecum*) has long had many uses in medicine and veterinary practice, and also in curry powders. The sprouts have a spicy taste and are very useful for giving distinctive flavour to soups and stews. It takes about four days to have the sprouts ready and they should be about 12 mm

(½ in) long – no more, or they may be tough! The yield is about eight times the weight of seed germinated. Various other seeds, and suited varieties, are now often offered by seedsmen, and more catalogue space is devoted to this important aspect of vegetable growing.

STRAWBERRY

Although really a frame crop, a few pots of strawberries in the home greenhouse are useful and decorative; also they fill the air with a delightful mouth-watering aroma. Plants are best bought each year and grown outdoors until early in the year when they should be brought inside. Pot into 13-cm (5-in) pots or strawberry urns, and give a temperature of about 7°C (45°F) minimum if possible. To ensure a good crop hand pollinatate the flowers, distributing pollen with a fluffed up piece of cotton wool. Consult a specialist nursery catalogue for descriptions of many fine modern varieties.

SWEET PEPPER (PIMIENTO)

This is sometimes incorrectly called capsicum and is now a frequent addition to both cooked and salad dishes. The modern varieties are very easy to grow much in the same way as tomato initially. Transfer the plants to about 18-cm (7-in) pots and give a cane for support. Although it is possible to get in the order of 30 fruits per plant, it is wise to restrict the number so that each fruit has room to swell and develop fully. The fruits are usually ready to pick in mid-summer. Green fruits will ripen after picking if stored in a warm place in the home, and it may be better to treat any late produced fruit in this way.

TOMATO

The tomato is undoubtedly the most popular and the most extensively grown of all home greenhouse crops. It can follow climbing French beans to give useful fruit from summer to autumn, without much expenditure on artificial heat, and can be cleared from the greenhouse in autumn to make room for late chrysanthemums if desired. With care, tomato

TABLE 4.   SELECTION OF RECOMMENDED FRUIT AND VEGETABLE VARIETIES

Plant/varieties	Characteristics and cultural hints
CUCUMBER*	
'Landora'	Early and superb quality and flavour.
'Femspot'	Similar to above.
'Fertila'	Similar to above. Very high disease resistance.
'Monique'	Specially suited to low-temperature greenhouses.
'Amslic'	Similar to above. Also suited to outdoors later.
LETTUCE	
'Kwiek'	Sow late summer. Crop winter. Cold greenhouse.
'Kloek'	Sow autumn. Crop spring. Cold greenhouse.
'Sea Queen'	Sow late summer or late winter. Crop winter or spring. Cold or cool greenhouse.
'Emerald'	Sow as above. Cold or cool greenhouse.
'May Queen'	Sow autumn or spring. Crop spring or summer. Cold or cool greenhouse.
'Dandie'	Sow autumn to early winter for cropping from late autumn to spring. Very fast maturing. Cool house.
'Marmer'	Similar to above, but also suited to cold house.
MELON	
CASSABAR MELON	
'Hero of Lockinge'	White flesh of splendid flavour.
'Emerald Gem'	Similar to above but green flesh.
'Superlative'	Red flesh. Attractive netted skin marking.
CANTALOUPE MELON	
'No Name'	Very easy for low temperatures. Fine flavour.
'Early Sweet' F_1	Large fruits for type. Netted skin. Pinkish flesh. Good flavour.
'Ogen'	Smallish, but excellent flavour and fruity aroma. Yellowish green flesh.
PIMIENTO†	
'Early Prolific' F_1	An award winner, for quality, earliness, and yield.
'New Ace'	Similar merit to above.
'Gypsy' F_1	Recently introduced. Early elongated fruits ripening to dark red.
'Goldstar'	Recently introduced. Cylindrical fruits ripening to unusual golden yellow colour. Fine flavour.
'Triton'	Recently introduced. Erect conical fruits ripening from yellow to dark red. An ornamental pot plant too.
TOMATO	
'Alicante'	Generally useful. Has exceeded 'Moneymaker' in popularity. Easy and good disease resistance.
'Shirley' F_1	General use. Very early, good disease resistance.
'Big Boy'	Enormous fruits. Fleshy and excellent for slicing and frying.
'Eurocross A'	Similar to 'Moneymaker', but superior in yield and vigour.
'Odine' F_1	Generally useful, but ideal for *small* greenhouse being short jointed.
'Yellow Perfection'	Superb flavour and fine quality fruit, but yellow colour causes prejudice.
'Mandel' F_1	Generally useful. Dark red. Very disease resistant.
'Growers Pride' F_1	Generally useful. Early. High yielding. A very good greenhouse-beginner's variety.
'Vibelco' F_1	Exceptional disease resistance.

*All female F_1 types † So-called sweet peppers and capsicums.

Plate 28 Tomato plants and other tall growing light lovers, set along the south side of one of the author's greenhouses. Note this house has a sliding door and and end-partitioned compartment for propagation.

plants can be grown in company with most of the other favourite edible and decorative plants suitable for the home greenhouse.

Although tomatoes can be sown in autumn and grown on over winter for very early cropping, this entails the expenditure necessary to maintain a very comfortable level of winter heating. Culture may also pose problems for the amateur and so, personally, I would not recommend the tomato as a winter subject for the ordinary home greenhouse.

On the other hand, it is extremely easy to raise splendid plants from seed sown from late winter onwards. Nowadays there is a very wide range of varieties to choose from, some of which are shown in Table 4. Fuller descriptions will be found in seed catalogues. Seed germinates well at about 16°C (61°F) when sown as described on p. 71. Prick out the seedlings into small pots and grow on for a few

weeks until sturdy well-rooted plants are obtained. Plants can of course be bought, but there is rarely much choice of variety. It is also possible to grow much better quality plants yourself – they should be sturdy, have a good green colour, and vigorous root system. Weak spindly and pale plants in an advanced stage of growth, should not be bought. Seedlings are best grown on in 7.5–10-cm (3–4-in) pots, to a height of about 15 cm (6 in), and then planted out permanently into the place where they are to be cropped.

Before planting the plants should be 'rogued'. This means throwing out any that show abnormality. Look for stunted development, excessive foliage, 'ferny' type leaves, an unusual proliferation of shoots, any deformity, and particularly yellowing and mottling of the foliage. It is wise to burn such plants; they may be affected by various viruses and are a source of infection.

When setting out the plants choose a bright part of the greenhouse; along the south side of an east-west orientated greenhouse is ideal (Plate 28). The inadvisability of using the ground soil has already been mentioned. However, if for some reason the soil must be employed, better results may be obtained if the tomato seedlings are grafted on to F_1 KNVF rootstock. This rootstock is resistant to the most important diseases liable to infect tomato roots, and can be easily grown from seed. Full instructions for the grafting operation – not at all difficult – is supplied with the special seed obtainable from Unwin Ltd (see Appendix).

In my own recent research in home tomato growing, I have found that the great majority of tomato problems the home gardener encounters are caused by wide, erratic and frequent changes in root moisture conditions, and often in feeding procedure. I have found that plants given a good root run do far better than those in relatively small pots. Often 23-cm (9-in) pots or rings are recommended, but I would suggest using larger if possible. Also, if growbags are employed, I would suggest not setting more than three plants to each bag. With a good bulk of soil for the roots, changes are 'buffered', but it is still important to keep moisture and temperature from fluctuating wildly.

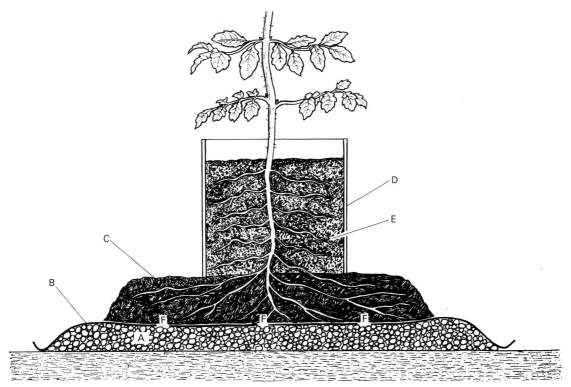

Fig. 34 Ring culture
(*A*) Shingle or gravel to ensure perfect drainage.
(*B*) Polythene sheeting with slits, (*F*) cut for
drainage. (*C*) Peat layer. (*D*) Ring pots – usually
fibre cylinders or similar. (*E*) Potting compost.

Ring culture has become very popular and does help to maintain more even conditions of root moisture. The method is shown diagrammatically in Fig. 34. It also lends itself well to a variety of methods for automatic watering, and is particularly useful for those who have to leave the greenhouse to fend for itself for long periods, such as the weekend gardener.

An ideal compost for pots or rings is genuine J.I. No. 3, but any of the proprietary types should give good results. Space plants about 38 cm (15 in) between stems. Canes or strings from floor to roof will be needed for support and as the plants grow they should be trained around in a clockwise direction, and tied as necessary with a rough soft string.

Side shoots that form at the joints between the leaves and the main stem, must be removed as a daily routine (Fig. 35). After the fourth truss has formed, it is customary to begin feeding with a special high potassium tomato feed – there are numerous proprietaries – according to instructions. Frequent weak feeds are better than infrequent high concentrations.

When the first truss has produced ripe fruit, the foliage below can be removed. This lessens the risk of disease problems. Some defoliation can be continued upwards as the trusses crop, but avoid unnecessary and drastic leaf removal. Remember that a leaf to a plant is as a lung is to us! Unhealthy foliage should, however, always be removed.

To ensure efficient pollination, and thus a good crop of full-size fruit, give the plants a sharp tap from time to time when they are flowering, to shake off and distribute pollen. Better, spray the flowers with a mist of water. Both operations are most effective if done when the greenhouse is bright and warm, preferably in the morning. If problems are encountered in pollination, and the fruit fails to form, falls when immature, or fails to reach proper size, a proprietary hormone 'tomato set' can be tried, and should be sprayed according to label instructions.

When the plants reach the greenhouse roof, usually about late summer, pinch off the tops to encourage fruit that is on the plants to

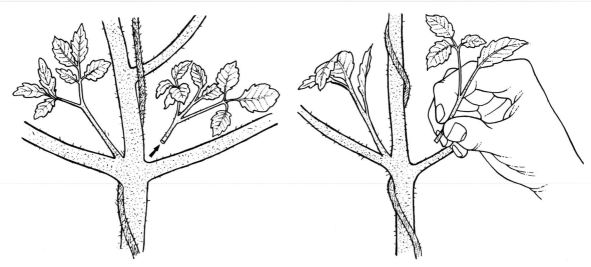

Fig. 35 De-shooting tomatoes.
The side shoots that grow from where the main leaves join the main stem must be promptly removed by carefully pulling sideways to give a clean break – do not cut to leave decaying stumps.

develop and ripen. In summer, try to keep the maximum greenhouse temperature below about 27°C (81°F). Higher than this the fruit fails to ripen properly since the red pigment does not form. You get patchy and blotchy fruit and, if there is too much sunlight, green or yellow tops, called greenback. Shade with Coolglass if there is very hot sun. Conversely, constant gloomy conditions are very unfavourable to tomato growing.

MISCELLANEOUS VEGETABLES

A number of vegetables make useful catch crops for the greenhouse and for early yield-

ing. For example, beetroot, carrot, turnip, radish, salad onions and turnip, but varieties suitable for the greenhouse or for forcing may be important; check with the seed catalogues. Some herbs can also be grown, or housed so that they can provide for winter. Typical are mint and parsley. Roots of these can be potted up in autumn and given greenhouse protection for winter production.

If there's enough warmth, the space under the staging can be blacked out with black polythene, and used to force and blanch vegetables like chicory, seakale and rhubarb. Details regarding varieties, culture and technique, are given in most general gardening books. Many gardeners like to use the greenhouse, or a frame, for forcing potatoes for Christmas. The seed potatoes are sprouted in autumn and potted up, about four to each 25-cm (10-in) pot. The plants can easily be tapped out of the pots for gathering the crop – which often is of unusually excellent flavour!

17 CACTI AND OTHER SUCCULENTS, FERNS AND AQUATICS

There are very many thousands of species of these fascinating plants, and it is an unenviable task to sort out a tiny fraction to suggest for the home greenhouse. Cacti are succulents but are distinguished by having structures called areoles. These are hairy or bristly tufts or sharp spines or prickles, that distribute themselves over the surface, often in patterns. Their formation or colouring often adds to the plant's attraction. Ordinary succulents usually have a more leaf-like structure, but are thick and, as in the cacti, are able to store much water in the tissues. Although the succulents do not object to being allowed to go dry from time to time, no plant can live without water indefinitely. In summer and when in active growth, they can be watered moderately. Indeed, some of the succulents may well begin to wilt if allowed to go too dry. However, in winter water is rarely needed, and if kept moist the plants may rot.

Nearly all the succulents like plenty of light, but a very large collection can be accommodated by a small all-glass house. A well-drained compost is essential, but they are not usually fussy about compost in other respects. A little extra grit may be appreciated. When potting the prickly cacti, it is usual to hold them with a strip of folded newspaper to avoid damage to the skin (Fig. 36). The bristles of some cacti, if they get under the skin, can cause prolonged and unpleasant irritation. Most cacti and succulents will have flowers at some time, and often these are brightly coloured and extremely showy. Certain species are worth singling out for special mention owing to their popular floral merit in the home greenhouse.

Fig. 36 Handling a spiny cactus.
The spines of some cacti can inflict unpleasant skin injuries and even some of the smaller bristles can cause irritation or dermatitis. A twist of newspaper can be used as a safe handle when potting.

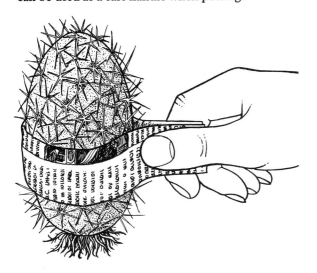

AEONIUM

Look out for *A. arboreum* 'Atropurpureum'. This succulent bears rosettes of leaves on trunk-like stems and they are beautifully tinted purple. It can reach about 90 cm (3 ft) in height and will do well in a greenhouse with a minimum of about 7°C (45°F). There are other forms without the purple colouration.

Of more spreading habit, and with green and cream leaves, is *A.* × *domesticum* 'Variegatum'. This is often sold as a house plant. So is *A. tabulaeforme* which has very flat rosettes and yellow flowers when the plants are two to three years' old. After flowering, the plant dies, but it's easy to keep going from leaf cuttings or from seed.

AGAVE

Several agaves make useful succulents· for the greenhouse, especially where temperatures are likely to become low. Perhaps the most impressive and best known is *A. americana*. This forms rosettes of thick fleshy sword-like leaves.

The types with ·variegated cream striped foliage are very beautiful, and can be used for sub-tropical bedding effects. In mild areas they may survive outdoors over winter, and they are fine for a frost-free conservatory that's reasonably spacious – the plants can develop leaves 90 cm (3 ft) long and will need large pots or small tubs when mature.

Two species for the small greenhouse are *A. filifera* with striped leaf rosettes bordered with filaments, and *A. victorae regina* with finely lined erect leaves tipped with a dark brown to black spine. Most agaves can be easily reproduced from offsets that form. They like a bright sunny airy position.

ALOE

This genus has many very attractive succulents, often with spikes or racemes of eye-catching flowers. They deserve to be much better known and more widely grown, especially since most will survive down to little more than frost-free conditions. Perhaps the best known because it's a house plant is *A. variegata* popularly called the partridge-breasted aloe because of its distinctive and lovely leaf markings. It usually sends up a tall orange-red spike of tubular flowers in spring. *A. microstigma* forms a rosette of thick succulent leaves that become magnificently tinted a rich maroon-red colour. *A. striata* is a beauty with very long grey-green, striped, red tinted leaves. *A. arborescens* is another house plant which, as the name suggests, has a more tree-like habit. Its leaves have toothed edges. *A. humilis* is rather pretty with clumpy thinnish bluish-grey-green foliage with whitish prickles and racemes of rose-pink flowers. All these species can be grown from seed and are easy to cultivate. However, some of the more spiny or prickly species can, apparently, inflict wounds, if you are not careful, that can cause severe irritation.

CEPHALOCEREUS SENILIS

This is a very striking cactus and, when grown to an appreciable size, it can look extremely beautiful. Unfortunately, it's sometimes unreliable in the greenhouse and needs a bright, airy position, where the minimum temperature does not fall below about 7°C (45°F). It grows as a tall cylindrical column, but it's smothered with dense long silky grey-white fine fibres. This leads to the very apt common name of old man cactus. When potting, incorporate some ground limestone or chalk into the compost to make it slightly alkaline. Water very sparingly in winter and, in summer, it's vital to keep water *off* the silky hair. Plants grown from seed, often do better than specimens that are brought and transferred to a strange (different) environment.

CEROPEGIA WOODII

This is a rather delightful *trailing* succulent. It grows from a quite large tuber, and sends out long thread-like stems. Well placed on the stems are pretty small marbled heart-shaped succulent leaves. These are silvery above and purplish below. It also produces strange pitcher-shaped dark reddish flowers, but they are curious rather than showy. It needs a winter minimum of about 10°C (50°F); if this is higher than you maintain, it's wise to transfer the plant to the home. It is fortunately happy with less light than most succulents. However, be very careful with watering, since the tubers are prone to rot if kept too damp. Make sure drainage is perfect. The plant is very effective grown in hanging pots.

CHAMAECEREUS SILVESTRII

This is a cactus that's seen everywhere and could well be called, like the Aspidistra, the cast iron plant – it's so difficult to kill. I have had specimens that have been frozen and neglected for months, but they have recovered quickly on being remembered again. It's also so easy to propagate by merely removing bits and sticking them in compost! The proper common name is peanut cactus, but it grows as a somewhat creeping mat of prickly stems about the thickness of the little finger. It flowers generously and well, with bright crimson-red starry flowers. These seem to be produced more generously if you are not too free with watering and give a bright sunny position.

CLEISTOCACTUS STRAUSII

This is a very popular window sill cactus, but it will be happy in a greenhouse with a 7°C (45°F) minimum. It forms a clump of tall slender cylindrical columns, covered with a woolly white down. It also produces showy tubular bright orange-red flowers almost as long as a finger. Water sparingly, if at all, over winter and give a bright position.

CRASSULA

Undoubtedly the best known crassula of this large group of succulents is *C. argentia*, called the jade plant. This is another plant hard to kill, and it will survive very low temperatures and no water for weeks. Plants that appear to be dead and that have lost all their leaves, often shoot again when cultivation is resumed. Old plants can acquire an almost 'bonsai' look, but if they have been well treated they become huge bushy specimens and may even bear clusters of flowers – flowering is however very unusual! The plant is grown for its jade-green shiny succulent oval foliage. Other crassulas that make good pot plants are *C. falcata* with velvety spoon-shaped elongated leaves, *C. perforata* with leaves of similar curious shape but much shorter and stems more branching, and the peculiar clump growing *C. lycopodiodes* with thin erect stems covered with scale-like leaves from which grow minute yellowish flowers in summer. The plants are easy provided they are given well drained compost and a bright position.

ECHEVERIA

The echeverias are easily grown succulents not demanding much warmth and generally happy in the home greenhouse. They are rosette forming and notable for subtle colouring. *E. derenbergii* is very low-growing forming a dense rosette with red tipped grey-green leaves coated with a whitish farina. The orange flowers are borne on a short stem in summer. A popular name is painted lady! *E. setosa* is rather similar in habit, but has larger leaves with white hair and a tinge of red at the tips. The flowers are red and on short stems in summer. Much taller, reaching 60 cm (2 ft) is *E. gibbifflora*. This is a striking species and forms rosettes of very large concave leaves tinted mauve-red. They are borne on longish leafless stems, because the lower leaves tend to fall off. This does not matter, because the effect is charming. Water generously in summer, very sparingly in winter, and keep water off the foliage as it is easily marked. The best winter minimum is about 5°C (40°F).

EPIPHYLLUMS

There are numerous named hybrids of this rather unusual cactus. It differs from most of those popularly grown in being a 'forest' cactus. It prefers slight shade and must never be allowed to go completely dry, even in winter. It is very free flowering and the blooms are enormous and beautifully coloured. Unfortunately its thick flattish succulent stems often grow in a grotesque manner and need careful supporting to prevent snapping off. The plants grow well with a winter minimum of about 5°C (40°F), and mine are quite happy in an ordinary potting compost, although special composts are often recommended. If taken into a warm home for winter, flowering may occur in spring as well as in summer. It is easy to raise new plants from pieces of the stem that may break off – the pieces root readily in a cutting compost during the warmer months of the year. Flowering plants need about 13-cm (5-in) pots or slightly larger.

KALANCHOE

This succulent is easy to raise from seed sown in spring, the plants flowering best the following late winter to spring. The species *K. blossfeldiana* is tall growing with very large flattish heads of small scarlet flowers and very showy. However, there are now many hybrid seed strains offered giving very much more compact plants, often sold as house plants. These are not nearly so spectacular, but the colour range includes shades of red, pink, yellow and white.

MAMMILLARIA

There are many desirable species of this cactus. They are generally globular and very spiny, and they usually become encircled with very beautiful flowers mostly cream or purplish-red. They are easy to grow too, and a winter minimum of about 5°C (40°F) is adequate. A particularly popular species is *M. bocasana*. It forms a dome-shaped blue-green clump smothered with fine whitish hair. A yellow or reddish tipped hooked spine emerges from each areole. It becomes covered with dainty cream flowers and these are followed by purple berries. The species is well worth collecting.

SANSEVERIA TRIFASCIATA

I am taking the liberty of including this delightful plant, well known as a house plant by the name of mother-in-law's tongue, in this section of succulents. This, in my opinion is where it should be, and it will certainly be grown more successfully if regarded as a succulent. The most attractive form is 'Laurentii'. This has the long erect green and grey banded leaves boldly bordered with cream. Well grown it will reach a height of at least 1 m (3½ ft).

The most common cause of failure with this plant is *overwatering*. Again I emphasize, if you treat it like most succulents, that is plenty of water in summer, and little, if any, in winter, there should be no problem. In fact, I keep my plants completely dry in winter. Provided this is done, the plants can survive surprisingly low temperatures. Ideally, however, about 7 to 10°C (45 to 50°F) should be the minimum. In summer the plants can grow quite rapidly in the warmth and humidity of the greenhouse. Often the pots given are too small, and the thick fleshy rhizome-like roots can burst them! A simple way to propagate is to plant up in a large pot – even in a greenhouse border. You will then get new plants coming up all around, and these can be severed and potted individually. By this method you are also sure of exact reproduction with retention of the cream

border variegation. This sanseveria sometimes produces a loose spike of small tubular creamy flowers, but they are not particularly decorative and rather short lived.

S. habnii is a low-growing species forming a rosette of leaves of similar appearance. It can be grown similarly, but is not seen very often.

SCHLUMBERGERA
(CHRISTMAS CACTUS)

Plants now given this name were once called *Zygocactus* and there is still some confusion over nomenclature. All are forest cacti and should not be allowed to go absolutely dry during their winter rest. The Christmas cactus is *S. × buckleyi* and produces its magenta flowers from early winter onwards. The crab cactus is *S. truncata* which is similar and winter flowering, but has a range of colours including shades of blue and white.

Once included in *Schlumbergera* is the Easter cactus, *Rhipsalidopsis gaertneri* with bright red flowers. Another pretty species is *R. rosea*.

All these cacti trail, although the Easter cactus is more erect. They can be grown in hanging containers or in wall pots. The ideal winter minimum is about 10°C (50°F), but they will usually survive a few degrees lower for short periods. The plants are very easily propagated by snapping off the flattish stems at a joint and rooting in the usual compost during summer. Better flowering is often achieved by standing out the plants in a slightly shaded place during summer.

SEMPERVIVUM

The houseleeks are a small group of succulents, but their Latin name which means 'always alive' well indicates why they are worth growing – some are perfectly hardy. A very beautiful pot plant is *S. arachnoideum tomentosum*. This can more conveniently be called the cobweb houseleek, but it's a specially fine form with large leaves generously 'spun' with white webbing. There are also some desirable hybrids of this species. Pretty carmine flowers are borne in summer and afterwards the mother rosette dies – there are plenty of others formed to replace her!

Other species worth collecting are the hybrid *S. × funckii* with webby rosettes (like its cobweb parent) and purplish-red flowers, *S.* × *marmoreum* known as 'Commander Hay' a fine hybrid of the common houseleek with very large reddish rosettes and pink to purple flowers, and *S. tectorum calcareum* with greyish green purple-tipped leaves, but flowering rarely. All these are ideal for a greenhouse little more than frost-free over winter.

GROWING SUCCULENTS FROM SEED

It does not seem to be generally appreciated that many of this group can be very easily grown from seed. Seed of an exciting range is now available from the leading seedsmen and from those specializing in the unusual. Moreover, the seed can be treated much in the same way as other ordinary plants, and it should be sown in a proper seed compost. Some people recommend adding a little extra grit, but I have not found this generally necessary at the germination stage. Succulent and cacti seed need exposure to light for best germination – although there is some difference of opinion about this! Just press the seed into the compost surface and water in with a *mist* of water from a sprayer. On average, good germination occurs at about 21 to 24°C (70 to 75°F).

Selection of Easy and Interesting Succulents to Grow from Seed
[(S) = succulent (C) = cactus]

Cotyledon (S): many species are easy from seed and make good pot plants, very varied in appearance and habit.

Echinocactus grusonii (C): a popular easy species, globular with attractive spines. Very slow growing, but after years can reach a considerable size and may then flower.

Echinocereus (C): very easy and practically hardy ribbed cacti, which freely bear glorious showy flowers. Some are fast growing, others slow.

Euphorbia obesa (S): a most intriguing and beautiful 'dome-like' structure with subtle colourings and markings, popularly called Turkish temple relating to its 'architecture'. Other species also worth growing.

Gasteria (S): rather like aloe, but leaves formed one above the other in opposite rows. Useful for more shady conditions.

Gymnocalycium (C): seed is sold with instructions for grafting. An astonishing brightly coloured globular cactus, but not quite so easy.

Haworthia (S): a number of species make attractive plants with interesting structure and markings – often suitable for home window sills too.

Lithops (S): called living stones. Prettily marked, pebble-like, with very showy large flowers, mostly white or yellow shades. Can make a fascinating collection.

Lophophora williamsii (C): the famous mescal button of Mexico. Not especially attractive, but a curiosity. Pretty shell-pink flowers. Very easy from seed and will survive quite low temperatures.

Opuntia (C): many popular species with lobed formation and attractive flowers – more likely to be produced in a greenhouse than on a home window sill!

Rebutia (C): globular cacti renowned for wonderfully showy flowers – plants for those who think cacti are not colourful.

Stapelia (S): these form strange angular stemmed clumps. The flowers are weird in colour and structure and sometimes of *enormous* size – they may smell unpleasant!

Ferns

GENERAL CULTURE

No greenhouse or conservatory is complete without some ferns. Most are ideal for shady places or for livening up an under-staging area often not bright enough for most of the favourite plants. The popular species are usually easy to grow. Some can, however, be extremely difficult. Plants of the less exacting species can be grown from spores. Usually seedsmen offer these as types suitable for warm conditions and for cool temperatures, packeted separately. For the home greenhouse, the latter may be better.

The spores are so fine as to be almost

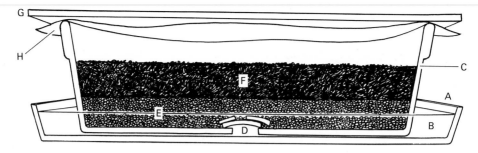

Fig. 37 Sowing fern spores.
(*A*) Shallow tray or bowl kept topped up with water, (*B*). (*C*) Seed pan or tray. (*D*) See that there are free drainage holes to allow moisture to reach the compost from the water tray. (*E*) Layer of sharp grit. (*F*) Seed compost. (*G*) Sheet of glass. (*H*) White paper under glass.

invisible. Mix with very fine sand before sowing to aid even distribution. Sow on the surface of a peat-based compost, in a pan stood in water, as shown in Fig. 37. Keep the water topped up during the entire germination precedure, which may be as long as a couple of months. The first stage of growth looks as though the compost is covered with a greenish lichen. Beginners may well think something has gone wrong, but on no account discard the containers. If you look closely you will see that the growth consists of tiny heart-shaped 'leaves' (Fig. 38). Leave the glass over the containers to maintain humidity – it is at this stage that true germination takes place and a film of moisture on the growths is necessary. When this has occurred, each tiny growth, called a prothallus, will sprout a leaf of typical fern frond type.

The plants can then be pricked out into small pots and grown on normally. Most of the easy ferns grow well in the usual potting composts, but they tend to like acid conditions. Peaty composts suit them well and the addition of sterilized leafmould may help some. Nicely moist conditions at all times should be maintained with few exceptions, and in summer most like a spray of water from time to time. Although most of the popular types grow well in shade, this does not mean murky perpetual gloom. Dry air must also be avoided. For these reasons, many of the so-called 'house plant' ferns will grow much better in the conditions of a cool greenhouse.

About 7°C (45°F) is ideal for most of the easier species.

Propagation of mature ferns can usually be simply done by division. Most form rhizome-like runner roots which can be cut off and potted up in spring.

SELECTED SPECIES

The hardy ferns are particularly useful for the chilly greenhouse or conservatory. The male fern, *Dryopteris filix-mas*, is very hardy and even weedy in some areas outdoors, but despite this makes a very handsome pot plant. The lady fern, *Athyrium filix-femina*, is similarly suited, but loses its fonds in winter. *Polypodium vulgare* is a hardy garden evergreen favourite, but there are some choice varieties particularly suited to pots. There are numerous evergreen species of *Polystichum*, all hardy in gardens, but most excellent for container growing. They thrive best in a leafmould compost.

Species of *Pteris* are very popular greenhouse ferns. Some, such as *P. cretica*, ribbon fern, were often used to decorate the windows of food shops. A very pretty species is *P. quadriaurita argyraea* which has silvery variegated fronds. Especially notable for hanging baskets is *Nephrolepis exaltata* the ladder fern. It must never be allowed to become dry, even when it has lost its fronds in winter.

Rather different in appearance is *Asplenium nidus*, the bird's nest fern. This has erect pale green spear-shaped glossy fronds. Another oddity is *Cyrtomium falcatum* the holly fern, the common name of which is an apt description; it had remarkably holly-like 'leaves' instead of the ferny fronds you might expect.

Davallia mariesii is sometimes sold under the name of Japanese fern ball. In this form its creeping rhizomes are wound in a ball of moss secured by thin wire. If the ball is hung and

168

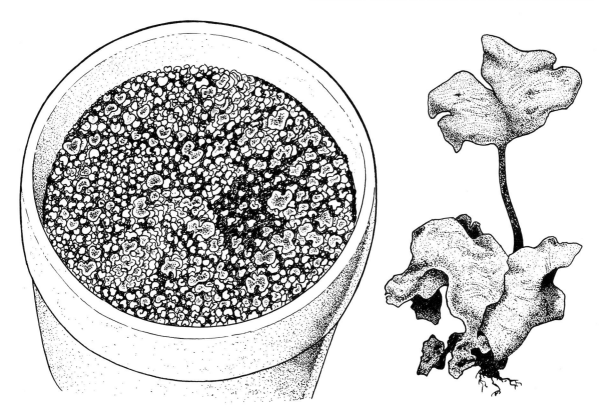

Fig. 38 Fern prothallus.
The first stage of a fern appears as a heart-shaped, filmy growth called a prothallus. The right-hand drawing shows a close look just before the first true frond is about to be formed.

kept sprayed with water it soon sprouts a mass of very pretty and dainty ferny fonds. Over winter it can be kept dry. However, it can be potted normally if desired.

Among the most graceful and beautiful of all the ferns are the various species of *Adiantum*, the maidenhair ferns. Unfortunately, they do not seem to rate high on the success list for the home greenhouse. Make sure the compost is well drained, but stays nicely moist, not wet. A moist atmosphere is also essential, but avoid directly spraying with water. A winter minimum of about 7°C (45°F) is usually desirable.

Aquatic Plants

The aquatics are just the thing for lending a distinctive character to a conservatory if you build a small indoor pool. This is easily done nowadays if you use a little artistic imagina-

tion, with the help of plastics, and with care and the use of easily handled materials such as Literoc (which has the appearance of natural-stone, but is lightweight and easily lifted), very natural-looking pools can be devised, complete with tinkling fountain and even fish. There are some especially delightful exotic aquatics, such as tropical *Nymphaea* (water lilies), but owing to the high temperatures they demand I have omitted them for practical reasons.

The following can be grown in pots stood in shallow pans or bowls kept topped up with water or, where stated, grown in a pool with the pots concealed or just covered with water. In all cases mix some crushed charcoal with the potting compost if possible.

ACORUS GRAMINEUS VARIEGATUS (Sweet flag)

This is clump growing with long sword-like erect leaves, striped along the centres with creamy white. It is hardy in the unheated greenhouse and can be used in pots or to decorate the edges of ornamental pools. It is very easy to propagate by simple division of the clumps in spring.

169

ASTILBE

The hybrids are beautiful decorative plants for pots, or the pool edge. In the greenhouse they produce their delightful feathery plumes in spring, outdoors in the summer. For pot culture be sure to obtain the low growing forms. If you wish to force plants, try to get the varieties 'Deutschland' (white) and 'Fanal' (red). These can be grown in 13-cm (5-in) pots. Pot in autumn and keep in a cold frame well watered. Take into the greenhouse at about Chrismas time and, if you wish to force, give a temperature of about 10°C (50°F) allowing this to rise a little over a few weeks if possible. Plants can be propagated by root division at repotting time.

CYPERUS

C. alternifolius, umbrella grass, is a dainty graceful pot plant, often grown as a house plant, with long stems bearing a spread of narrow foliage at the top like the spines of an umbrella. It is quite easy to raise from seed sown in spring by the usual methods. It can also be propagated by root division in spring. There are variegated varieties that can only be propagated by the latter method. In the greenhouse the plants are evergreen, but they can be used for pool edging outdoors during summer.

EICHHORNIA SPECIOSA

This is a weed in its native habitat and is known here as the water hyacinth, owing to the hyacinth-like spikes of lavender-blue flowers. It is extremely decorative and floats on water by means of its inflated leaf bases. The glossy heart-shaped foliage is also very attractive. Plants are often obtainable from shops specializing in tropical fish, and should be purchased from spring onwards. They can be floated on a pool or grown in water tubs or bowls. They can be put in an outdoor pool in early summer.

Overwinter the plants in bowls of wet potting compost making sure the fibrous roots are covered. The plant does best when, during summer, it is floated in shallow water so that the roots can reach down to the bottom layer of soil or compost. In the right conditions the plants multiply themselves readily and can be divided for propagation. If the greenhouse falls below about 10°C (50°F) in winter, it is best to overwinter plants in the home.

LOBELIA CARDINALIS

It is not generally known that this attracive tall spiky scarlet flowered lobelia with reddish foliage makes a good semi-aquatic. It overwinters well in an unheated greenhouse, but can be unreliable when grown outdoors. It is very easy to raise from seed sown in early spring, usually flowering the first year. Best flowers are usually seen on the clumpy plants that develop by the second year; older specimens may deteriorate. Best grown in large pots of very moist compost. Can also be planted in the moist soil around natural outdoor pools.

MIMULUS (MUSK)

The recently introduced dwarf F_1 hybrids, such as 'Royal Velvet' are very easy to raise from seed and make wonderful, extremely exotic flowering pot plants. The flowers are freely formed, very large and strikingly marked in contrasting colours. The flowering is also fast, and fine plants will be obtained in a few weeks from seed sown in spring. To prolong the display, it is wise to stagger sowings. Grow about three seedlings to each 13-cm pot. Pots can be stood in shallow water.

ZANTEDESCHIA AETHIOPICA (ARUM or CALLA LILY)

This well known florist's flower is *not* a lily, although commonly thought to be by the layman. Pot the rhizomes, one to each 15-cm (6-in) pot – or three to a 25-cm-(10-in) pot – in autumn. Just cover the rhizomes with compost and keep quite moist in the greenhouse. Flowering time depends on overall greenhouse temperature, but is usually in spring or early summer. After flowering, put the pots outdoors and gradually reduce watering. In autumn let the pots go quite dry and turn them out to separate the rhizomes which should have reproduced. During the growing period, the pots can be stood in a pool with the water just covering the rim if desired.

18 PLANTS FOR UNHEATED GREENHOUSES

In recent years the conservation of energy has aroused much interest, and certainly avoiding waste makes sense. Conservation apart, many people may be reluctant to spend money on heating for financial reasons and, it must be admitted, to provide even only frost-free conditions in a *large* greenhouse can cost a sum that most of us might consider a serious expenditure. For this reason, if you have a sizeable greenhouse, it is worth thinking about running it as an unheated greenhouse. Moreover, it is not often realized that there are many plants you can grow without heating artificially, that would actually be *unhappy* if you had winter warmth. Even if you have a heated house in operation, it may sometimes be well worth having an extra greenhouse without heat.

The point is that very many plants will thrive, and can be grown to perfection, with only protection from the sort of weather that causes mechanical damage – heavy rain, snow, hail, excessive frost, wind, and sometimes the depredations of birds and rodents and the like. Moreover, although the unheated greenhouse may get no artificial warmth from us, it still traps considerable free warmth from the sun. Plants often do better than when grown out in the open and certainly flower or crop earlier.

MAKING THE MOST OF AN UNHEATED GREENHOUSE

The great majority of perfectly hardy plants are suitable for the unheated greenhouse. Particularly suited too, in most areas, are those plants that are slightly tender but grow outdoors where the winter is mild, and in sheltered spots.

When grown in a greenhouse nearly all such plants will object to excessively high temperatures, which may spoil growth and interfere with flowering and cropping in many cases. They need airy conditions and very many need plenty of light.

The best site for an unheated house is an open bright one, and there should be provision for very generous ventilation. To keep temperature down in summer, some shading is nearly always essential. The simplest and cheapest way to shade, also extremely effective, is to paint the glass with white Coolglass electrostatic shading. The density of this can be adjusted to suit the type of plants being grown.

An unheated greenhouse to be used as a general utility house or as a conservatory is best made from glass. Plastic houses are, however, often especially useful for specific flowers or crops, but ventilation facilities must be up to standard. Many flowers grown for cutting make ideal subjects for growing without heat in plastic tunnels that give only weather protection. Many of the hardy vegetables can be grown similarly with great advantage. Hardy pot plants, like polyanthus and the multi-coloured primroses, bowls and pots of the spring flowering bulbs, and the like, are often best given a cold glass or plastic structure.

A wide range of the plants described in this book are possible to grow without any artificial heat, provided they are started into growth later. In many cases this is not a great hardship. Indeed, with rising fuel costs and the need for conservation, more gardeners now probably shut down their greenhouse for the mid-winter months. During this period, an unheated house is still extremely useful for overwintering the more tender outdoor garden plants, that perhaps may be unreliable if left out during a severe winter (see p. 10). When to bring an unheated greenhouse into full use depends on the climate of your area. However, in most places, by mid-spring, there is usually enough natural heat trapped by a glass house to start into growth and maintain most of the popular bedding plants, crops and pot plants.

A disadvantage with a heated greenhouse is that it has to be kept small for economic reasons. If you want an unheated house it is wise to get the largest you can afford or fit into your space – you do not have to worry about heating costs. You can then enjoy the opportunity of growing larger wall shrubs, shrubby plants, climbers, and even small trees in tubs, many of which, when of a type suited to greenhouse culture, make a most impressive and beautiful sight. These are especially delightful too when grown in an unheated conservatory, and some will also provide welcome winter colour.

Selection of Plants for Unheated Greenhouses

(See Index for relevant pages giving cultural instructions.)

Acacias: a number of species can be grown from seed to give attractive foliage and flowers, including *A. dealbata*, mimosa.

Actinidia chinensis: Chinese gooseberry. Wall shrub with delicious fruit. Grow a male and female together.

Agapanthus: cold conservatory.

Annuals: very many. Sow hardies in autumn, more tender types in spring.

Azalea: very many for conservatory.

Bergenia: exotic early flowers when grown in pots.

Broccoli: grow varieties for autumn sowing.

Bulbs (hardy and tender): very many to give colour nearly the year round.

Cabbage: 'May Star' and 'Hispi' are good varieties.

Callistemon: several species of bottle brushes are ideal for unheated greenhouse. *C. linearis* very hardy.

Camellia: one of the most beautiful evergreens with exotic flowers ideal for the unheated house.

Cauliflower: grow varieties for autumn sowing.

Chrysanthemums: very many types.

Clianthus puniceus: lobster claw. Unusual wall shrub with usually scarlet claw-like flowers and dainty foliage.

Conifers: many dwarf types make good pot plants and are excellent evergreens for the unheated conservatory.

Cut flowers: a number can be raised for winter picking.

Daphne: several species. *D. odora* is neat evergreen with very fragrant winter flowers. Variegated form best.

Delphinium: the new variety 'Blue Fountains' easy from seed, makes neat compact pot plant. Handsome spikes.

Eucalyptus: many species easy from seed. Very attractive often fragrant foliage.

Euonymus: very useful hardy evergreen.

Ericas: many heathers can be grown to give colour almost the year round. Grow in acid compost.

Fatsia japonica: useful to give a tropical look, although perfectly hardy. Ideal for conservatory.

Ferns: choose evergreen types for an unheated conservatory.

Fig: can be grown as a wall plant or in tubs.

French bean: 'Masterpiece' is a particularly good variety.

Fuchsias: the more hardy types are excellent permanent residents for the cold conservatory.

Grapes: can be grown in pots for ornament.

Hebe: many species and varieties are dwarf and fine for pots. Both foliage and flowers are attractive.

Hedera: a wide range of ivies can be grown.

Helleborus: Christmas rose. Indispensable winter cut flower. *H. orientalis*, cream to crimson flowers, may retain foliage over winter in the greenhouse and makes a good pot plant.

Hydrangea: excellent for large pots in the unheated conservatory. Numerous named forms. Acid compost.

Incarvillea delavayi: beautiful pot plant with large showy streptocarpus-like flowers. Very easy.

Lapageria rosea: especially suited to the unheated conservatory, especially if shady.

Lettuce: choose suitable varieties.

Lilies: absolutely ideal for the unheated greenhouse or conservatory since they do not like heat at any time. Both tall and low growing types do well in pots. Modern hybrids are very exotic.

Melon: cantaloupes are suitable for unheated greenhouses. Avoid large Cassabar types.

Palms: hardy types indispensable for unheated conservatories to give a tropical touch.

Many crocus species make ideal plants for the alpine house. Some of the finest ones flower in mid winter when their flowers would be ruined by weather out of doors.

(**Left**) F$_1$ hybrid *Mimulus*. Easy from seed, this is an ideal plant for those who tend to overwater – it can be grown as a semi-aquatic. Several forms with flowers exotically marked with rich red and yellow are now available to grow as annuals.

Pleome reflexa 'Song of India', a very fine variegated form of this slow-growing greenhouse shrub.

The ladder fern, *Nephrolepsis exaltata*, makes an impressive basket plant.

The author's conservatory. This illustration exemplifies the various points discussed in Chapter 20. Note the mosaic-patterned vinyl floor, the tiled inner base wall; there is somewhere to sit and relax. Plants include many grown from seed in the greenhouse, such as *Musa ensete* (Abyssinian banana), *Coleus*, *Schefflera*, and *Strelitzia*. Plants likely to shed debris are avoided, and all pots are given decorative containers.

Pansies: it is not generally realized that the winter flowering types make marvellous and very colourful pot plants.

Passiflora: good for where there is space.

Peach and other stone fruits: pots or walls.

Polyanthus and primroses: brilliant for pots.

Roses: the miniature roses are also excellent pot plants for the unheated house, and some can be grown from seed offered by most seedsmen.

Shrubs and climbers generally: many can be found to give character and colour the year round. A useful source of suitable types are nurseries situated in the south and west. Write for descriptive catalogues.

Sparmannia africana: easy from seed, flowering second year. Whitish flowers with sensitive stamens.

Strawberry: for cold, 'Grandee' recommended.

Tomatoes and cucumbers: sow late or buy plants. F_1 hybrids especially suited to cool house. 'Ida' F_1 is a 1983 introduction recommended for unheated greenhouses.

Alpines

A vast number of alpine plants can be grown ideally in the unheated greenhouse, but conditions must be as bright as possible and *ventilation extra generous*. Special alpine houses are available, and these usually have extra high staging to bring the dainty plants nearer to the eye. However, many gardeners will find that a special house is not really necessary unless you wish to become a serious collector of many different species. Very often, alpine plants can be taken into the ordinary home greenhouse for flowering, and given frames for the rest of the time but always ventilate as freely as possible.

All alpines must have a well-drained compost. The usual potting compost can be employed with the addition of some extra grit. In some cases some stone chips, or limestone for those needing alkaline compost, may need to be added. All pots must be free draining and it is nearly always best to employ half-pots or drained pans – most of the plants are quite shallow rooting.

The main flowering period is from spring to early summer. If the plants are housed in frames for the rest of the time the greenhouse can be used for any other purpose after the plants have been taken out. For example growing annuals in pots, or for the numerous other popular pot plants described in this book, giving their display from summer to late autumn.

While alpines are in flower under glass, although the conditions should be bright, some protection from full intense sunlight will prolong the time the flowers remain in good condition. A slight shading with white Coolglass is ideal for these plants, and will also help to keep temperature down. To make a display of alpines more attractive and interesting, other plants can be used to create effect. The dwarf conifers are splendid natural companions. A great many of the dwarf spring flowering bulbs also blend well.

Most alpines are very easy to propagate by simple division of the roots – best done after flowering – or from cuttings. Many can be grown easily from seed, but in some cases the seed must be exposed to frost before it will germinate, a technique called stratification. Seed can also be put in a domestic refrigerator for a few weeks, if this is known to be necessary.

Although good drainage is essential, there must be no lack of water during the growing period and during flowering. In winter, when the plants may be housed in frames, only sufficient water should be given to prevent complete drying out. In summer the best times to water are in the morning and in the evening.

Selection of Alpines for Unheated Greenhouses

Anacyclus depressus: very dainty greyish foliage, pretty daisy-like flowers, petals crimson below, white above.

Anchusa caespitosa: tuft-like foliage forming a background to brilliant blue starry flowers with white eye.

Asperula suberosa: greyish woolly foliage and beautiful pale pink, trumpet-shaped flowers.

Campanula: very many species and named varieties. *C. vidalii* is a choice species for the alpine house, but should be protected from frost. Very pretty tubular cream to pink waxy flowers.

Carduncellus rhaponticoides: striking rosette forming green foliage with maroon markings, large blue thistle-like blooms.

Convolvulus cneorum: grows as small shrub, 60 cm (2 ft), silvery leaves and stems, masses of large pinkish flowers for a long period in summer. Striking.

Corydalis wilsonii: very dainty fern-like foliage and spikes of bright yellow flowers over an exceptionally long period. 30 cm (1 ft). A good pot plant generally.

Crassula sarcocaulis: shrubby growth reaching 30 cm (1 ft), masses of rose pink flowers late summer.

Draba polytricha: cushion-like, greyish foliage and bright yellow flowers in clusters. Do not overwater.

Erodium chamaedrioides 'Roseum': very low mat-like growth of crinkled foliage, masses of veined rose-pink flowers almost the entire summer. Very pretty.

Lewisia cotyledon hybrids: foliage rosette-like and rather succulent in texture, lovely flowers in deep red and shades of rose red and pink. Long blooming.

Linaria tristis 'Lurida': bluish foliage of waxy texture, striking flowers coloured in a combination of green and maroon.

Lithospermum oleifolium: miniature shrubby growth with greyish foliage and large attractive bluish flowers.

Nierembergia caerulea: very easy from seed sown in spring by normal methods, flowering same year, better second year. Cut back and keep almost dry over winter. Masses of blue campanula-like flowers. Variety 'Purple Robe' sold by most seedsmen.

Primula auricula: many hybrids with delightful, fascinating flowers with beautiful colours and markings. Plants tempting to collectors.

Saxifraga (Kabschia types): those suited to the alpine house are slow growing and form cushions of silvery foliage. There are numerous hybrids and named varieties with a wide range of beautiful flower colours. Give slightly more shade during summer.

Teucrium subspinosum: forms mats of spiky growth and greyish foliage and become smothered with tiny contrasting red flowers. Very unusual.

Thymus cilicicus: minature shrub with greyish hairy foliage, large bright pink flowers in late summer.

Thymus membranaceus: cushions of delightfully thyme-scented foliage, pink flowers with white bracts. Not quite so easy as the other alpines described here.

Verbascum dumulosum: minature shrub with grey woolly foliage, spikes of large yellow flowers. The hybrid 'Letitia' is a more compact and finer form which originated by chance at the R.H.S. Wisley garden.

Veronica bombycina: mounds of silvery velvety foliage and spikes of pale blue flowers. Another less easy plant.

Viola hederacea: roundish foliage in tuft-like formation and charming violet and white flowers over a very long period. There are a few choice named varieties.

19 BROMELIADS AND ORCHIDS

Both the bromeliads, which are members of the pineapple family, and the orchids, have many species with a common characteristic – they are epiphytic. This means that in their native habitat they grow *above ground*, usually in the moss of tree trunks or rocks, or in the decaying plant debris caught in the forks of branches or in hollows.

Bromeliads

In recent years these have become very popular house plants. Despite their often very exotic appearance, a large number of species are perfectly happy with a winter minimum of about 10°C (50°F) and for some it can be considerably lower. I have chosen such species to describe here for practical reasons. The true pineapple, *Ananas comosus*, is not usually practical for serious growing, although people do sometimes root the spiky tops and grow on the plants in warmth for a while. It needs considerable space to develop fully, and constant warmth and humidity.

Most of the more suited bromeliads are from Central America or the mountains of South America. The latter are particularly easy, since they naturally grow where there are wide temperature changes.

As well as the epiphytic bromeliads there are also those that are terrestrial, i.e. root in the ground like normal plants. Those nearly always have leaves with *barbed edges*, like the pineapple top. The epiphytics have leaves with *smooth edges*. In both cases the leaves are formed as a rosette, and are very exotically coloured or variegated. In many species there is a depression at the centre of the leaf rosette forming a cup. This is called the 'urn' and should be kept topped up with water. In nature, this urn traps and drowns insects which are subsequently digested by the plant to give a useful source of nitrogen, rather like insectivorous plants. From our point of view, the urn makes watering an easy procedure for beginners; you merely need to keep it full.

In the bromeliads can be found some of the most extraordinary and spectacular 'flowers', often actually bracts. Frequently it is the species with the least interesting foliage that produce the most showy flowers. After flowering, which it does only once, a bromeliad forms baby plants around its base. To maintain a stock of plants it is essential to remove and pot these individually.

A general compost suitable for all bromeliads is a mixture of peat and sterilized leafmould with a little grit and bonemeal added. If pine needles can be obtained, use these instead of leafmould. I personally prefer clay pots for bromeliads, but slatted wooden baskets, as used for epiphytic orchids, can be used when the plants are hung.

A specially effective natural way to grow and display the epiphytic types, and indeed many of the terrestrials, is to plant on a mossy pole or tree branch. A pole, or preferably a Y-shaped tree branch, cleaned to free it from any possible pests it may harbour, is wrapped with sphagnum moss secured with inconspicuous florist's wire. Next the young bromeliads have a wad of moss mixed with some recommended compost, wound around their roots with wire. They are then secured to the moss on the pole or tree branch at artistically and randomly positioned intervals – where you might find them if nature had placed them there (Fig. 39). Further watering is done by application with a sprayer, and feeding can be done with the special foliar types to which bromeliads respond very well.

Fig. 39 Growing bromeliads on a tree branch. (A) Choose a piece of tree with lots of branching and with attractive bark if possible. This need not be entirely covered with moss. Make sure there are no undesirable pests or fungi present. If necessary sterilize (see p. 99) but do not use the branch for some weeks, until the disinfectant has cleared. (B) Bromeliads with a well defined 'urn' are usually most suited and the urn should be kept filled with water. (C) Before securing to the branch, wrap the bromeliad roots which should be surrounded with a suitable compost in a wad of sphagnum moss.

During summer most bromeliads like slight shade and a good air humidity. In winter, keep on the dry side, especially if conditions are chilly. Although the plants can often be grown from seed, this is not easy for beginners; it is best to get them from a specialist nursery.

Introductory selection of bromeliads for low temperatures to grow in pots or epiphytically

(Minimum temperature given)

Aechmea fasciata: leaves with grey and green striping across. Very long lasting blue and pink flowers. (10°C).

Aechmea × 'Foster's Favourite': (*A. victoriana × A. racine*) wine-red leaves, pendent clusters of coral berries, very long lasting and attractive. (10°C).

Aechmea multicaulis: dark green foliage and short spike of yellow flowers with red bracts. (7°C).

Billbergia nutans: very popular. Grassy silvery green foliage, stems bearing pendent scapes of greenish-purple flowers with rose red bracts. (5°C).

Billbergia × 'Santa Barbara': (*B. nutans × B. distachya × B. pyramidalis*) paler flowers, but leaves beautifully banded dark green and cream. (10°C).

Billbergia × 'Windii': (*B. decora × B. nutans*) a larger and more impressive form of *B. nutans*. (7°C).

Cryptanthus bivittatus 'Roseus Pictus': chameleon plant. This is a popular bromeliad for bottle gardens, but will grow to a moderate size given space. It grows as a star-shaped rosette. In shade the leaves are pale green with central dark stripe. In a bright position the colours change to pink and maroon, hence popular name. Attractive and interesting. (10°C).

× Cryptbergia rubra: (*Cryptanthus babianus × Billbergia nutans*) notable for its very bright red foliage, the colour developing best in a position of good light. (10°C).

Neoregelia marmorata: beautiful leaf variegation with red and green marbling. Lavender blue flowers. (10°C).

Nidularium burchellii: neat grower with leaves purple below, green above. White flowers followed by a very long lasting spike of orange berries. (10°C).

Pitcairnia flavescens: grassy foliage. Erect spike of pale yellow flowers in early summer. Easy. (7°C).

Tillandsia: most tillandsias are best grown epiphytically. They can be grown in hanging orchid baskets, or in moss secured to a piece of cork or bark suspended or fastened to a wall. However, the rosette species will do well if given small pots. All like to be watered by a fine spray and respond especially well to foliar feeding.

BROMELIAD FLOWERING

For some unknown reason bromeliads are sometimes reluctant to produce flowers. It has been found that flowering can be induced by treatment with ethylene, a process used to ripen certain fruits. This gas is evolved by *very ripe* apples. If you have a reluctant bromeliad try putting it in a transparent polythene bag in company with an apple for a few days. Plants have been claimed to flower within six months after such treatment.

Orchids

The world of orchids is one of enchantment, but it is also one that the ordinary gardener with the average home greenhouse can freely enter. The types described here will be perfectly happy with a winter minimum of about 7°C (45°F) and will often survive considerably lower for short periods. Moreover, there is no need to put the orchids in a special greenhouse of their own. They will grow well in the company of other ordinary plants.

There are a few special cultural requirements, but these need present no difficulty. In fact the orchids described in this chapter are often difficult to kill unless one is guilty of gross carelessness or negligence. There are far more difficult plants to cultivate than orchids.

The most important essential is potting compost. This must be of open texture to let plenty of air to the roots, but hold the maximum amount of moisture without waterlogging. In the past, composts were composed of osmunda fibre (from the osmunda fern), sphagnum moss, various types of leafmould, and fibrous peat and sometimes loam. Nowadays formulations are very different and may even contain plastics in the form of shavings or chips. It is best for the home gardener to get orchid compost *ready-made* from an orchid nursery. Composition may vary slightly to suit different orchid types.

When watering orchids, do so generously to make sure the compost is thoroughly soaked, but do not water again until the compost has almost dried. Constantly wet conditions may lead to rotting. In winter, most like plenty of light. During flowering slight shading, preferably with white Coolglass, will keep blooms in good condition – the flowers often last for weeks, so the plants are an excellent investment. A good orchid compost contains enough plant food to last until next potting time, but most plants can be fed with soluble feeds according to the supplier's instructions. Orchids also respond very well to foliar feeds.

There is often a difference of opinion about the use of hard and soft water. Ideally use *clean* rainwater, not collected from roofs or open butts. If clean water is not available, it is, in my opinion, better to use mains tap water – even if it is hard. I have employed such a source of water on orchids of my own with no apparent ill effects. Dirty water, however, is liable to contain diseases and pests that can do very serious damage.

RECOMMENDED ORCHIDS

The vast majority of orchids we grow are produced by man, by hybridization, and given fancy names; there are hundreds with such names and the number increases each year. The best way to start growing is to visit an orchid nursery if possible and see the plants in flower. The best time to visit is from winter to spring, but avoid buying plants that are in flower. Transportation of flowering plants can be risky, even if they are only in the flower spike stage, and they are also more expensive. If you note the names of the plants that please you, young plants or seedlings may be avail-

Fig. 40 Potting an orchid (cymbidium).
(A) 'Back bulb' from which new growth is
developing (B). Note that the planting is *one-sided*
in the pot, the old pseudobulb being set against the
rim. This gives the new growth maximum area to
spread across.

able which you can grow on By doing this,
you save money and get greate satisfaction.

In my opinion, by far the most important
orchid for the home greenhouse, and particularly for the beginner, is the CYMBIDIUM. It is
extremely easy to manage, yet has all the
wonderful exotic characters you expect from
the orchid family. There is a wide variety of
colouring and marking, and the long spikes of
bloom can be cut to last ages in water. The
individual butterfly-like flowers can also be
picked for buttonholes or corsage. A winter
minimum of about 7°C (45°F) is ideal. During
summer, many growers put the plants outside
to make more room in the greenhouse. A
bright position, even in full sun, often encourages plants to flower better later on, but
exposure should be gradual. In mid-summer,
when the sun is very intense, a more shaded
site should be found. The effect of light on

flowering is sometimes not appreciated, and
gloomy conditions all the year round is often
the cause of disappointment.

From late summer to autumn, when flowering sized plants begin to form their flower
spikes, greater care is needed. It is a disaster if
the young spikes become damaged. This is
also the time when new pseudobulbs, as the
swollen base stems of orchids are called, begin
to grow (Fig. 40). It may be difficult to
distinguish the two at first. When the flower
spike has formed a well-defined stem, it should
be given a cane for support. The cane will also
be needed to hold the heavy spray of flowers
that will subsequently develop. Recently the
miniature cymbidiums have gained much publicity. These are excellent for the very small
greenhouse but, personally, I do not find them
nearly so satisfying as the full size hybrids.

Many other orchids have forms that can be
grown in both cool and warm conditions, and
the catalogues of orchid nurseries should be
carefully consulted before buying. PAPHIOPE-
DILUMS have plain green leaved forms and
types with mottled foliage. The former are
usually – not always – happy in cool conditions, but require more shade than cymbidiums. These orchids are quite fascinating,
however, because of their quaint slipper-
shaped blooms held boldly erect and having a
wide range of remarkable colourings and
markings. Unlike most orchids they do not
have pseudobulbs. They need generally quite
humid conditions and in my opinion are not so
happy in the company of ordinary plants.

Numerous other orchids are often suggested
for the cool home greenhouse, such as the
lovely odontoglossums, miltonias (pansy
orchids), and even the very exotic cattleyas. In
my opinion this is rather unwise; few home
greenhouses today have sufficient winter
warmth to keep such orchids happy for long.

POTTING

The best time to pot cymbidiums and most
other orchids is after flowering, or in spring.
With orchids that form pseudobulbs growth is
often very one-sided. Divide plants by turning
them out of their pots and cutting through the
roots with a very sharp blade to avoid bruising
them. Old pseudobulbs that have flowered

Plate 29 Potting a cymbidium showing use of a potting stick to push pieces of compost between the roots. Note one-sided potting procedure.

well, and may be a little shrivelled, can be repotted so that the side from which growth is *not* developing is placed almost against the pot's rim. Further development will then take place across the pot. An inspection of the roots will usually disclose old shrivelled ones that can be cut out. New succulent roots must be carefully handled to avoid damage. When potting, hold the pseudobulbs in the position required with one hand, and press down the fibrous compost around the roots with the other. Using a potting stick, carefully push pieces of compost between the roots (Plate 29), and finally use the fingers to firm down the compost from above, again carefully. Firm potting is often recommended, but take care not to crush or damage the new roots. It should be possible to lift the plant, compost, and pots, by the pseudobulbs, without the whole lot falling away. After potting, water very sparingly and cautiously at first. If the compost was moist at the outset, do not water for a week or so. This is to lessen the risk of rotting if any damage to the roots has occurred.

HARDY ORCHIDS

By far the best, the most exotic, and the easiest hardy orchid is the *Pleione*. Most popular are

several named varieties of *P. formosana*. These are quite hardy, but greatly benefit from the protection of a greenhouse or frame – there is no need for artificial heat in winter. The plant forms pseudobulbs, and these should be planted in half pots or pans as used for alpines (p. 177). An easy to make DIY compost gives excellent results: equal parts of loam, grit, peat, and leafmould. A single pseudobulb will multiply if left undisturbed, so that the best effect will be seen after a few years when a group has formed and a cluster of flowers will be produced. They are typically orchid shaped and resemble small cattleyas.

When the flowers fade the pseudobulb produces new ones by its side, and eventually shrivels. Previous to this some baby pseudobulbs are often formed at the tip of the old. These can be detached and planted in the same pan if it is large enough; otherwise plant in individual pots.

During winter the bulbs should be kept dry. Increase watering as growth commences, generously in summer, but reduce as the foliage begins to fade. Give airy conditions and slight shade in summer and during flowering which is usually in spring. There is a certain amount of disagreement among botanists about the naming of pleiones.

183

20 THE CONSERVATORY

I like to think of the conservatory as a place where plants and people can enjoy each other's company. This concept should also be borne in mind when planning and designing. Gone are the days of the grand ornamental structures of the Victorian era, but in recent years conservatories have returned to fashion in a more modern design, and sometimes in the form of 'garden room' type structures.

Basically the conservatory should be a place where you can *enjoy* your plants, where they are displayed with regard to eye appeal, and preferably where you can sit and relax among them. In Victorian times the conservatory was often used to entertain visitors, or to partake of morning coffee or afternoon tea. This is still possible, even if the structure has shrunk in size.

THE SITE

A site giving communication with the dwelling house is obviously extremely desirable, otherwise it should certainly be as near as possible to the home. If it is possible to choose, a place that is not *too* sunny will give conditions more comfortable for you and most of the beautiful plants suited to the conservatory. If the site has to be very shady or very sunny, what you can grow must be much more carefully chosen. Conditions too shady can become gloomy and depressing, and little can be done about it. On the other hand, a very bright site, such as facing full south, can be shaded by blinds or a shading paint like Coolglass during the summer; this is, however, an added chore and complication. If left unshaded, a south facing lean-to conservatory, for example, can become far too hot for comfort – plants and yourself included. If the aspect is clear both on the west and east sides, a north facing conservatory is often ideal. You get morning and afternoon-to-evening sun, but miss the midday excessive heat.

A conservatory set against a dwelling is usually warmer than a free standing one, even if there is no artificial heating. However, sometimes it may be possible to extend the home central heating system to the conservatory. A professional heating engineer must always be consulted before such an extension is made.

TEMPERATURE AND HUMIDITY

Very high temperatures are unnecessary and expensive if they are maintained in winter. Although there are lots of exotic plants that will revel in the heat and humidity, most people will not! A winter minimum of from just frost free (if you have to watch your spending) to about 7°C (45°F) will give enormous scope. However, if artificial heating is not possible, there is much that can be done with an unheated conservatory.

Since a high humidity is very uncomfortable to most people, plants liking a damp atmosphere should be avoided.

CHOOSING AND DISPLAYING THE PLANTS

If there are to be permanent plant residents in the conservatory, they should be of the type to give interest the year round. Plenty of evergreens are essential. Many of those described in Chapter 14 are suitable. A selection of plants that will give winter colour is also very desirable; include some variegated foliage plants, for example.

Fatsia japonica has a rather 'tropical' look, and is useful for creating the psychological effect of a warm climate, even though it is practically hardy.

Representatives of the palms were invariably found in conservatories, but most of the best do need moderate winter warmth. Not demanding too much warmth – about 7°C (45°F) winter minimum – are *Howea belmoreana* curly palm, and *H. fosteriana* the flat palm. Both are often sold as house plants. Another possibility is *Chamaedora elegans* (also called *Neanthebella*) which is compact and neat growing. Quite hardy are *Trachycarpus fortunei* and *Chamaerops humilis* often grown outdoors in mild areas, but usually getting scruffy looking through weather damage. Both these palms make good tub subjects when young but may outgrow their usefulness. Very easy to raise from seed, and handsome for frost-free conditions, is *Phoenix canariensis*. This too, will eventually grow to a considerable height, but its ease from seed means that young specimens can always be at hand.

Many of the climbers and wall shrubs described in Chapter 15 will give distinction to the conservatory, and some hanging and trailing plants are also essential for character. For a very sunny site the succulents are useful. If you have another utility greenhouse – or even some frames – most of the plants for colourful flowers, described in Chapter 12, can be displayed in the conservatory when they have reached the decorative stage. The conservatory is *not* a place where all the visually uninteresting cultural jobs and growing-on stages are done!

Permanent plants in the home conservatory are best grown in containers. There is a wide choice of ornamental pots and tubs, to suit individual taste, sold by garden centres and shops. However, many improvised containers can be easily disguised and made to look attractive by such coverings as sphagnum moss, or pieces of cork or thin natural stone. The plastic growbags, now very popular, can be similarly hidden from view. If a natural border effect is wanted, a trough can be sunk into the floor and lined with polythene sheeting slit for drainage. This should be filled with

peat and the plants grown in pots then plunged up to their rims in the peat. For this purpose, clay pots are very convenient since they will allow moisture from the peat to pass through to the roots. Try to arrange and set out your conservatory plants with the same care and artistic consideration that you would give to a floral arrangement. If the conservatory is large enough, a tiny pool and tinkling fountain makes an attractive feature. Many ideas for this will be found in good garden centres, and the plants described in Chapter 17 will be especially useful.

FURNISHING THE CONSERVATORY

Personally I prefer a conservatory to be in the form of a greenhouse basically – rather than of the form of a home extension. The latter is often too dark to keep plants happy, but may be all right where the site is south facing and very sunny. Another problem with many home extensions is that they may have a translucent corrugated plastic roof, with hardly any slope. Condensation often collects along the corrugations and drips on your head and your furnishings!

However, in all cases, furnishings resistant to damp and water are essential. a pleasing and comfortable floor is also important. There is no need for elaborate and expensive tiling – most of the modern vinyl type flooring serves perfectly well and many designs ideal for conservatories can be found. Natural stone, or more ornamental mosaic, patterns are particularly suited. Bright garish colours are best avoided. I have had vinyl flooring on test in a conservatory for very many years and am amazed how resistant it is to wet, upset pots, and the treading-in of garden mud – but always make sure it is put down on a *perfectly level and smooth cement base*.

For furniture, again a wide choice is possible. For a modern setting, plate glass and steel tables and chairs, and stands for plants, are usually extremely damp resistant and easy to clean. For an 'olde worlde' look, period style cast aluminium alloy is expensive but very attractive. Bamboo furniture also often blends beautifully, but it might be advisable to give the bamboo an extra coat of polyurethane varnish when leaving it in the damp atmosphere of a conservatory the year round.

Many flowering plants have the habit of shedding bits and pieces of fading petals and need to be sited to avoid these spoiling furniture or treading them into the home.

WINTER COLOUR

One of the objectives desired by most people with a conservatory is to have plenty of winter colour. This is not difficult to achieve – particularly if you have another greenhouse in which to do the basic growing or propagation. Many of the plants already described in previous chapters will provide colour. Important are the early flowering cinerarias, such as 'Spring Glory' and calceolarias like 'Jewel Cluster' and 'Anytime'. These alone make a dazzling display. Add a selection of the primulas, such as *P. obconica*, *P. praenitens* (*P. sinensis*), *P. malacoides* and polyanthus if sown early, and some of the new multi-coloured primroses, and you are well away. Particularly seasonal for the Christmas period are the brightly berried ardisias, the capsicums and solanums. The latter are best sown in February, if wanted for Christmas. Various plants that are sold in the shops at around Christmas time can be housed in the conservatory, but unfortunately most have been tricked into out-of-season performance and it may not

be posssible to keep them easily after they have passed over. The chrysanthemums have been artificially dwarfed with chemicals and treated with artificial light to induce flowering; also forced are the Indian azaleas; many bulbs, *Erica gracilis* and the Christmas cactus; poinsettia and kalanchoe have been light and possibly chemically treated. However, all these should give colour in cool conditions for a long time, and will usually do this longer in a conservatory than in a warm room of the home. Cyclamen, whether raised yourself or bought, do not like chill. They need a steady 10°C (50°F) or so. African violets also need *at least* this temperature too – preferably a few degrees higher. They may not make good company for the cool-condition lovers!

Some crocus and other early flowering bulbs are easy for winter colour and popular. The 'prepared' lilies, however, are not well known – yet they are quite spectacular. Try especially 'Brandywine', 'Enchantment', 'Prosperity', and 'Paprika', but do check that they are *specially treated* for *early flowering*.

A number of shrubby plants or climbers can give a beautiful winter show. Some camellias will flower quite early under glass making a very beautiful display, and do well in a conservatory, even if in small pots. *Jasminum polyanthum* is a well known climber that becomes smothered with flowers and fills the house with fragrance. You will find many other possibilities described in this book, so the winter months should never be dull!

PART IV

APPENDIX – USEFUL INFORMATION

To make small quantity of John Innes compost (easy to mix)

Use a 13-cm (5-in) pot, filled to 2.5 cm (1 in) below the rim as a standard measure. Use small diabetic balance for weighing fertilizers.

Seed compost (sufficient for four 23 × 15-cm (9 × 6-in) seed trays):
    2 measures sterilized loam (see below)
    1 measure peat
    1 measure sharp sand
Add and mix well:
    calcium superphosphate 7 g (¼ ounce)
    chalk 5 g (1/5 oz)
Potting compost (one large bucketful):
    7 measures loam
    3 measures peat
    2 measures sharp sand or washed grit
Add and mix well:
    John Innes base fertilizer (garden shops) 28 g (1 oz)
    chalk 5 g (1/5 oz) (omit for lime-hating plants,).

John Innes base: 2 parts hoof and horn 3 mm (1/8 in) grist, 2 parts calcium superphosphate (18% phosphoric acid), 1 part potassium sulphate – all parts by weight.

To sterilize loam (a good garden soil can be substituted): A domestic saucepan can be used for small quantities. Place 12 mm (½ inch) water on bottom. Add *dry* sifted soil nearly to the brim and simmer for 15 minutes.

Useful products and materials

ALGOFEN: Generally safe-to-use greenhouse disinfectant. Controls algae and slimes. Macpenny International Ltd.

BENLATE: Controls wide range of moulds and mildews. Most garden shops.

BUBBLE PLASTIC FOR INSULATION: Two Wests & Elliot Ltd. Transatlantic Plastics Ltd.

CALGON: Safe glass cleaner. Most pharmacists.

CAPILLARY MATTING: Two Wests & Elliot Ltd.

CHEMPAK DIY COMPOST MIX: Ready-mixed fertilizers to add to your own peat/grit or peat/perlite. Chempak Products.

CHESUNT COMPOUND: Useful in deterring damping-off of seedlings. Tins of concentrate available from most garden shops.

CLEAN-UP: Very useful cresol based sterilizing agent for greenhouse soils and structure. ICI garden shops.

COOLGLASS: Invaluable electrostatic type shading. PBI garden shops and centres.

FILLIP: Excellent foliar feed also containing hormones and vitamins. PBI garden shops and centres.

FUMITE: TCNB fumigant invaluable for botrytis control. May & Baker Ltd. Most garden shops.

HEXYL: Combined insecticide/fungicide. Especially useful for chrysanthemums. Most garden shops.

HORTAG: Very water-absorbent mineral material for covering staging. Thomas Butcher.

KETTLE DESCALER: Invaluable for cleaning very dirty and lime-covered glass. Most household stores.

LEAFSHINE: Wax emulsion for giving brilliant lustre to certain foliage plants. Most garden shops.

LEVINGTON COMPOST: Excellent wide ranging composts. Potting compost, in my tests, is also suitable for germinating most popular *seeds*.

MAGNESIUM SULPHATE (EPSOM SALTS): For correcting magnesium deficiency. Most pharmacists.

MOISTURE METER: A reliable instrument is the J.M.A. type. J.M.A. Scientific Co, 152 Nelson Rd, Twickenham, TW2 7BX.

PERLITE: Very useful compost ingredient. Can replace sand or grit and is more reliably sterile. Silvaperl Products Ltd, P.O. Box 8, Harrogate, North Yorkshire, HG2 8JW.

PHOSTROGEN: Invaluable general fertilizer also useful for making a DIY compost. Special pack also available for this purpose. Most garden shops and centres.

PLASTICS: Plastic sheeting, film and materials for many greenhouse uses. Transatlantic Plastics Ltd, Garden Estate, Ventnor, I.O.W.

SPRAYDAY: Very safe insecticide for most plants, especially good for whitefly, aphids and similar pests.

SULPHUR: Fumigant for complete sterilization. Most pharmacists.

THERMOMETERS AND INSTRUMENTS (INCLUDING FROST FORECASTERS): Diplex Ltd, P.O. Box 172, Watford, Hertfordshire, WD1 1BX.

TUMBLEBUG: Extremely useful systemic insecticide controlling most greenhouse pests and safe for most plants, including cucumber family. Murphy Chemical Co. Most garden shops and centres.

Greenhouse suppliers

(Note: It is wise to patronize *long established* firms with extensive experience.)

Alitex Ltd, Station Road, Alton, Hants (unique cross-sectional glazing bars give exceptional strength).

Alton Cedar Greenhouses: Banbury Homes and Gardens Ltd, P.O. Box 17, Banbury, Oxfordshire, OX17 3NS.

Baco Leisure Products Ltd, Windover Road, Huntingdon, Cambs, PE18 7EH.

Crittall Warmlife Ltd, Crittall Road, Witham, Essex, CM8 3AW.

Edenlite Products, Wern Works, Briton Ferry, Neath, West Glamorgan, SA11 2JS.

Europa Manor Engineers Ltd, Oxford Road, Brackley, Northamptonshire, NN13 5EQ.

Halls Homes and Gardens Ltd, Church Road, Paddock Wood, Kent, TN12 6EU.

Hartley Greenhouses: Clear Span Ltd, Greenfield, Oldham, Lancs, OL3 7BR.

A. E. Headen Ltd, 218 High Street, Potters Bar, Hertfordshire, EN6 5BJ.

Park Lines (Buildings) Ltd, Park House, 501 Green Lanes, Palmers Green, London, N13 4BS.

F. Pratten & Co. Ltd, Charlton Road, Midsomer Norton, Bath, BA3 4AG.

Robinsons of Winchester Ltd, Robinson House, Winnall Industrial Estate, Winchester, SO23 8LH.

Rosedale Engineers Ltd, Rosedale Works, Hunmanby, Filey, Yorkshire.

C. H. Whitehouse Ltd, Buckhurst Works, Frant, Tunbridge Wells, TN3 9BN.

General equipment and fittings

Alite Metals (Bristol) Co. Ltd, Maze Street, Barton Hill Trading Estate, Bristol. Aluminium glazing bars and other components for DIY construction, replacement or alteration.

Bentall Simplex Ltd, Heybridge Works, Maldon, Essex, CM9 7NW. Wide range of heating and automation equipment and instrumentation.

Chempak Products, Bingley Road, Hoddesdon, Herts., EN11 0LR. Wide range of horticultural chemicals and fertilizers.

George H. Elt Ltd, Eltex Works, Worcester. Paraffin heaters and propagators, also natural gas heaters.

House and Garden Automation, Leahurst Nursery, 36A Galley Lane, Arkley, Barnet, Herts. Automatic aids of all kinds.

Macpenny International Ltd, Gore Road Industrial Estate, New Milton, Hampshire, BH25 6SF. Electric heating, propagators, wide range of automatic watering, much other important equipment.

Tube Heat Ltd, 123 High Street, Bordesley, Birmingham, B12 0JO. Electrical heaters, heating tubes, warming cables, thermostats, etc.

Two Wests & Elliot Ltd, Unit 4, Carrwood Road, Sheepbridge Industrial Estate, Chesterfield, Derbyshire, S41 9RH. Wide range of accessories and staging types.

Seedsmen

Bees and Webbs Seeds, Temana Bees Ltd, Sealand, Chester, CH1 6BA.

J. W. Boyce, 67 Station Road, Soham, Ely, Cambridgeshire, CB7 5ED.

Chiltern Seeds, Bortree Stile, Ulverston, Cumbria. Rare and unusual seeds.

Samuel Dobie & Son Ltd, Upper Dee Mills, Llangollen, Denbighshire, LL20 8SD.

Fothergill's Seeds, Regal Lodge, Gazeley Road, Kentford, Newmarket, Suffolk, CB8 7QB.

M. Holtzhausen, 14 High Cross Street, St Austell, Cornwall. Rare and unusual seeds.

Hurst Gunson Cooper Taber Ltd, Avenue Road, Witham, Essex, CM8 2DX.

Marshalls Seeds Ltd, Regal Road, Wisbech, Cambs, PE13 2RF.

Suttons Seeds Ltd, Hele Road, Torquay, Devon, TQ2 7QJ.

Thompson & Morgan Ltd, London Road, Ipswich, Suffolk, IP2 0BA.

W. J. Unwin Ltd, Histon, Cambridge, CB4 4LE.

Specialist nurserymen

Steven Bailey Ltd, Eden Nurseries, Sway, Hants. Carnation and gerbera specialist.

Blackmore & Langdon Ltd, Bath, Somerset. Begonias, cyclamen and gloxinias.

Walter Blom & Son Ltd, Leavesden, Watford, Herts. General bulb supplier.

Burnham Nurseries Ltd, Kingsteignton, Newton Abbot, Devon. Orchids especially suited to home growers.

Thomas Butcher Ltd, Shirley, Croydon, Surrey. Wide range of greenhouse plants, seeds, and exotics, palms etc.

Clifton Geranium Nursery, Cherry Orchard Road, Whyke, Chichester, PO19 2BX. Pelargoniums – all kinds.

Deacons Nursery, Godshill, Isle of Wight. Fruit trees and bushes of all kinds.

Efenechtyd Nurseries, Efenechtyd, Ruthin, Clwyd, LL15 2PW. Streptocarpus.

C. G. Hollett, Green Bank Nursery, Sedbergh, Cumbria, LA10 5AG. Wide range of alpines and primulas.

Holly Gate Nurseries Ltd, Billingshurst Lane, Ashington, Sussex. Cacti and other succulents.

Michael Jefferson-Brown, Maylite, Martley, Worcester. Grapes, lilies.

Ken Muir, Honeypot Farm, Weeley Heath, Clacton-on-Sea, CO16 9BJ. Strawberries.

Nerine Nurseries, Welland, Worcestershire. Nerines.

K. J. Townsend, 17 Valerie Close, St Albans, Herts., AL1 5JD. Achimenes.

B. Wall, 4 Selbourne Close, New Haw, Weybridge, Surrey. Bromeliads, and begonia species and other exotics.

Wallace & Barr Ltd, Marden, Kent. Bulbs generally including many rare types.

Wills Fuchsias Ltd, The Fuchsia Nursery, Chapel Lane, West Wittering, Chichester, Sussex.

H. Woolman Ltd, Grange Road, Dorridge, Solihull, B90 3NQ. Chrysanthemum specialists, but wide range of popular greenhouse plants of outstanding quality.

INDEX